Arabic Instruction in Israel

Social, Economic and Political Studies of the Middle East and Asia

VOLUME 117

The titles published in this series are listed at *brill.com/seps*

Arabic Instruction in Israel

Lessons in Conflict, Cognition and Failure

By

Allon J. Uhlmann

BRILL

LEIDEN | BOSTON

Cover illustration: Learning Arabic Calligraphy. Photo by Aieman Khimji.

Library of Congress Cataloging-in-Publication Data

Names: Uhlmann, Allon J.
Title: Arabic instruction in Israel : lessons in conflict, cognition and failure / by Allon J. Uhlmann.
Description: Leiden ; Boston : Brill, 2017. | Series: Social, economic and political studies of the Middle East and Asia ; volume 117 | Includes bibliographical references and index.
Identifiers: LCCN 2017023188 (print) | LCCN 2017025420 (ebook) | ISBN 9789004349957 (E-book) | ISBN 9789004323810 (hardback : alk. paper)
Subjects: LCSH: Arabic language–Study and teaching–Israel. | Language policy–Israel. | Sociolinguistics–Israel. | Palestinian Arabs–Israel–Languages. | Hebrew language–Influence on Arabic.
Classification: LCC PJ6068.18 (ebook) | LCC PJ6068.18 U94 2017 (print) | DDC 492.7/8007105694–dc23
LC record available at https://lccn.loc.gov/2017023188

Typeface for the Latin, Greek, and Cyrillic scripts: "Brill". See and download: brill.com/brill-typeface.

ISSN 1385-3376
ISBN 978-90-04-32381-0 (hardback)
ISBN 978-90-04-34995-7 (e-book)

This book is printed on acid-free paper and produced in a sustainable manner.

To Ella J., Charlotte H. and Jennifer R.

Contents

Preface

Arabic instruction in Israel struggles with two wicked challenges. The first is the elusive nature of Arabic proficiency in the Jewish school sector. By "proficiency" I mean sufficient competence or mastery that allows for effective use of the language. (This broad definition will be elaborated later.) There is an explicit commitment to the promotion of Arabic instruction that is rooted in the immediate institutional self-interest of powerful stakeholders in Israel. There is also an abundance of resources that could greatly support and enhance Arabic instruction. Nevertheless, Arabic instruction in the Jewish school sector remains stubbornly ineffective.

The other seemingly inexplicable oddity is the intractable underperformance of Arab university students, proficient in Arabic as they are, at Arabic grammar. This is odd both in absolute terms as Arab students struggle through what they experience as a profoundly bewildering and often impenetrable material, and in relative terms as Arab students' attainment is overshadowed by the superior performance of Jewish students who are nowhere nearly as proficient in Arabic as are underperforming Arab students.

The persistence of these problems suggests that they are not coincidental, but somehow inherently related to the structure and function of Arabic language instruction in Israel. This book seeks to account for the endurance of these unintended consequences of Arabic instruction. Arabic instruction in Israel is obviously not unique in betraying the effects of unintended consequences that are at odds with the articulated intention of all dominant stakeholders. The discussion that follows examines specific practices of Arabic instruction in their specific contexts, but the implications of this analysis extend beyond the unique, conflicted contexts of Arabic instruction in Israel.

The multifaceted failure of Arabic instruction for Jewish students in Israel can be traced back to the effects of the Zionist project of de-Arabising the nation and the land. Ironically, the Zionist project serves as the very impetus for Arabic instruction in the first place, even as it condemns Arabic instruction to failure. But the analysis cannot stop with this general statement. Humans respond to the environment around them. Therefore, a comprehensive explanation of how Arabic instruction for Israeli Jews fails to achieve its intended results also needs to include an account of how and why it is allowed to continuously flounder. The answer has to do with the debased value of Arabic in the broad economy of knowledge in Israel, and this debased value ultimately accounts for the fact that the field continues to function the way it does.

Even more perplexing than the sorry state of Jewish Arabic literacy is the poor performance of Arab university students in Arabic grammar. The political economy of Israel is clearly implicated in this, as are the dynamics of schooling in the Arab world, the structures of Arabic grammatical scholarship, Arabic's sociolinguistic reality and the dynamics of Arabic language instruction.

Arabs and Jews think and learn about Arabic grammar differently. They acquire different habits of learning and thinking grammar in the course of their primary and secondary schooling. The grammatical knowledge that is taught in Arab and Jewish education systems is radically divergent, as are the styles of Arabic grammatical instruction. These differences are pervasive. Once orchestrated by the political economy of Arabic instruction in the Zionist state, they produce a situation whereby Jewish knowledge predominates, marginalising Arabs and their knowledge. Specifically, universities, with one partial exception, teach Arabic grammar the way it is taught in Jewish schools, leaving Arab students struggling. These effects accentuate an already fraught relationship between Arabs and Arabic grammar, itself a core feature of the history and political economy of Arabic scholarship in the Arab world.

In a nutshell, both instances of pedagogical underachievement, namely Jewish failure to achieve Arabic proficiency and Arab underperformance in university-taught Arabic grammar, are not haphazard. They are unintended consequences of the very way Arabic instruction unfolds. To understand the systemic logic of Arabic instruction and the dynamics that produce and reproduce these unintended consequences, this book approach the whole set of stakeholders, practices and dynamics that shape Arabic instruction in Israel as a field of practice. Both the Jewish failure to attain proficiency in Arabic and Arab intellectual alienation from Arabic grammar result from the field's very structure and function even as they are entirely unintended and unplanned by any of the participants in the field.

Earlier Studies

Until recently, Arabic instruction in Israel did not receive much attention. Two collections of articles and papers have appeared over the years, charting the development and dilemmas of Arabic instruction in Israel's Jewish education stream (Landau 1962, Yonai 1992). Sporadic articles have also addressed some specific issues such as whether Arabic should be approached in Jewish schools as a second or foreign language, and the place of colloquial Arabic in the curriculum (e.g. Brosh 1997). Otherwise the topic has not attracted much scholarly attention.

Research into language policy provides something of a systematic perspective on Arabic instruction. Spolsky and Shohamy's authoritative overview of the field (1999) offers a refreshingly critical perspective on Arabic instruction policy and practice. The discussions of Arabic instruction in this vein, however, have been marked by the application to Arabic of a generalised framework of language politics. They have usefully treated Arabic as an instance of a minority language, as an instance of a second language, or as an instance of a heritage language. But such treatments have tended to ignore the peculiarities of Arabic and the idiosyncrasies of its place among Israeli Arabs. Thus, Arabic's diglossia has been acknowledged in this literature, but the idiosyncratic character of Arabic's diglossia and its pedagogical significance, for both Arabs and Jews, has not been elaborated (cf. Spolsky and Shohamy 1999, 143–146). This omission detracts from the interpretation of substantial language education policy dilemmas. For instance, to understand the debate on whether to focus Arabic instruction in Jewish schools on Modern Standard Arabic or colloquial Arabic, one must understand that the Standard variety is morphologically more stable than the colloquial one, and that it is easier to rely on knowledge of Standard Arabic to acquire colloquial Arabic than vice versa. But Spolsky and Shohamy, ignoring the actual grammatical character of Arabic, ascribe the argument in favour of Modern Standard Arabic to poor command among Jewish academics of colloquial Arabic (1999, 145). Spolsky and Shohamy miss a critical point. Arabic is not just a generic language type. To understand its sociolinguistic character and the way Arabic is learned and taught one must also consider its historical and linguistic specificities. This book advances the critical analysis of language policy by going beyond a treatment of Arabic as merely an "instance of" a language type, and considering the critical significance of the peculiarities of the language.

Moreover, language policy research has focused primarily on government policies towards language, and has avoided a consideration of the actual learning processes and classroom interactions, or the way policy formulation and implementation are affected from below, as it were, by students, parents, teachers, and other interested parties. These are all crucial components of the field of Arabic instruction. Furthermore, to understand classroom dynamics it is important to take into account the broad symbolic economics of language proficiency that drives attitudes and behaviours of learners and teachers of Arabic in Israel. The chapters that follow offer a broader alternative purview by focusing on the educational process, the logic that drives different stakeholders in the process, and how policies and intentional action are modified and subverted as they are being executed, culminating in perplexing, unintended consequences.

The scholars of language policy (e.g. Spolsky and Shohamy 1999, chapters 5 and 6) have followed the institutional structure of language instruction policy in carving up their subject matter. They have broken up the challenges of Arabic instruction into distinct policy issues. These include Arabic as a minority mother tongue for Arabs; Arabic as a second language for Jews; and, to a lesser extent, Arabic as a heritage Jewish language. Different bureaucracies address these policy issues, and the policies they engender are targeted at different segments of the population. It is easy to see why the literature on language policy treats them as distinct sets of policy problematics.

Yet, these seemingly disparate policy challenges are linked through a common, pervasive imperative which is embodied in Zionism's inherent Orientalist outlook. Gil Eyal (2005) traces the emergence of an externalising discourse that came to dominate Zionism. Jewish ethnicity was demarcated in part by means of this externalising discourse that constituted Arabs as a distinct, non-Jewish and alien collective that threatens the Zionist enterprise, both as an external enemy, and as an internal one. This duality was embodied in both Palestinian Arabs and the Arab Jews.[1] The former were to be externalised or contained and controlled. The latter were to be exorcised of their Arabness and civilised (cf. Shenhav 2003; Shohat 1999). Institutional policies towards Arabic—be it as the heritage language of Jews or as the language of the Arab minority—are greatly influenced by this project of constituting Jewishness as an ethnically distinct, Hebraic identity.

In recent years, Arabic instruction in Israel has enjoyed growing scholarly attention that extends beyond the question of policy and has investigated the educational processes involved. Zvi Bekerman and his collaborators (e.g. Bekerman 2009) studied instruction in mixed Arab-Jewish schools using observational methods and interviews. Mixed schools like those studied by Bekerman are rare. They are effectively social experiments in Israel, reflecting a liberal drive among a minuscule fragment of the population. Nonetheless, by challenging the segregation that runs through Israeli schooling these schools bring into view some of the normally latent dynamics that reinforce the segregation of Israeli education. For example, the studies have highlighted such pertinent issues as the demotivating effects of the perceived uselessness of Arabic, and

1 By Arab Jews I mean Jews from the Arab world. This is much narrower than the concept of Mizrahi (i.e. Oriental) Jews, which includes Jews from some non-Arab regions (e.g. Iran). The concept of Arab Jews is equivalent to the Hebrew *yᵉhudey ʿarav*. I am not implying here a meaningful category of self-identity, even though some people may identify, if only for reasons of discursive politics, as Arab Jews or Jewish Arabs.

the persistent inability of Jewish students to achieve proficiency in Arabic (Bekerman 2009, 241–243). These conform to the observations described below that are derived from my study of the broad, ethnolinguistically segregated, public school system.

The discussion in this book concerning Arabic instruction to Jews in Israel has had some parallels in other lines of research into "enemy" language instruction, most notably a series of studies on Turkish instruction to Greek Cypriots (Charalambous 2012; 2013; Rampton, Charalambous and Charalambous 2014). Some of the similarities between the Cypriot and Israeli contexts are striking. The psychological effects of identifying the language with a hostile speaker pose similar challenges to both teachers of Turkish to native Greek speakers in Cyprus and teachers of Arabic to Jews in Israel. Not surprisingly, equivalent pedagogical dilemmas confront both groups of teachers.

In a similar vein, a different emerging line of research into Arabic instruction in Israel focuses on securitisation and language instruction. Yonatan Mendel (2011, 2013, 2014) examined the role of Israel's security apparatus in shaping Arabic instruction at schools over the years. Mendel draws also on contemporary scholarship into the political economy of contemporary Arabic history, most notably Yasir Suleiman's analysis of the way the development of Arabic instruction in the modern Arab world was implicated in the broader cultural politics of the era (2004, 2006a). Mendel's work illuminates the historical and administrative processes through which the security apparatus and its needs came to define the scope and content of Arabic instruction to Jews in Israel, and shaped its administrative control.

My research project (e.g. Uhlmann 2008; 2010) shares many of the concerns and themes that are raised by Mendel and Suleiman. It highlights the centrality of the political context and the Zionist project to the formation of Arabic instruction at school. My angle is different, though. I define the two conundrums of Arabic instruction and proceed to explain the systemic logic that accounts for these intractable, clearly unintended consequences of Arabic instruction. I do not treat these unintended consequences as haphazard or accidental, but rather as an integral aspect of the field. My question is not "how is Arabic instruction subverted?" but rather "how are the two elements of underachievement achieved?" Moreover, my primary aim is not to discover new facts about Arabic and its instruction, but rather to put together both established and novel facts in a way that would make sense of the underachievements under consideration.

The recent academic interest in Arabic instruction to Jews has crossed over to the semi-governmental research sector. This has been reflected in a series of government-funded, policy-related research and publications (e.g. Eickelman et al. 2010; Hayam-Yonas and Malka 2006; Landau-Tasseron, Olshtain, et al. 2012). However, because this research is framed in support of policy formulation and implementation, it tends to exclude the political context that both shapes the field of Arabic instruction and subverts much of the pedagogical intentions of official educational policy.

This book shares some common themes with this policy-driven line of research, most notably an interest in what affects the effectiveness of Arabic instruction and what shapes the demand for Arabic instruction among students. But this book differs from policy-driven research in significant ways. Policy-driven research has focused on courses of action that institutional players can adopt, but has shunned a consideration of unintended secondary consequences of policy implementation, and the broad systemic consequences of different stakeholders pursuing different, often contradictory, aims. This leaves little space for a critical investigation of such broad themes as the political economy of linguistic capacity—a crucial part of the picture that is not foregrounded in research that is produced to support and improve policy implementation by the Ministry of Education, for example.

The different lines of research that I have just discussed pertain primarily to the study of Arabic instruction to Jews. But the book covers another substantial and related issue, namely the educational experience of Arabs undergoing Arabic instruction at Israeli universities. As I hope my book shows, these are different aspects of the same field, yet they draw on distinct, bodies of research.

Scholarship on Arab education in Mandatory Palestine and the Jewish state is not abundant and focuses on the use of education as a means of political control (e.g. Al-Haj 1995; Abu-Saad 2006). One major focus of the research has been the effect on Arab schooling of the power relations in Israel, and especially the marginalisation of Israeli Arabs. For quite some time, now, Arab intellectuals have decried the poor level of Arabic instruction in Arab schools in Israel, and more generally, the status of Arabic among Palestinians (e.g. Amara and Marʾi 2002; Bawardi 2012a; 2012b).

These concerns are picked up in the discussion that follows, but from a different angle. I do not have much to add on the premeditated attempts by the state to marginalise and contain Arabs, and control Arab education. In fact, my research did not directly target Arab schools. Rather, chapters three and four that discuss Arab experiences of Arabic-grammar instruction revolve around a subtle, unintended, marginalisation of Arabs at the academic level. Nonetheless, the realities of university Arabic-grammar instruction reveal plenty about Arab schools in Israel. Moreover, what happens in university Arabic-grammar classrooms has significant flow-on effects on schools, and the book suggests some of them.

Another line of research that is relevant to the issue of Arabic instruction to Arabs in Israel is the literature on the Arabic Linguistic Tradition (e.g. Carter 1981; Owens 1988; 1990; 1997; Bohas, Guillaume and Kouloughli [1990] 2006; Versteegh 1997a; Suleiman 1999b; Baalbaki 2008), Arabic revival in the modern era (Blau 1981; Landau 1987; Shraybom-Shivtiel 1999; 2006; Suleiman 1994; 2006a), and the debate over Arabic grammar and its instruction in the Arab world (e.g. Suleiman 2006b). What emerges from the literature is a picture of a golden age of indigenous Arabic grammatical scholarship that petered out by the fifteenth century as Arabic was gradually displaced in high culture and official contexts by Turkish and Persian, only to struggle with great difficulty to re-emerge in the modern era along with the rise of Arab nationalism, the spread of literacy, and the evolution of mass media. Contemporary indigenous Arabic linguistics and grammar instruction are portrayed in the literature as moribund and irrelevant, fixed in place by the Arab intellectual class's inability to formulate a shared program of reform in linguistics and its instruction.

This is very significant to the theme of Arab students' underachievement in Arabic grammar. This book describes a cultural clash between the grammar that is taught in the Arab sector—a contemporary variant of the Arabic Linguistic Tradition—and the Western-orientated grammar of Arabic that prevails in Jewish schools and at Israeli universities. The specific history of the Arabic Linguistic Tradition conditions much of the clash between the two grammatical approaches.

Interestingly, the current debates in the Arab world about linguistic instruction and language policy seem to be quite irrelevant to the problems facing Israeli Arabs. This is due to the fact that Palestinians in Israel are still very much a colonised minority, marginalised both within Israel and in the Arab world, and with little control over their own educational and linguistic destinies. Debates in the Arab world on the fate of Arabic are predicated on an assumption that the public speaks a dialect of Arabic in which it is fully immersed, and confronts a bureaucratic imperative to formally communicate in Standard Arabic. By contrast, Israeli Arabs must contend with the general irrelevance of Standard Arabic, and the penetration of Hebrew into their dialects.

This book's analysis of the Arab experience of Arabic instruction goes well beyond the issue of language acquisition, though, and raises the question of knowledge and learning as cultural, historically specific processes. I argue that Arab Arabic grammar and Jewish Arabic grammar are two distinct bodies of knowledge that differ in their cognitive organisation and in the instructional modalities that they require. This is a particularly interesting situation in that both seek to apprehend what is nominally the same slice of reality, namely the structures and regularities of the Arabic language. In other words, we are dealing with two distinct conceptualisations that are embedded in different cultural circumstances, of a single, common object—two distinct grammars of the one language. Can the differences between the two approaches tell us something about cultural differences in cognition, learning, reasoning and thought?

The question of the cultural variability in knowledge and modes of thought is by no means new. Its modern formulation in the Western academic tradition goes back to Lucien Lévy-Bruhl's work in the early 20th century. Lévy-Bruhl argued that culture determines cognition. So much so, in fact, that empathy across cultures may be impaired, or even impossible. Lévy-Bruhl's pioneering cultural relativism came up against the dominant position of cognitive universality, which argued in essence that humans in different cultural settings may differ in what they know, but not in how they know. The underlying cognitive processes of knowledge, in this view, are identical across cultures (Cazeneuve 1972, and see Lloyd 2007 for a broad overview of some of the main issues in this debate). Lévy-Bruhl further stood ahead of his time when he ventured to consider the affective nature of thought as an explanation for some of the cross-cultural differences that he postulated (see discussion and references in Cazeneuve 1972, 11 ff.).

Lévy-Bruhl's specific formulations have long been discarded, but the fundamental issue has not yet been resolved. Are knowledge acquisition and organisation dependent on the cultural and historical context in which they are formulated, or do they transcend the immediate social context of their production? To what extent is the knowledge of reality determined by reality, and to what extent is it affected by the cultural and social environments of the knower? Are logic, thought, and cognition universal, or do they differ across societies and culture?

Ethnographic and linguistic comparisons of systems of knowledge attest to the variability in tropes and underlying cognitive constructs (scripts, schemas etc.) that organise knowledge (e.g. Mandler 1984; Keen 1995; Lakoff and Johnson 1980; Lakoff 1987; Weiss 1996; Uhlmann 2006, chapter 4). This variability provides a useful angle to explore the way in which practices of Arabic-grammar instruction in the Jewish sector alienate Arab students who are exposed to it at university. It focuses our gaze on the tropes that are used to construct grammatical knowledge, and on the conceptual organisation of this knowledge. If Jewish and Arab knowledges of Arabic grammar differ in the way they are structured and in the tropes that are used to concretise abstract notions, this difference could account for the alienation of Arab students from Arabic grammar at Israeli universities (Uhlmann 2012; 2015).

In dealing with the questions of commonalities and differences in habits of learning and thinking grammar, this book advances the discussion of cognition and its possible variability across cultures and society. It joins inductive anthropological and sociological approaches to cognition that seek to discover broad generalisations through the accumulation of knowledge that is derived from contextualised studies of cognition *in situ*. The book also adds support to those who seek to challenge the view of cognition as a set of computational processes that occur inside circumscribed minds or brains of individual people.

The Current Study

Chapter One gives a more detailed account of the perplexing nature of the two conundrums of Arabic instruction, and situates them within the context of Israel's schooling system. The chapter then details the evolution of the research project and the methodology that underlies the subsequent analysis.

Chapter Two discusses Arabic instruction in the dominant, Jewish sector. It describes the systemic logic of Arabic instruction in the Jewish stream, specifically the mainstream Hebrew public school system and the universities. It identifies the major stakeholders involved, most notably Jewish Arabic teachers, the security apparatus, students and their families, and the different sets of interests that such stakeholders pursue in the field.

The chapter further identifies some critical external influences on the field that affect the relationships between social agents, and the dynamics of practice within the field. The linguistic political economy in Israel is one of these critical conditions. Arabic is generally greatly devalued with profound consequences for the practice of social agents throughout the field. The collective project of de-Arabising Arab Jews—or probably more accurately, Jewish Arabs—is another example of an external condition which has further detracted from the symbolic value of Arabic. The influence of factors such as these can be seen in the practice of local school communities, both Jewish and Arab.

The security apparatus, in its drive to promote Arabic as strategically vital, has influenced the development of a very specific educational approach. This has backfired, not least because of limits to the malleability of effective language learning. Some constructions of the context of language instruction appear to greatly hinder language acquisition. More specifically, in this case, construing Arabic as an enemy language and approaching its instruction as the inculcation of decoding skills rather than linguistic and cultural proficiencies inevitably detracts from student motivation and capacity to effectively acquire the language.

The ubiquity of the Jewish-Arab communal conflict affects other institutions as well, including those whose very *raison d'être* is the promulgation of Arabic literacy, academia being a case in point. The academic sphere is dominated by a self-image that is both Jewish and Western. The academic approach and the scholarship of Arabic linguistics at Israeli universities are distinctly Western. Moreover, they are driven by a significant imperative of maintaining Jewish dominance. The lack of Arab universities in Israel means that Arab schools, along with Jewish schools, feed their graduates into the Hebrew university system. Arabs have a natural advantage in departments of Arabic language and culture, namely their mastery of Arabic. It is primarily for this reason that even at university departments of Arabic, Arabic is artificially devalued to the point that Arabic proficiency is not essential for success in Arabic either as a student or as an academic.

Chapter Three carries the analysis to Arabic instruction in the marginalised, Arab sector. Arab students in Israel typically follow a parallel trajectory to Jewish students, but with significant differences. The school system in the Arab sector is run in Arabic. Whereas Jews learn a Westernised grammar of Arabic which is conceptually identical to the grammar of Hebrew, Arabs learn a contemporary version of the Arabic Linguistic Tradition at school. Those who continue their studies at university and enrol in Arabic as one of their majors find themselves, sooner or later, in Arabic grammar classes which are taught along Western lines.

The chapter focuses on tertiary education and traces some of the dynamics that alienate Arabs from Arabic. It examines how Arabs in Israel are prevented from achieving any measure of autonomous control over their own linguistic destiny, or addressing any of these alienating dynamics.

Israeli Arabs are doubly marginalised. They are often viewed with suspicion in the Arab world and are bound to adhere to educational conventions in the Arab world, conventions over which they have little influence and which do not reflect their own specific educational concerns. They are marginalised within Israel, too, where there is no Arab university, where Arabs are generally relegated to subordinate positions in academia, and where there is a lack of an educational and institutional context to support the elaboration, formulation and implementation of substantial reform to Arabic instruction in the Arab sector.

This political alienation adds to an already strained relationship between Arabs and Arabic grammar that has marred the relationships between Arabs and their grammarians for centuries. This general alienation has become a great source of anxiety in modernity, and is linked to the processes of Arabic revival (*al-nahḍa*—النهضة), and to the creation of a modern, logocentric universal school education.

All of this is further aggravated by the segmented nature of Israel's market of linguistic exchange (cf. Bourdieu 1977) where Arabic proficiency is generally devalued, but particularly so for Arabs. Unlike Arabs, Jews can still cash in on knowledge of Arabic through prestigious, well paid jobs with the security apparatus and state bureaucracy in ways that are closed off to Arabs.

Moreover, Arab linguists and teachers in Israel are becoming increasingly concerned not only about the progressive loss and dilution of Standard Arabic, but even about the very integrity of colloquial Arabic. The substantial penetration of Hebrew and English into common usage, coupled with the poor view many Arab students have of Arabic, has led a few Arab intellectuals to warn that Arabic in Israel is subject to gradual glottophagia, whereby it is being displaced and progressively driven to extinction by Hebrew.

The challenges to Israel's Arab intellectual leadership are thus great. Israeli Arabs face the full range of common problems that typify the state of Arabic throughout the Arab world, on top of which pile up the great unique problems that strain the relationship between Arabs and Arabic within Israel. The resources available to the Arab educational leadership to confront these challenges are limited.

Chapter four extends the discussion of Arabs and Arabic instruction in Israel. It dissects specific aspects of Arabic-grammar instruction in order to account for the jarring effect of the field whereby Arab university students struggle with Arabic grammar and are outperformed by Jewish students. The analysis in chapter four focuses on the incommensurability of the two systems of knowledge inculcation, the Westernised grammar that I refer to as the Israeli-Jewish grammar of Arabic on the one hand, and on the other hand the variety of the Arabic Grammatical Tradition that I refer to as the Israeli-Arab grammar of Arabic. The latter is the Arabic grammar that is taught at Arab schools, while the former is the Arabic grammar that is taught at Jewish schools as well as at universities. The chapter analyses the educational encounter and inevitable cognitive clash at universities, where Jewish and Arab students share the benches in Arabic grammar classes. The analysis shows how this encounter produces Arab underachievement at Arabic grammar.

The incommensurability of the two systems of grammar is comprehensive. The different conceptual frameworks cannot be translated into each other. The two frameworks are further motivated by different analytic tropes. In fact, the different scientific traditions seek to achieve different intellectual goals, and measure their success in different ways altogether. Even the emotive tonality and intellectual structure of instruction are quite different, and are further complicated by the undercurrent of hostility and suspicion between Arab students and Jewish-dominated instruction that inflects all aspects of Arabic-grammar instruction at Israeli universities.

What makes this comprehensive incommensurability all the more decisive is a combination of irrelevance and metacognitive blindness. The material that is canvassed in Arabic grammar courses at Israeli universities is alienating in large part because it is irrelevant to Arab students. They have not learnt it that way at school, and those who will become school teachers of Arabic will not be teaching it that way. And due to the pervasive lack of metacognitive self-awareness, the extent of the incommensurability between the Jewish and Arab ways of thinking grammar is universally overlooked by both Jews and Arabs who fail to appreciate that when they talk about grammar they are not discussing the same things. Pragmatic, opportunistic translation of terms from one system to the other gives a false gloss of commonality to the two systems. Most participants in the educational processes remain oblivious to the differences in the habitual ways Arabs and Jews think about grammar.

Consequently, the difficulties that Arabs face in grammar are experienced as personal failure rather than systemic incommensurability. Stylistic differences and political inequality thus combine to alienate Arabs from an integral aspect of their lived cultural identity. This personalisation of failure also prevents stakeholders from searching for possible systemic remedies for the situation.

The discussions in Chapters Two, Three and Four touch on different aspects of the field of Arabic instruction in Israel. They deal with different issues, ranging from cognitive habits to institutional dynamics, and with different groups of stakeholders. Yet all these elements are bound together and affect each other. This is why they can be analysed as a single field of practice. Moreover, some noteworthy ubiquitous themes run through the different aspects of the one field. Most notable among them is Zionism which is at one and the same time a set of ideological imperatives, a set of institutional practices, a collective project, and an organising principle of social divisions. The influence of Zionism is indeed decisive, but it is contradictory and negotiable too. This gives the field of Arabic instruction much of its autonomy. Similarly, the differences in styles of Arabic grammar and its instruction are in a way pregiven. But the multiple ways they are articulated, and the consequences of these differences, are not. Here, too, we see the autonomous nature of the field. Recognising the autonomy may open up avenues for change at the local level, without having to wait for broad revolutionary transformations in the political order at large. In the way of conclusion, Chapter Five considers the systemic nature of fields like Arabic instruction and evaluates the analytic benefits of considering learning and instruction as fields of social practice. The preponderance of unintended consequences is salient in the discussion.

The chapter then moves to consider the cognitive dynamics that underlie learning. Cognition is obviously a significant theme for studies of knowledge formation and distribution. In fact, cognitive dynamics must be an integral aspect of any account of systems that involve humans. Human cognition mediates the perception of reality and governs intentional practice. It imposes and enables some dynamics and constrains others. The profound hold that learning and analytic habits have on Arab students are a case in point. The negative effect of a teaching agenda that is hostile to Arabs on Jewish students' capacity to acquire cultural and linguistic proficiency is another. Both are significant causes of the endemic, persistent educational failure of Arabic instruction in Israel.

Ultimately, if change is to be contemplated, it is necessary to understand what keeps the field the way it is. I therefore canvass some options for change and discuss the forces that stand in the way of such change. This has the dual aim of further outlining the dynamics of the field that resist change, while possibly suggesting some avenues for intentional transformation.

Acknowledgments

This book is the culmination of a long and tortuous research project. It benefited from the generosity of many people, far too numerous to thank here. These have included educators, administrators, students, researchers, parents, and other interested people. Most should recognise their contributions in the book, even though I suspect some would initially baulk at the analysis. I hope that upon reflection scepticism will give way to recognition of the book as a true and fair account of a complex slice of reality, albeit from an unusual perspective—one that seeks to make explicit what in the normal run of things remains implicit, taken for granted and invisible.

The following pages address some highly contested and controversial issues. Some of those who helped me along the path would prefer not to be publicly associated with the project, and some have been concerned about possible recriminations. I have therefore been at pains to protect the identity of many who have contributed to the project.

The enthusiastic encouragement of many of my collaborators has been invaluable in helping me stay the course over may years. But such supportive enthusiasm has not been universal, and the political implications, both imagined and real, of the analysis that follows have caused some anxiety and consternation.

Some Arabic teachers in the Jewish sector have expressed unease about the way my research has challenged much of what they do and how they do it. I would like to emphasise that the analysis in the following pages does not seek to pass moral judgments on educators or bureaucrats. I am rather trying to identify the logic of the system that drives Arabic instruction in Israel—a system that is not controlled by any of the participants in the field.

Systemic constraints notwithstanding, Arabic teachers in the Jewish sector in Israel stand out for some remarkable personal choices. These people have crossed, for whatever reason, into the existential other's linguistic territory. It is not always a very comfortable place to be. Some of these people have charted much of the path that I myself took into the same linguistic liminal space, and I am truly grateful to them for it. In fact, if there is a tone of urgency and indignation that comes through in the book, it is testament to the great expectations that they inspired in me when they set me on that path and waved me off. They never quite told me how much more than a mere academic subject Arabic would be.

Some Arab teachers, scholars and administrators may also feel uncomfortable at some of the discussion in the following chapters. Unsolicited opinions from outsiders about highly emotive internal controversies rarely meet with unqualified acceptance. Indeed, some of those whose help has been critical to my project might feel that I have transgressed the role of a polite guest in their world. Indeed I have, and I hope that they find my unsolicited opinionated contribution useful. In any event, I hope they do not doubt the sincerity of my intention.

I would like to thank the book's series editor, Dale Eickelman, and the editorial staff at Brill for their patience, their faith in the book, their accommodation of numerous delays, and their support through the process of its production. I would also like to thank the anonymous reviewers of the original manuscript for their honest feedback. It greatly improved this book.

Charlotte, Ella and Jennifer have borne with me the brunt of the ongoing project. Their help was enormous, and probably, on balance, outweighs the disruptions that they have caused. This book is dedicated to them.

List of Illustrations

Tables

Figure

CHAPTER 1

Conundrums of Arabic Instruction in Israel

The Israeli public school system is split into distinct streams with separate administrations within the Ministry of Education. The most elementary division is between the Hebrew-language streams, which cater predominantly to Israel's dominant Jewish population, and the Arabic-language streams which cater to Israel's Arab citizens and residents.[1] Arabic is taught in the Jewish sector as a second foreign language after English, normally from seventh grade, and is available as a matriculation major. Arabic is the language of instruction in Arab-sector schools and kindergartens.

While the school systems that cater to Jews and Arabs are distinct, both lead to the one integrated tertiary education system. In fact, the tertiary education system in Israel is essentially an integral part of the Jewish education trajectory which Arabs must join for lack of an alternative equivalent Arab tertiary education.

Israel's tertiary education system is tiered with universities forming the top tier, and colleges—including teacher colleges—forming the second tier. The universities and most colleges teach in Hebrew and are effectively extensions of the Jewish school system, while a few teacher colleges that specialise in training Arab teachers for the Arab school sector carry out their instruction in Arabic. There is no Arabic-language university accredited in Israel (Amara and Mar'i 2002), and advanced, graduate-level academic Arabic instruction is monopolised by departments of Arabic language and literature at the top-tier universities.

This education system hinders Arabic instruction to both Jewish and Arab students, albeit in different ways. Jewish students, even those who major in Arabic at the matriculation level, do not achieve even elementary proficiency. Notwithstanding an entire educational career in Arabic, Arab undergraduates tend to do poorly at university grammar of Arabic both in absolute terms and in relative terms in comparison with their non-proficient Jewish peers.

That Arabic instruction should be fraught with such problems as Arab incomprehension of Arabic grammar and Jewish incapacity to gain proficiency

1 Druze schools are administered separately from other Arab schools for reasons that have nothing to do with pedagogy. Jewish schools comprise the National Stream and the National Religious Stream as well as the autonomous/independent ultra-orthodox stream.

 | DOI: 10.1163/9789004349957_002

is puzzling. The educational potential for successful Arabic instruction in the Jewish school sector is clear. Arabs form a large part of Israel's citizenry. There is therefore a large population of native speakers of Arabic in Israel who can provide a natural pool of Arabic teachers, along with meaningful contexts to use the language, rendering it a second rather than a foreign language. There is also a large number of Jews for whom Arabic is a heritage language, something that might lead us to expect students to have high levels of motivation, and the pursuit of Arabic to be meaningful in its own right. And of course, the great linguistic affinity between Arabic and Hebrew, a fact emphasised in Arabic instruction in the Jewish sector and vigorously flagged for a couple of centuries with the unfolding of the Hebrew revival, should make the acquisition of Arabic somewhat easier for Hebrew speakers than the acquisition of more substantially different languages such as English.

Furthermore, Arabic instruction in Jewish schools has always been of utmost strategic importance in Israel. It is backed by very powerful, highly prestigious and well-resourced stakeholders, not least of which is the security apparatus which continuously asserts that Arabic instruction at school is vital (Mendel 2011, 2014). These stakeholders have poured additional funds and provided extra personnel and other instructional resources to support and enhance Arabic instruction in the Jewish school sector.

The will to improve Arabic language instruction is there, the resources are there, the conditions are ripe, and the framework exists to deploy resources in pursuit of the goal. Yet the goal remains elusive. Not enough Jewish students study Arabic and those who do fail to achieve proficiency. Even graduates who major in Arabic tend to leave school with a greater proficiency in English than in Arabic. This situation has been a source of consternation ever since the inception of Arabic instruction in the nascent Jewish public school system in the days of the British Mandate over Palestine (cf. Yonai, 1992; Landau 1961). This is not to suggest that there are absolutely no Jews in Israel who are proficient in Arabic. Some are, but they are remarkably few, and none of those whom I have encountered had acquired his or her proficiency exclusively, or even primarily, through Israel's formal education system.

The failure of Arabs at university Arabic grammar is no less perplexing. Arabs undergo their schooling in Arabic and have full command of the language, or at least they should if they earn a matriculation certificate—a prerequisite for university admission. They also study Arabic grammar at school, and do so at a much higher level and intensity than do Jewish students of Arabic. Yet Arab university students struggle, seemingly inexplicably, to translate their linguistic advantage into superior performance in the most basic descriptive aspects of Arabic grammar. By contrast, the Jews who outperform their Arab peers at grammar have typically studied Arabic as a second foreign language and have nothing approaching a native command of the language.

Arab intellectuals have expressed great concern over the general level of Arabic proficiency and literacy among Arab youth, and the population more generally (e.g. Bawardi 2012a, 2012b). However justified these concerns are, the state of Arab students' proficiency does not explain the difficulties they face in the university Arabic grammar classroom. Arab students' Arabic proficiency—unsatisfactory as it may be—remains immeasurably superior to that of the Jewish students who nonetheless excel in Arabic grammar and syntax classes. Simply put, educational attainment in Arabic grammar at university correlates first and foremost with Jewishness versus Arabness rather than with Arabic proficiency.

The fact that instruction in Arabic grammar classes at universities is usually conducted in Hebrew is insufficient in itself to account for this situation. Arab university students successfully study other subjects in Hebrew. Moreover, the concepts of grammar in Hebrew should be familiar to Arab students from their own studies of Hebrew at school, as Arab schools in Israel teach Hebrew as a second language from the early years of primary school.

Like the Jewish failure to achieve Arabic proficiency, Arab underperformance at university Arabic grammar has been a permanent fixture of the education system at least since the Jewish state assumed control over Arab schooling in the aftermath of the Catastrophe (*Nakba*) of 1948. A veteran Arabic teacher and senior administrator with Israel's Department of Education recounted how Arab students had always "fallen like flies" in exams over such elementary tasks as verb conjugation. I raised with several Arab academics in departments of Arabic the troubles that beset Arab university students' comprehension of grammar. They all related to the phenomenon from their own experience. A prominent young Arab academic at one of the universities recounted how he entered into undergraduate studies in Arabic with a keen interest in grammar and love for the language, only to be hit by the grammar classes which he somehow scraped through. He then abandoned his interest in Arabic grammar, and continued on an academic trajectory specialising in literature and culture and in Islamic studies. When I tried to delve deeper into the specific difficulties he might have faced in the grammar course, he could not identify particular areas of incomprehension. The material in class on the whole was alien and incomprehensible, and the entire experience quite traumatic, especially as he had thought he was good at grammar and expected to do well in the class. This account was rather typical. A common leitmotif among Arab graduates of Arabic who pursued an academic career is precisely that completely unexpected, incomprehensible, debilitating encounter with Arabic grammar at university. Of all the sub-specialisations of Arabic language and literature, Arabic grammar, usually bundled with dialectology, is arguably the most Jewish-dominated field, more so in fact than the study of medieval Jewish Arabic texts.

We are faced, then, with two educational conundrums where the results of the classroom engagement are diametrically opposed to the professed intended outcomes of the educational process. The continuous pervasive reproduction of failure in instruction indicates the systemic nature of the problem. It is not a matter of particular teachers, students or textbooks.

The Origins of This Research Project

I initially experienced the two mysteries of Jewish and Arab underachievement in Arabic in my own personal trajectory in Israel as a student at school and later at university, only to subsequently discover that they are permanent, systemic features of Arabic instruction in Israel.

I first encountered Arabic instruction at my primary school, a small elementary school in the northern part of the then sleepy town of Rehovot. There was a short-lived attempt to add Arabic to the after-hours activities that were offered to school children along with various arts and crafts. The class was given by one of the English teachers who had originally come from Egypt, and included a few phrases in Arabic and a general outline of the Arabic alphabet. The initiative did not last long. I was unable to find out later what the intention was behind offering this course and why it was not continued.

My next encounter with Arabic instruction came at the beginning of junior high school at year seven. Students were required to choose one of two second foreign languages—Arabic or French. Early in the year students were summoned *en masse* and told they had to choose between the two. The overwhelming majority chose to study Arabic. French was perceived as useless and unduly complex. Arabic had the prestige of a language required for national security. This was in 1977. Later in the year Arabic became even more popular with the short-lived euphoria that accompanied Egyptian President Sadat's visit to Jerusalem and the subsequent peace deal between Egypt and Israel in 1979.

The subject coordinator who oversaw Arabic instruction was also the deputy principal of my high school. He was an Iraqi-born Jew who had been a reserve officer in military intelligence. He was the only Arabic teacher who lasted for the duration of my studies at the school and for many subsequent years thereafter. There were other teachers brought in, some were young graduates of teacher colleges, one was an Iraqi-born and raised man who did not have a teaching credential. None stayed for long, and the program was always starved for qualified, experienced teachers.

In year nine, in part in response to the shortage of teachers, the Arabic class was streamed. The stronger students were taught by the lead Arabic teacher and learned Standard Arabic, in line with the curricular schedule for the year. The weaker ones were taught colloquial Arabic by casual relief teachers. These students were marking time, were not expected to continue with Arabic at high school, and most were not expected to continue in the academic high school stream but rather shift to one of the town's vocational high schools.

By this stage some oddities had already become obvious to me and to my fellow high school students. Students from Arabic-speaking backgrounds were more likely to be in the colloquial-cum-inferior stream. Within the Standard Arabic stream the dominant achievers were Ashkenazi males, that is, boys with no family background in Arabic.

It is hard to reconstruct the decision-making process that culminated in my decision at year ten to major in Arabic. The attraction of Arabic included the gratification of mastering a code, along with the seduction of courting danger. Media from Egypt started arriving in Israel, and I could buy Egyptian newspapers and weekly magazines at the news agency at the central bus station. Struggling through those was quite rewarding.

Not all aspects of language use were accepted as legitimate. Listening to Arabic music was definitely crossing a line of legitimacy. The late 1970s was the time when Oriental Jewish music broke into the mainstream, receiving an increasing amount of airtime on pop-music radio programs. But even then, being caught listening to Arabic music was embarrassing. I suppose that while reading Arabic magazines put one in a position of power—one can read *their* language and understand what *they* say—being captivated by *their* music put one in a subordinate or dependent position. The difference lies in the contrast between a cold intellective response on the one hand, and an affective response on the other. By this logic, being captivated by Arabic art or music requires one to cede control to captivating Arab artists or musicians and implies identification with or subservience to them. At any rate, acquiring and sharing Arabs' aesthetics, be it in music, poetry or prose, was not as acceptable as mastering their language.

While the choice of Arabic as a second language was rather popular, few continued with Arabic as a major in the matriculation. Arabic was considered difficult, yet it lacked the rewards that accompanied other difficult subjects. It was not the natural choice for aspiring, career-minded students. Mathematics was the most prestigious choice, considered the hardest subject, followed by sciences. I did indeed have some concerned teachers question my choice to major in Arabic and take mathematics as a minor.

I ended up specialising in Arabic at the unprecedented extension of twelve matriculation units (more than twice the five-unit normal extension of a major).[2] The specialisation included five units of Standard Arabic, one unit of colloquial Arabic, two units of history of Arabs and Islam, and four units of a matriculation thesis that I chose to write on political trends among Israeli Arabs under the guidance of an external academic supervisor. It is worth noting the inclusion of the non-linguistic components in the major in Arabic.

This level of extension in Arabic was only possible because of the strong support from my Arabic teacher who enjoyed the privileges that come with also being the deputy principal and the subject coordinator at school. I was the only student at my school (and the first in the entire country, for that matter) to study Arabic at that level of extension. I participated in classroom instruction with other students who majored in Arabic up to an extension of five units of Standard Arabic, and then had additional classes on an individual basis with the Arabic teacher, mostly covering classical texts and other material which was outside the scope of the five-unit specialisation. There was no teacher in town who taught the history component for one of the years I was studying it, so I ended up cycling on a weekly basis to one of the kibbutzim nearby where a teacher was running a class on the history of Arabs and Islam.

I complemented this classroom activity with extra-curricular activities, such as participation in Tel Aviv University's extension program for academically minded youth that focused on the contemporary Middle East. In hindsight I would emphasise the significance of such programs to building motivation in students. The instructors in the course were the very same academic pundits who regularly appeared on television current-affairs programs and were quoted in the media.

As a measure of my success, and the desperate need for teachers in the system, I came to stand in during my high school years for Arabic teachers at the junior high school where I had studied.

I graduated from high school in 1982. By all measures of academic success I did well. With the highest possible grade at the highest possible extension of

2 The Matriculation Certificate is a qualification that is normally awarded upon completion of high school to qualifying students, and is essential for university admission. Matriculation grades are calculated based on the performance in uniform national tests for different subjects, which are weighted against school exams and normal grades obtained at high school. Matriculation units are standardised measures of contact hours across different subjects. To be awarded a Matriculation Certificate, students must complete a minimum number of 21 units, including one or more majors (at a minimum extension of five units), electives at a lower extension and a number of mandatory subjects.

Arabic studies, my Arabic was as good as it could possibly get at school. Yet while I had a solid grounding in morphology and elementary syntax, I was not proficient, nor was I heading towards any capacity at a proficient interaction with Arabic texts beyond narrow decoding, or with Arab interlocutors beyond superficial and highly stylised contexts such as greetings and introductions. I lacked both strict linguistic proficiency as well as cultural proficiency.

At university I initially enrolled in a double major of Middle Eastern History and Arabic Language and Literature. I was somewhat apprehensive about enrolling in Arabic assuming I would face major difficulties given I was not proficient at Arabic, and looking forward to sweating my way through to proficiency. I expected that because the program was (or so I naively believed) aimed at already-proficient students rather than at language learners, that Arab students would lead the pack with their native proficiency, a bit like native speakers of English enjoy a substantial advantage in undergraduate studies at university departments of English language and literature where non-proficient students would be ill-advised to enrol.

Reality was quite different from what I had envisaged. To my surprise, classroom instruction in Arabic language and literature was conducted in Hebrew which for me was no disadvantage. The amount of required reading in Arabic was minimal, and rarely if ever were we required to seriously engage with what contemporary Arab scholars would consider "hard" or "challenging" texts. Similarly, essays were submitted in Hebrew, and exams were conducted in Hebrew, with the minor exception of grammar classes where the illustrative examples or sample texts were rendered in Arabic, but still even then the analysis that followed and subsequent grammatical elaborations were presented and discussed in Hebrew. Some instructors who felt confident and competent enough allowed Arab students the option of submitting essays in Arabic, but the option of submitting work in Arabic was not universally available and essay writing in Arabic was never a requirement.

By normal indicators of academic success I continued to do well. In grammar classes for instance, I could conjugate any radical (root) imaginable (real or hypothetical), and took great pleasure in trying to push grammatical logic to its limit and construct the most complicated possible combination of radical, paradigm and pronoun. I might not have been able to use these verbs idiomatically, but idiomatic usage was never an issue.

I was by no means unusual in the class. Those who were doing best at grammar were all Jews. By contrast, Arab students who were taking the same courses were struggling and often failed or barely scraped through in their assignments. They did not seem to be familiar with the conceptual framework that we, the Jewish students, took for granted. They appeared to be unable to follow the logic of instruction or see the point of the conceptual apparatus we applied in class, and otherwise seemed disorientated. In conversations we had as fellow students during the semester it seemed impossible to pinpoint any specific problem they had. They rather exhibited a general incomprehension of the entire analytic framework or how and why it was deployed.

Jewish students and instructors would normally ascribe Arab students' difficulties to a complete lack of elementary background knowledge of grammar, itself the result of a supposedly inferior schooling in the Arab sector. It was never quite clear what specific aspects of background knowledge were missing. The disorientation appeared to be comprehensive and general. Collaboration among students, such as sharing notes or joint studies for exams did not usually cut across the divide between Arabs and Jews, so that the two sides could remain ignorant of the exact nature of the pedagogic incommensurability.

Some instructors endeavoured to improve the lagging Arabic proficiency of Jewish students by enhancing, however minimally, the extent of Arabic usage in the classroom. This occurred in such classes as Arabic literature, rather than grammar classes.[3] Not all academic instructors felt sufficiently comfortable teaching in Arabic, but one instructor who did—an Iraqi-born scholar of literature—instituted periods during the lesson when he would speak slowly in Standard Arabic. This caused consternation among Jewish students who were struggling to keep up, and felt at a disadvantage compared with Arab students, who were themselves bemused at having to waste much time bearing witness to strained communications in very basic standard Arabic between instructors and Jewish students, that did nothing to advance the lesson or add much to their own learning. Jewish students were quick to organise to fight this initiative tooth and nail. Similar initiatives on the part of academics to integrate Arabic into the instruction continued on a sporadic and haphazard basis with no substantial continuity and little significant effect.

---

3 It is probably not reasonable to expect individual instructors to be able to teach in Arabic the Arabic grammar that is taught at Israeli universities because the originally European grammatical approach that prevails in Israeli universities is fundamentally different from the Arab grammatical approach to Arabic, to the point that the one cannot be rendered with the terminology that prevails in the other. In chapter four I highlight the problems in translating across the conceptual divide between the grammatical framework that is taught in Arabic in Arab schools, and the European-orientated grammar that is taught in Hebrew in Jewish schools and at universities in Israel. For the European-orientated grammatical approach at universities to be taught in Arabic would require a concerted effort at a systematic translation of the whole framework. This is an enormous task, much greater than merely rendering information in different languages.

Disappointed with this state of affairs, and having lost hope of gaining substantial linguistic or cultural proficiency, I shifted to the Single-Major track of Middle Eastern History. Having been attracted to social and cultural history in the course of my undergraduate studies, I continued to pursue an interest in social sciences, and subsequently moved to study anthropology in Australia.

But the two oddities of unattainable Jewish proficiency and of Arab grammatical incomprehension stayed with me. It became clear over the years, as I grew more familiar with academic life and as I discussed the matter with others, that both are immutable, systemic features of Arabic instruction in Israel.

Having completed an MA in anthropology, I undertook studies in education and qualified as a school teacher. I toyed with the idea of returning to advanced studies in anthropology and conducting my PhD research on a Middle Eastern topic. In 1993 I explored this option in a preliminary fieldwork of about half a year in Cairo, where I improved my Arabic considerably. Having crossed to the other side, as it were, I found the realities of the Middle East confronting and decided that I had not yet reached the necessary intellectual distance to be able to engage in a considered, even-handed way with the realities of the region. I decided to proceed with PhD research into White Australian kinship, family and gender—pursuing anthropology, a distinctly Western science, in a distinctly Western cultural context. I promised myself to return to a Middle Eastern topic in subsequent research.

In 2003, two decades after I was first struck by the two stark unintended consequences of Arabic instruction in Israel, I took up the topic as an object of research. I marshalled the analytic arsenal that I had acquired in the intervening years in the course of that Sisyphean pursuit of advanced academic education, and sought to make sense of my own experience and the bewildering realities I encountered firsthand, namely how it was that I did so well, but failed to achieve Arabic proficiency throughout my studies (the conundrum of elusive Jewish proficiency); and how it was that I failed to achieve proficiency, yet did so well compared with proficient Arab peers at university (the conundrum of Arab underachievement). Not much had changed in the intervening years. Stakeholders were still bemoaning the poor state of Arabic education, curricula were reformed, initiatives announced, but all with little effect. Jews were failing to achieve proficiency. Arabs were underperforming at university Arabic grammar.

Methodological Disclosures

My reengagement with the undesired yet seemingly inevitable results of Arabic instruction is the formal beginning of the research project that has culminated in this book. But this starting point is more imagined than real. I had obviously thought about the issue in the preceding decades, and had formed a general sense of what the questions were and where the answers lay. In fact, those formal scholastic frameworks that separate data collection from analysis are entirely inappropriate models to describe the study that has unfolded since 2003.

My research did not separate the stages of data collection and analysis, but rather unfolded in an iterative way. Data collection shaped analysis at the very same time that analysis shaped the data collection. The two aspects were never entirely separable. This was particularly so as my interlocutors were not only research subjects, but also conscious participants in the field and, very often, subject matter experts too. So, for example, in discussions with academic researchers and instructors of Arabic grammar, it is not always possible to distinguish between an interview of how grammar instruction is being conducted and an analytic exploration of the implications of different aspects of grammar instruction.

My formal research was, in fact, a process of continuous elaboration and refinement of my answers to the two conundrums that have been set out above. New "data" and experiences were generated in response to the issues I was considering at any given time and helped generate further questions and empirical explorations. Theories drove data collection and interpretation to no less an extent than the data drove the theories. The processes of theoretical elaboration and empirical research largely intertwined.

I can therefore cite no formal methodological procedural standard—to the extent that there is such a beast in qualitative research—that can assure that this research is somehow objectively valid or scientifically sound. Is this study, then, anything more than a prejudicial hypothesis justified through opportunistic data collection? I claim that it is, but I cannot substantiate the claim on procedural grounds. Rather, the legitimacy of the claims in the pages that follow must rely on the extent to which they help make sense of the realities they describe, that is, the extent to which they account for the persistence of the unintended and undesired consequences of Arabic instruction, and the extent to which they make social practice understandable within the prevalent terms by which we account for social practice.

I emerged from the research incubation period—that is the period preceding 2003—with a sense that the status of Arabic and the underlying agenda of

Arabic instruction militate against the mastery by Jews of the Arabic language. The question that emerged was how it was that this underlying agenda, a seemingly external factor to classroom interaction, came to hinder the acquisition of Arabic. I also had a sense that there was something in the way Arabic was taught that alienated Arab students. I could not otherwise explain how some excellent Arab students with a masterful command of Arabic struggled with basic Arabic grammar and syntax.

My formal academic research into Arabic instruction began in late 2003 with a two-year postdoctoral fellowship at the Hebrew University of Jerusalem. This period gave me the opportunity to conduct interviews and observations, and to collect other research material (such as correspondence, exam sheets, teaching material and curricular literature). This period of research was followed by six months of research *in situ* at the Department of Arabic at Haifa University in the first half of 2007, where I continued with interviews, observations and other material collection, but also intensified the presentation of my analysis, and reformulated it in line with the feedback from those who were kind enough to listen. A further research fellowship at Cambridge University's Centre of Islamic Studies in the summer of 2009 gave me a further sounding board to develop the analysis, and gave me the opportunity to return to Israel for a brief visit to consult some additional archives and conduct a few more interviews. I later returned to Israel yet again for two weeks of final research and interviews in the summer of 2010.

Research into Arab Underperformance in Arabic Grammar

At the beginning my postdoctoral affiliation at the Hebrew University in 2003, I pored over Arab textbooks to gauge the extent to which Arabic instruction to Arabs differs from the way Arabic is taught to Jews. The difference between the two approaches was stark. Having been schooled in Arabic grammar in the Jewish sector, I found myself utterly disorientated when I tried to follow the logic of the presentation in the textbook.

This led me down the path of examining textbooks and curricular documents of Arabic on both the Jewish and Arab sides. I examined traditional and novel textbooks at the high school level and at universities (the textbooks are described below in chapters two and four). I also examined some of the primary school Arabic textbooks that were used in Arab schools in Israel. I consulted the curriculum material of both the Jewish and Arab streams, looking both at the way the educational process was conceptualised, at the rationale that was offered for instruction, and at the pedagogical formulation that it offered.

I relied initially on my own intuition in identifying areas of difference, and then proceeded to look for systematic differences in the way the material is taught and systemic differences in the way Arabic syntax and grammar are conceptualised. I looked for both variance and consistency within and between the two educational streams—the Jewish and the Arab. I examined such issues as the order in which topics were introduced (noting, for example, the attempt to push desinential inflection to later years in a recent curriculum in the Arab school system), and the way comparable aspects of language (e.g. the material covered in the Jewish textbooks as verb morphology) were carved up, formulated and presented in the two streams. What emerged was a picture of broad difference across various dimensions such as the way language is conceptualised, the way the learning process is conceptualised, the way the linguistic phenomena are broken down into topics, the tropes that are used to make sense of language, and the way the science of grammar is conceptualised and visualised. Furthermore, a difference in the emotional tonality that underlies grammar and its instruction emerged as well. I ascribed these differences to a large extent to the differences between the two distinct scholarly traditions that inform Arabic instruction in the two streams, namely the Arabic linguistic tradition that undergirds instruction on the Arab side, and the European Orientalist tradition that lies behind Arabic instruction on the Jewish side.

As my research unfolded, I interviewed several scholars, academic instructors and school teachers in the two streams to try to get a further grasp of the curricular approach that underlay the different curricula. These interlocutors contributed insights in two significant ways. They offered comments based on their unique vantage points which derived from the particular position they held within the field of Arabic instruction. But they were also participants who had been processed, as it were, within the field, and to varying degrees have experienced the workings of the field firsthand as students and learners. Interviewees included the following.

- *Three of the Arab scholars who had been involved in writing the textbook series*—al-ǧadīd fī qawāʿid al-luġa al-ʿarabīya (Abu Khadra et al 2000)—*that was introduced in the 1990s into Arab schools to replace the old textbooks that had been used since the early twentieth century:* These scholars gave me particular insights into the complexity of maintaining student interest in an unpopular subject, and of trying to chart a useful grammatic and pedagogic approach that would be of use to Arab students at schools, would be more relevant to young Arabs in the late twentieth century, would be acceptable to the intellectual elites in the Arab world, would be acceptable to the Israeli Ministry of Education, and would embrace a grammatic approach that was less distant from the Orientalist grammar that was taught at universities.
- *Two Arab grammarians holding junior academic positions:* Both had under-

gone their schooling in the Arab stream and held marginal academic positions, one as an adjunct instructor teaching grammar to Arab university students, and one a teaching assistant who had closely worked with senior grammarians of Arabic on research and instruction. Both were invaluable sources of information on the incommensurability of the approaches that prevailed in Jewish and Arab instruction into Arabic, and both exemplified the way the power relations between Jewish and Arab grammars of Arabic are inscribed into academic institutions and academics' career paths.

- *Seven academics, mostly Jewish but also Arab, who taught Arabic grammar at Israeli universities:* These provided deep insight into grammar instruction and into the extent of Arab underperformance. Interestingly, while the Jewish academics could clearly account for areas where Arab students had particular difficulties, they were unaware of the extent of incommensurability between what was taught in their classrooms and in the Jewish stream more generally, and what Arab students had learnt beforehand. While Jewish grammarians were fully aware of the nuances of classical grammatical theory and medieval Arabic grammar instruction, they were not aware of the curriculum or textbooks that were used in the Arab schools from which their Arab students and colleagues had graduated. No less interesting, the most dismissive attitude towards the grammar that was taught to Arabs at schools came from one of the Arab academics, himself a graduate of a Druze school whose wife taught at an Arab school in central Israel. His critique of the grammar that was taught at Arab schools and its demotivating effect was scathing, and he favoured its complete replacement with the approach that prevailed in Jewish schools.
- *Arab academics in departments of Arabic who did not teach grammar:* These academics had successfully passed through the educational systems from Arab schools through Arabic programs at universities all the way to advanced study and research in Arabic. They could reflect on their experiences studying and teaching Arabic in general, and their experiences studying grammar in particular. A common theme that ran through all their accounts was the alienating experience of encountering Arabic grammar at university. They could not quite account for why or how Arabic grammar was so alienating. But the experience was odious enough to drive quite a few to specialise in other aspects of Arabic programs, namely literature and Islamic culture, instead of grammar.
- *Arab intellectuals and instructors at Arab colleges:* These could attest to the relationship between Arab student teachers and grammar in their own programs, which differed from that of Arab university students. But what is more, they could attest, through their own personal careers, to the institu-

tional marginalisation of the Arab tradition of Arabic grammatical scholarship which is confined to the second-tier institutions.

- *Six Arab teachers at Arab schools:* These included teachers in the Haifa region, Jaffa and central Israel, and a principal of a private Arab school in Jerusalem.
- *Arab and Jewish university students of Arabic:* These students recounted some of their own dilemmas and problems with grammar.[4]

This outline of interlocutors should not be taken as suggesting that my observations somehow reflect a universal or commonly held understanding among my interlocutors. I set the agenda for the discussions. The interviews and discussions were usually in the form of a collaborative attempt to evaluate my tentative hypotheses, and to make sense of my observations. This was necessary primarily because there are very few people indeed who have been systematically exposed to the two approaches to Arabic-grammar instruction. Most of the specialists on the Jewish side, including those who have engaged with the history of Arabic-grammar instruction in the Arab world, have a limited view of the texts and approaches that inform contemporary Arabic instruction on the Arab side. By the same token, few specialists on the Arab side have had a comprehensive exposure to grammar instruction on the Jewish side. This is true even of those Arab scholars who endured and survived Arabic-grammar instruction at university. In other words, the interviews served mostly to help me refine and expand my observations. The conclusions that are drawn from them are my own interpretation, and they cannot be taken as adding validity through an independent concurrence of peers in the field of Arabic instruction.

In the course of my affiliation at Haifa University in 2007 I observed university classes of Arabic grammar there and at other tertiary education institutions. Most classes were mixed Jewish-Arab ones. At Haifa University grammar classes in the first two years of the undergraduate Arabic degree were taught separately to graduates of Jewish and Arab schools, allowing the university to

---

4 Lave and her colleagues (1984) followed shoppers in action and recorded the shoppers' running commentaries on their shopping decision making. This gave the researchers insight into the mental processes that shoppers use to make decisions about relative pricing and maximum utility. A similar approach to learning and thinking grammar, whereby a student would vocalise his/her thought processes as s/he engages with a grammatical task, might shed further light on the different ways students think and process Arabic grammar. However due to the sensitivities involved—both institutional and personal—I did not engage in that kind of direct interactive observation of students thinking and learning grammar. Rather, I confined myself to in-class observations and to interviews.

deliver different curricula. Over the semester that I spent at Haifa University I closely followed one of the Arab Arabic grammar courses.

The second-year grammar course was a serendipitous and enormously useful opportunity. As I describe in chapter four below, a confluence of unlikely events led to an unprecedented situation whereby three Jewish students were tacked onto the course that was taught by an Arab instructor to a class of Arab students and followed the distinctive Arab way of conceptualising grammar. This situation amounted to a role reversal. Jewish students were now learning grammar the Arab way from an Arab teacher in a classroom dominated by Arab students. These Jewish students exhibited, quite remarkably, the very disorientation that typified Arab students of Arabic in the normal course of events.

As I was clarifying my perception of the exact nature of the differences between the two ways of conceptualising and teaching Arabic grammar, I found it useful to explore the broader traditions that inform the two distinct systems of Arabic-grammar instruction, namely the Arabic Linguistic Tradition that informs Arabic instruction in Arab schools, and the European Orientalist tradition that manifests in curricula in Jewish schools and Israel's universities. I further relied on conversations with scholars and grammar instructors to help trace how the broad scholarly traditions inhere in the different curricula in the two educational systems. These scholars and instructors included researchers who worked at universities and published within the European-orientated tradition of Arabic grammar as well as researchers in the Arab sectors who published in Arabic and operated within the perimeters of the prevalent approach in the Arab world. These scholars' teaching also covered the two sectors, teaching at universities, Hebrew-language colleges and Arabic colleges. Some of these expert practitioners also held administrative positions in the education system, including inspectors and subject superintendents within the Department of Education, and this added a different dimension to their perspective.

In my limited participation in the life of the department of Arabic at Haifa, and my visits to other departments, I observed firsthand the significance of the overall political context for alienating both Jews and Arabs from Arabic. Jewish lecturers of Arabic, for example, have a niggling fear that Arab students and colleagues are waiting for them to "slip up" when they use Arabic. These fears are entirely justified. By the same token, some Arab students feel uncomfortable when required to communicate in Standard Arabic rather than dialect, especially in the presence of Jewish instructors or fellow students. The undercurrent of suspicion further inflects the Arab reception of grammatic ideas that are presented by Jews and are at odds with common Arab truisms (such as the uniqueness of the consonant ض (*ḍ*) to Arabic—see chapter three). These tensions rarely, if ever, come to the fore, and would be impervious to objective observational research. Their suppression is essential for all those who are involved in the educational exchange to function. Yet they emerged in private conversations, at moments of slippage in image management, sniggers, facial expressions, meaningful exchanges of looks and the like. Although rarely acknowledged, these ubiquitous tensions affect the experience of Arabs and Jews in Arabic departments at a very fundamental and visceral way.

During both *in situ* research periods—in Jerusalem and in Haifa—my family and I lived in Arab neighbourhoods. Living on the Arab side of town, especially in Haifa, I had ample opportunity to discuss schooling and Arabic with students, parents, teachers and others around. These included former teachers and academics, students in primary, secondary and tertiary institutions and their parents, and some instructors in Arab teacher colleges. This gave me a particularly powerful insight into the fraught relationships between Arabs and Arabic. The poor value of Arabic as an academic subject emerged as did a ubiquitous latent antagonism among Arab interlocutors towards grammatic pedantry.

Moreover, the penetration of Hebrew into Arabic and the consequent anxieties about the fate of Arabic were made abundantly clear to me, as well. Hebrew words invade normal conversations between people speaking Arabic, and provide one source of obscenities—a rather ironic situation given the common reliance by Hebrew speakers on Arabic for obscenities. The penetration of Hebrew becomes even more pronounced in SMS and email exchanges.

Unfortunately, I was unable to observe Arabic-grammar instruction in Arab primary and high schools. My contacts were not enthusiastic about such participant observation. Arab participants in Arabic instruction are wary of being perceived by fellow Arabs as collaborators, or by the Israeli authorities as trouble makers. Officialdom was not very encouraging either. Given the politically charged nature of Arab schooling, the high level of heavy-handed surveillance of Arab schools on the part of Israel's security apparatus, and the inevitable suspicions that would surround my request to observe classes at school, I judged it unlikely that I would be able to penetrate the bureaucratic barriers to such a study, and successfully manage the concerns of Arab teachers and bureaucrats whose collaboration I would need to enable me to undertake the research.

Cambridge University's Centre for Islamic Studies offered an opportunity to further engage with a community of Arabic scholars in relative freedom from the immediate circumstances of Arabic instruction in Israel. This distance allowed me to gain a broader perspective on the fraught relationship between Arabs and Arabic—a relationship that is strained independently of the complex realities in Israel. With a cadre of scholars, many of whom hailed from the Arab world, who were keenly interested in the politics of Arabic, yet removed from the stifling communal conflicts in the region, I was able to receive critical feedback, as well as highly relevant observations rooted in biographic experiences from different parts of the Arab world. I suppose that it is the unique nature of the topic that made these scholars at Cambridge play the dual role of subject matter experts and ethnographic informants.

Before embarking on the affiliation I had already started considering the significance of the problematic relationship between Arabs and Arabic grammar that is reflected in writings such as Ramzi Baalbaki's (e.g. 1995), but it was only through discussions with Yasir Suleiman and other fellows at the Centre of Islamic Studies at Cambridge who recounted their own grammatical and linguistic biographies that I came to appreciate the full significance of the overall ongoing crisis of Arabic instruction throughout the Arab world.

In the course of my research affiliation in Cambridge I also further developed my appreciation of the profundity of the differences between the European and the Arab traditions in styles of learning and teaching grammar. This, too, was possible because of the multifaceted expertise and activities at the Centre, where scholarship of classical linguistic theory coincided with research into contemporary educational policy and language curricula in the Arab world.

Research into Jewish Underachievement of Arabic Proficiency

It was when I first attended university that the depth of the disparity between my achievement and proficiency became clear to me, as did the fact that this was typical of Jewish students of Arabic. Over the years I had further opportunities to improve my Arabic, not least in a six-month ethnographic foray in Cairo in 1993. I could draw on a good grasp of formal grammar that I had acquired in the course of my studies at high school and university, but I otherwise had to cover a lot of ground.

Most significantly, I had to adopt a communicative persona in Arabic that relates to Arabs in a meaningful way. It occurred to me then that I had never in the course of my formal Arabic learning at school had to insert myself into a communicative engagement in Arabic with Arabs. During my school years I had neither the opportunity nor the reason to engage much with Arabs, other than in highly scripted, stereotypical roles, such as a buyer in a market. At university, effective communication between Jews and Arabs was mostly carried out in Hebrew. If Arabic was used, the context was brief and superficial, tending quickly back to Hebrew the moment mutual comprehension was in doubt. This applied to personal conversational interaction and, to a lesser extent, to reading. Texts of Arabic that I had read till then were read for the purpose of learning Arabic, but nothing else. In the course of my subsequent fieldwork in Cairo, perhaps for the first time, I had to engage with texts in a different way—

filling out endless bureaucratic forms, for example, or reading newspapers to glean immediate, important information about what was happening in town. Finding pleasure in reading Arabic texts for their own sake, rather than for the purpose of improving my Arabic, only came later.

My PhD course in anthropology followed shortly after. I set aside the subject of Arabic and turned to the quintessentially anthropological themes of kinship, gender and family. The tension between a view of humans as enacting rules, and a counterview of humans as free agents, had coloured much of the debate in the field. In making sense of the logic of my informants' lived experience I came to focus on cognition as historically constructed and situated. In other words, the way people perceive and judge the world around them and the way they respond to the world are largely affected by their experiences and social locations. Hence people who occupy similar social locations tend to share a common sense, and act in mutually comprehensible ways, giving rise to spontaneous behaviour of seemingly free-willed people who nonetheless adhere to regular patterns of conduct. It was then that I started thinking of my Arabic learning experience as a useful angle to study cognition as embedded in fields of practice.

With this in mind I later began my postdoctoral affiliation at the Hebrew University. At first, I thought of my project as a dual project. One component was the Arab underperformance at grammar instruction at University. The other was the failure of schools to develop Arabic proficiency in Jewish students of Arabic. I was not at all clear as to how the two would link up, and it was only as the project evolved that I came to see the two as different aspects of a similar configuration of power. But for the most part, I researched them separately.

Thus, in parallel with my deep dive into Arab textbooks of Arabic grammar that I mentioned above, I sought to gain a general view of Arabic instruction in the Jewish sector, and to understand my own personal experience learning Arabic within its historical context. I engaged with senior officials in the Ministry of Education, with academics in departments of Arabic at different universities and colleges, and with teachers at several schools in the Jewish public school stream. In these discussions I sought to delve into the evolution of Arabic instruction in Israel.

My contacts gave me access to curricular documents and administrative material relating to the administration of Arabic instruction. I also reviewed material used for professional development of teachers, most notably the many volumes of the journal that was issued by the Ministry of Education's Arabic Inspectorate for teachers of Arabic in the Jewish stream.

I attended ten classes of Arabic instruction at high schools in central Israel, and attended a conference of teachers of Arabic that was conducted at Haifa

University and gave me an insight from another angle into the leitmotifs of the saga of Arabic instruction in Israel. The one-day conference brought together Arab and Jewish teachers of Arabic to discuss Arabic instruction in both the Jewish and Arab sectors. But the joint nature of the event was evidently inauthentic and forced. The first half of the day was dedicated to instruction in the Jewish sector, was conducted predominantly in Hebrew, and had no relevance to the Arab participants. The second half of the day was dedicated to instruction in the Arab sector, was conducted predominantly in Arabic, and was irrelevant to the Jewish teachers, almost all of whom fizzled out shortly after the second half of the day began. There was no cross-over of themes from the Jewish to the Arab halves of the day. During the Arab half of the day some of the early speakers tried to speak in Hebrew to include the Jewish participants most of whose command of Arabic was insufficient to handle Arabic presentations. But as the Jews dissipated, and the Arab teachers—whose frustration had simmered as they sat through the irrelevant, Hebrew-speaking Jewish half of the day—insisted on moving to Arabic, the presenters moved to Arabic as well.

This conference was important not only in enacting some of the unpleasant truths about Arabic instruction in Israel, but also in allowing me to talk to teachers, administrators and academics, raise some hypotheses—most notably the problems of poor Arabic proficiency among Jewish teachers, and the centrality of the security agenda to shaping Arabic instruction in Jewish schools—and get an overwhelmingly candid confirmation of many of these observations. I suppose this was in part the result of my being a part insider, having majored in Arabic at school and undertaken Arabic courses at university, and this might have helped go beyond some of the obfuscation that might be encountered by a complete outsider.

I also discussed Arabic instruction with high school students that I met during my observations at schools, and with parents of Arabic students that I met socially or casually. The people I spoke with were not a representative sample, and the discussions were not standardised interviews. But the conversations reiterated some common themes such as the notion of Arabic being useful for a career with the intelligence apparatus, but not much more, and that returns on educational investment in Arabic were quite low given how demanding Arabic was, especially when compared with other low-value subjects like literature.

In early 2005 I delivered a seminar presentation at Beit Berl College to students who were training to become teachers of Arabic in the Jewish sector, and to their instructors. I raised the mysteriously elusive proficiency in Arabic and canvassed my analysis of the construction of Arabic as a subject matter at school. A lengthy discussion followed. The response was overwhelmingly positive especially to my provocative use of the term "Latinisation" to describe how the political underpinnings of Arabic instruction in Israel combine to produce a curriculum that constitutes Arabic as a dead language and drives a wedge of alienation between the student and the language. Students recounted their own personal experiences and frustrations, some of which were illuminating and were used in subsequent papers. I was struck by the emphatic confirmation of my evolving understanding of the situation. Moreover, my contention that the alienating aspects of Arabic instruction were an inherent aspect of the field of Arabic instruction rather than an accidental, haphazard outcome, was strengthened by the fact that Arabic had remained just as Latinised, and proficiency just as elusive to Jewish students of Arabic as it had been in my time at school over two decades earlier, and in fact since the inception of Arabic instruction in secular Jewish schools (see chapter two).

By the end of my postdoctoral affiliation with the Hebrew University of Jerusalem, my basic understanding of the contours of the field of Arabic instruction was set. The nuances kept on being worked out in the subsequent affiliation I had at Haifa University in 2007, and then the research affiliation at Cambridge.

One issue that stood out to me during my 2007 sojourn at Haifa University was the uneven level of Arabic proficiency among Jewish academics. It was in this period that I followed Jewish academic specialists in Arabic who were not proficient in Arabic. I was particularly struck by an academic who specialised in medieval Arabic texts who was admittedly not proficient in Arabic and who did not feel the need to become proficient. That particular academic was quite right-leaning politically and maintained a hostilely suspicious attitude towards Arab students.

My research period at Haifa raised some other themes. A series of informal conversations and formal interviews with Professor Reuven Snir and others brought into sharp relief the obsolescent place of the Arab Jew, as it were, or the Arabic cultural production of autochthonous Middle Eastern Jews. Snir wrote about Iraqi Jews (1985). He also pointed out the missing place of Arabic in much of the agenda of radical Mizrahi Jews—Israeli Jewish intellectuals and activists who hail from Arab countries who seek to claim their space within Israeli culture, although some have subsequently discovered the Arabness of their Mizrahi heritage.

During that period I also presented a paper about my research at a departmental colloquium. The series was organised that semester by one of the department's Arab academics. I asked him if I could present in Arabic. He was amused by the suggestion and said he thought it would be a good idea. I did. I had originally intended this as an act of personal development—presenting a paper in Arabic in public. It turned out to be an act of political subversion. It was the only paper presented in Arabic in the series that semester, and the dynamics during and following the presentation allowed for much of the normally implicit politics of language usage in the department to come to the fore (as I discuss in the next chapter).

My subsequent stay in Cambridge coincided with Mendel's historical research into the securitisation of Arabic and its instruction in Israel (e.g. 2011, 2014). Discussing some of the commonalities of our experiences learning Arabic in Israel was powerfully reassuring, and his detailed historical study of the securitisation of Arabic instruction in Israel helped me fill in gaps and nuance my understanding of the bureaucratic machinations that underlay the evolution of Arabic instruction in Israel.

Fields as Systems

The two conundrums of Arabic instruction are "wicked" analytic problems (cf. Rittel & Webber 1973, 160). The definition of the problem, the identity of the components involved, the inherent dynamics of the field, the boundaries of the issues and the shape of the "solution" must all be constructed as part of the analysis of the problem. They are not pregiven.

The analysis in this book develops a unified conceptualisation of the structures of the field of Arabic instruction and of the subjectivity of agents in the field. It builds on Bourdieu's conceptualisation of field and habitus. It treats the apparent elements of underachievement—the two conundrums—as products of a system rather than as aberrations. It proceeds to identify the agents that cooperate to produce these products, albeit unwittingly, and the relationships between them. The heuristic nature of the concept of field, at least the way I deploy it here, allows for the field to be constructed in a way that can serve to account for the remarkable persistence of two unintended and undesired consequences.[5] The boundaries of the field do not overlap with administrative or institutional boundaries. For example, the security apparatus is not part of the formal structure of Arabic instruction, yet it is included in the field because it affects the way the field functions. Similarly, the labour market and its segmen-

5 By heuristic approach I mean to say that I use concepts as heuristic devices. For example, I am not relying on an abstract definition of field and asking whether Arabic instruction is a field. Rather, I am asking what we can learn about Arabic instruction by treating it as if it were a field. The heuristic approach makes it easy to reconcile Bourdieu's sociology of practice with systems approaches. Indeed, as Dale Eickelman pointed out (1979), Bourdieu's conceptual arsenal is most effective when embedded in ethnographic reality rather than when reified and elaborated in abstract.

tation are not part of the formal structure of Arabic instruction, yet one cannot understand the dynamics of Arabic instruction if one ignores the effects of the labour market and its segmentation.

The framework of social fields also allows for the specific relationships between the elements that make up the field to be captured as they are negotiated through practice. For example, the values that are attached to skills and knowledge—Arabic literacy being a case in point—can be conceptualised as symbolic capital, and this allows for a consideration of how their value can shift across society, and how it is determined by the web of social and economic relationships.

By seeking to explain how the system of Arabic instruction produces the two species of underachievement—the Jewish and Arab—I sought to tie together the broad political processes, close interpersonal interactions, and subjective experience. The notion of habitus helped bridge the conceptual gap between social structure and subjectivity. The principle of habitus sees the subjectivity of social agents as formed by the specific positions they occupy within the field. These agents' subjectivity, in turn, serves to affect the structure of the field in which they operate.

The dynamics of the field of Arabic instruction in Israel conform to some dynamics that have been identified in the various branches of systems studies (e.g. cybernetics and system dynamics—Heylighen and Joslyn 2001, Forrester 1990). For example, I describe the cycle of non-proficiency of Arabic instruction in the Jewish sector in chapter two below. This cycle is an example of a reinforcing feedback cycle.

It was by drawing on Bourdieu's sociology of practice, and on the logic of systems thinking that I was able to develop a unitary approach to confront the two seemingly disparate riddles that drive the book—that of Jewish failure to achieve proficiency in Arabic notwithstanding a genuine, well-resourced drive to promote Arabic proficiency among Jews, and the alienation of Arabs from Arabic grammar. Overlapping forces seem to drive both instances of underachievement. The next few chapters describe these forces in action.

CHAPTER 2

The Field of Arabic Instruction in Israel: Underachievement in the Jewish Sector

Chapter 1 discussed two related factors that have conditioned the evolution of Arabic instruction in Israel in various, often contradictory ways.[1] One is the modernist Zionist project of inventing a Jewish nation by bracketing off Jews from gentiles and reconstituting them as a distinct Hebraic ethno-linguistic community. The other is the project of securing historic Palestine as an exclusive national homeland for this newly invented nation (cf. Eyal 2005). Both elements—the constitution of Jews as an ethno-linguistic community and the establishment of an exclusive national homeland in Palestine—are essential constituents of modern Zionist particularism. The influence of both elements on Arabic pedagogy has been decisive and pervasive, yet contradictory and unpredictable, demonstrating the autonomous nature of fields of practice.

This chapter focuses on the teaching of Arabic in the mainstream Jewish educational trajectory, that is, in Hebrew state schools that cater to Jews, and in the academic system, where Jewish and Arab educational trajectories typically overlap. English instruction serves as a notional yardstick to help highlight pedagogical choices in Arabic instruction. After identifying some differences in the ways English and Arabic are taught in Israel, I use the concept of cultural capital to outline the systemic significance of these differences. Bourdieu's conceptualisation of "field" then helps explain the systemic logic of Arabic instruction in Jewish schools.

Bourdieu's field is a construct that makes it possible to model specific contexts of social interaction as a set of positions that people or groups may occupy as they confront each other in what can be constituted as struggles over stakes that are inherent in the field. In other words, field is an analytic metaphor that accounts for social interaction as if it were a game of sorts, only the rules and the stakes of the game are themselves also part of the game itself and are not pregiven (see e.g. Bourdieu and Wacquant 1992, 94–115). This analytic approach

1 This chapter builds upon the analysis in "Arabic Instruction in Jewish Schools and in Universities in Israel: Contradictions, Subversion, and the Politics of Pedagogy," *International Journal of Middle East Studies*, 2010, 42(2):291–309, doi:10.1017/S0020743810000061.

 | DOI: 10.1163/9789004349957_003

aims not only to describe the way the field works, but also to account for the intractability of some of its features and the way the complex realities of the field impose themselves on participants in the field, thereby determining the range and limits of stakeholders' possible action and shaping the outcomes of specific courses of action, although not necessarily in a predictable or controllable way.

Language Instruction in the Jewish Sector: English versus Arabic

It is instructive to juxtapose the pedagogical choices made in developing the teaching of English and Arabic as foreign languages in Israel. This comparison reveals the different imperatives and constraints that shape English and Arabic instruction in Israeli Jewish schools. While English is taught as a living second language, Arabic is Latinised, as it were. It is generally taught in the Jewish sector as if it were a textually bound, dead language, to be decoded and interpreted rather than creatively used for communicative purposes.

Thus, Arabic classes are taught in Hebrew. In fact, most of the schoolteachers of Arabic in the Jewish sector and a substantial number of university lecturers in Arabic are not sufficiently proficient to teach Arabic classes in Arabic (Hayam-Yonas and Malka 2006; Brosh 1997, 111–131; Lustigman 2008, 174; Spolsky and Shohamy 1999, 128, 144–149; Spolsky, Shohamy and Donitsa-Schmit 1995, 23–25). By contrast, schoolteachers and university lecturers of English are usually fluent speakers of English, many are native speakers, and teaching is generally conducted in English. In many schools, English teachers have a policy of speaking only English with students, even outside of class, although this is by no means universal (Spolsky and Shohamy 1999, chapter 7; cf. Spolsky, Shohamy and Wald 1995).[2]

Arabic instruction is focused on Modern Standard Arabic. This is not in itself an aspect of the Latinisation I am discussing here. Unlike Latin, Standard Arabic is a living linguistic register the proficient mastery of which requires the full set of linguistic skills, both receptive and generative. However, the very pedagogical approach that has in fact been adopted in teaching Standard Arabic neglects generative participatory skills in favour of non-participatory

2 It is hard to estimate the ratio of native-speaking English teachers in Israeli schools. Spolsky and his colleagues surveyed schools in the mid-1990s and put the figure at 40 percent for Jewish high schools. This varies widely by region and by the socioeconomic standing of the school catchment areas (Spolsky, Shohamy and Wald 1995).

receptivity and a narrow focus on decoding skills. This is facilitated by the way Arabic's diglossia is often misinterpreted sociolinguistically (cf. Ferguson 1959).

It is easy to slip into the misconception of Standard Arabic as a purely textual language, and ascribe its Latinisation to its linguistic nature. But the notion of Standard Arabic as the frozen language of reading and writing and of colloquial Arabic as the living language of speech is misleading for two reasons. First, writing and reading are integral living aspects of the linguistic lives of contemporary Arabic speakers. Second, neither the registers nor their contextual use are clearly demarcated in practice. Modern Standard Arabic is used throughout the Arab world in speech in many living contexts, and likewise, colloquial Arabic is integrated into many texts for different effects and for various reasons. In fact, all linguistic events draw to some extent on both registers, even in the minimal situation when only one register is apparently used. For instance, in a literary text or a speech delivered entirely in Standard Arabic the distance between chosen turns of phrase and their colloquial equivalents are crucial in making expressions turgid and arcane or straightforward and plain. Ultimately, a full proficiency in Arabic is predicated not only on the mastery of both registers (or more accurately, both families of registers), but also on the art of their integration (Ferguson 1963). Diglossia is merely a partial alibi for Arabic's pedagogical Latinisation in Israel, not its cause.

In contrast with Arabic instruction, English classes emphasise generative usage and cultural competency through such assignments as compositions and conversational exercises in order to develop and enhance the capacity of pupils to express themselves in the language. By comparison, school instruction and matriculation examinations in Arabic emphasise passive understanding and overvalue grammatical skills such as the conjugation of decontextualised verbs and basic desinential inflection, while undervaluing the capacity to construct meaningful utterances and express ideas (Brosh 1997, 117–121. See also Spolsky and Shohamy 1999, 174 ff.).

This duality also exists in university instruction. A comparison of departments of English language and literature with departments of Arabic language and literature is revealing. Nominally, both sets of departments assume that the students have largely mastered the target language before enrolment. However, advanced English instruction at university assumes a much higher level of mastery than does advanced Arabic instruction. The amount of reading, writing, and spoken presentation required in the target language in departments of Arabic is incomparably less than that required in departments of English.

This state of affairs is remarkable, given Israel's linguistic demography. More Israeli citizens and residents are native speakers of Arabic than English. These are mostly non-Jewish Arabs, but also autochthonous and immigrant Jews from the Arab world (Amara and Mar'i 2002; Spolsky and Shohamy 1999).[3] There is therefore a large pool of potential teachers who are proficient in Arabic and who can sustain the instruction of Arabic as a living language. Moreover, university standards for Arabic proficiency need not be less than for English in order to accommodate students' prior proficiency. In fact, the number of Israelis who could sustain an Arabic-saturated university program is greater than those whose mother tongue is English. But crucially, the former are predominantly non-Jewish Arabs and the latter are predominantly Jews.

In addition to the curricular choices, the different value attached to Arabic and English is made clear by the extent of their instruction at different points on the school trajectory. In Jewish schools, English is taught as a compulsory subject from primary school, normally third grade. It is usually only at seventh grade that Arabic is introduced into Jewish schools, when pupils are given the choice between Arabic and French as a second foreign language. English is a compulsory subject for all matriculating students and is normally taught at a level equivalent to a major or near major at those high schools that follow the matriculation curriculum. By contrast, the second foreign language is typically taught from seventh to only ninth or tenth grade. It is not, at least in practice, a required matriculation subject, although it is available for matriculation both as a major and as an elective.

School practices further reflect the stark difference between the value of English and Arabic instruction. Schools invest considerably in maintaining and supporting immigrant English-speaking students' native knowledge. Many schools run special classes for English speakers or, at the very least, support English speakers with special assignments, and help English-speaking children maintain and develop their native proficiency. By contrast, knowledge of Arabic from home meets with no support in Jewish schools (Spolsky and Shohamy 1999, 140, 151ff.).

Clearly there is a marked difference in the standards and approach to language and its pedagogy between English and Arabic instruction. English is prioritised in the allocation of curricular and instructional resources, intensely promoted, and taught as a vibrant, vital skill. By contrast, Arabic is of greatly reduced urgency and is inculcated as a set of passive, receptive skills rather than as a crucial communicative asset. This difference runs through all levels of instruction in the Jewish sector and at universities in Israel.

---

3 While the ratio of school-age Jews who currently speak Arabic at home is low, the educational situation was not substantially different a generation or two ago when the ratio was much higher.

Arabic as Cultural Capital

Language proficiency is an element of what Bourdieu has dubbed cultural capital, that is, the knowledge, skills, and dispositions that are acquired through social interactions (Bourdieu 1986). These are conceptualised as capital because they carry with them value which is ultimately interchangeable with other forms of capital.

Pedagogical policy and practice carry profound implications for the differential valuations of literacy and fluency. In the case of Arabic in Israel, educational practice devalues native knowledge of the language while, by contrast, native fluency in English is highly valued. Moreover, university departments of Arabic language and literature carry out instruction primarily in Hebrew (Cf. Spolsky, and Shohamy 1999, 128, 144–149; Spolsky, Shohamy, and Donitsa-Schmit 1995, 23–25), thereby creating a strong overvaluation of Hebrew proficiency as against Arabic proficiency. In fact, the capacity to speak Hebrew and the capacity to write English are the two verifiable linguistic prerequisites for appointments and promotion in university departments of Arabic. Command of Arabic is neither essential nor regularly demonstrable because university instructors of Arabic language and literature are not normally called upon to communicate in Arabic. There are no proficiency tests for graduates or faculty in university departments of Arabic, nor are there any for Arabic school teachers. Departmental business, seminars, and conferences are usually conducted in Hebrew and, when foreign scholars are involved, in English. While there is some variation depending on the preference and capacity of the instructor, and on the student composition of the class, Arabic classes are taught overwhelmingly in Hebrew. I have observed some exceptional situations where instructors sought to employ slow and simple Standard Arabic interspersed with Hebrew summaries, and other situations where Arab instructors would use formal speech in an intermediate register that combines colloquial and Standard Arabic. Initiatives like these often meet with suspicion and resistance from Jewish students who struggle to keep up with the Arabic, and from Arab students who struggle to put up with the much slower pace and simplistic level of Arabic discourse. This was true of the time I was an undergraduate student of Arabic (chapter 1), and continued in the time of my research. Such sporadic exceptions notwithstanding, Arabic use in instruction remains rare and is mostly confined to instructors whose native tongue is Arabic.

In this way not only is the native knowledge of Arabs devalued, but so is the diasporic knowledge of Arab Jews, in contrast with the equivalent diasporic knowledge of substantial groups of European Jews. This reflects two processes.

One is the overvaluation by the global political economy of European colonial languages, and English in particular. These languages are the international languages of commerce, technology, science, and of power in general (cf. Fishman, Cooper and Conrad 1977). Even though Arabic is nominally an official language in Israel and English is not, English carries far greater currency than does Arabic. This reality of global political economy is amplified by segregation within Israeli society, and by the work of bureaucracies with an exclusive Jewish outlook. The segregation of Israeli society is such that very few Jews have the opportunity to interact with Arabic speakers beyond superficial, laconic exchanges (Spolsky and Shohamy, 1999; Brosh, 1997; Lustigman 2008). The moment they operate outside the narrow confines of Arab society, Arabs, too, normally use Hebrew. The forces of the linguistic market are further amplified and reinforced by bureaucratic imperatives. In calculating university entrance scores, universities add bonus points for preferred matriculation subjects such as mathematics and English. Arabic attracts no bonus (Amara and Mar'i 2002, 83). This means that Arabic is of greatly reduced value as cultural capital, a vicarious measure of the marginalisation of Arabs in the Jewish state.

The other process is the broader project of de-Arabising Arab Jews. Core to this process is what Suleiman calls language subtraction (Suleiman 2006a). Suleiman suggests that the subtraction of Arabic was strongly motivated by the European outlook of the early Zionist elite, coupled with the existential conflict with Palestine's non-Jewish majority. But I believe language subtraction and cultural differentiation were even more fundamental than that, as demonstrated by the collapse of some other diasporic languages such as German. The urgency of language subtraction stemmed from the ideological void left by Zionism's radical secularism and its rejection of diasporic religiosity as a basis for national identity. The newly constituted Jewish nation was left without a positive definition or a shared, common identity. The reconstitution of Jewishness as a secular ethno-linguistic identity required the immediate establishment of Hebrew as its exclusive language in conjunction with secularisation, modernisation, and separation from both the gentile and the religious, diasporic environments. Hence the urgent and radical nature of the de-Arabisation of autochthonous Middle Eastern Jews. Hence, too, the absence of any assimilation or "civilising" interest in non-Jewish Arabs.[4] De-Arabisation has been further reinforced by some oppositional trends and moods in the Arab world

4 Jew and Arab as national or ethnic categories have been bureaucratically reified through a system that defines a person as a Jew or Arab explicitly (through the population registry) and effectively (through the differential deployment of law and bureaucracy), so that nearly all in Israel (with but a handful of exceptions) know their "place" regardless of whether they accept

that embrace Zionism's basic dichotomous distinction between Arab and Jew, all but eliminating the place of the Jewish Arab (Brosh and Ben-Rafael 1994; cf. Shohat 1999; Shenhav 2003; Snir 2005).

The revaluation of cultural capital reproduces in the realm of linguistic proficiency the social structure and the hegemonic self-image—that is, the dominant vision of social division—of Israeli society. It is a Zionist self-image of a distinctly Western and modern, Hebrew-speaking, Jewish, Israeli nation, an image that reduces Jewish Arabs and Israeli Palestinians to oxymorons (cf. Eyal 2005).

Arabic Educational Policy and Practice

The prevailing social order greatly conditions the place of Arabic and the patterns of its instruction, but it does not determine these patterns. To account for the systemic nature of the seemingly fluctuating yet little changing practice of Arabic instruction I will incorporate Bourdieu's notion of field, a heuristic device that serves to identify the specific dynamics that shape particular segments of social reality (e.g. Bourdieu 1985). Being a relatively distinct area of practice, Arabic instruction lends itself to the application of the concept of field. The field's origins can be traced back to the period of autonomous Jewish schooling in Mandatory Palestine. In fact, most of the contours of the field had been established by the 1940s, and have held relatively constant regardless of changing circumstances.[5]

The Politics of Schooling

One originary trait of the field is the subversion of official policy at the local level of practice. For instance, there seems to have always been a general consensus among policymakers that Arabic should be made compulsory for Hebrew-speaking students, and that Arabic is best taught at school in Arabic (see the collection of policy documents and pedagogical debates in Yonai 1992 and Landau 1962). Yet no less remarkable than this ongoing consensus is its

---

it or identify with it. Moreover, this invention has been largely successful, as demonstrated by the active popular participation of Jews in Zionist particularism.

5 Spolsky and Shohamy's comprehensive review describes much of this reality, without, however, accounting for its intractability. While highlighting the major deficiencies in Arabic instruction, they do not account for the systemic compulsions and constraints that have shaped this field independently of the volition of any of the stakeholders, and that have made such deficiencies recalcitrant (Spolsky and Shohamy 1999).

failure to materialise in practice. Such policies are repeatedly subverted at various levels. A 1976 decision by a Knesset Committee to make Arabic compulsory throughout high school was ignored, and then a 1988 policy decision by Minister of Education Yitzhak Navon to make Arabic universally compulsory from seventh to twelfth grade was not acted upon by his own ministry. When policy steps were, in fact, adopted by the ministry, they were subsequently subverted, or severely diluted, at the local level of schools (State Comptroller 1996; cf. Hayam-Yonas and Malka 2006, chapter 1). Policymakers have so far been unwilling or unable to force the issue.

This state of affairs is remarkable given the impressive weight of the forces that push for the expansion of Arabic instruction. These have included academics, functionaries involved in teaching Arabic such as supervisors at the Ministry of Education and Arabic teachers, and some sympathetic ministers of education. In this they have been allied with the very powerful security apparatus—most importantly, Military Intelligence—with its enormous resources and insatiable need for loyal—that is, Jewish—Arabic speakers.

The Intelligence Takeover of Arabic Instruction

Military Intelligence is probably the most powerful driving force in the promotion of Arabic instruction in Jewish schools (cf. Mendel 2011, 2014). Military representatives have participated in virtually all commissions of inquiry into Arabic since the 1960s. The military is also represented on the Arabic Language Subject Committee, which steers Arabic instruction within the Ministry of Education.[6]

The rationale provided by Military Intelligence for the promotion of Arabic at schools is straightforward: Israel needs Jews who understand Arabic to help protect the Jewish State from the Arab threat, and also to facilitate at the national level a strategic engagement with the peoples of the region. This need

6 See Military Intelligence (I.D.F.). *T.L.M.* (Section on development of the study of Orientalism), https://www.aman.idf.il/modiin/general.aspx?catId=60384 (accessed 4 February 2017). As an indication of the hegemonic domination of the military in this area, one might also note that the State Comptroller's staff, in formulating their report on Arabic instruction, consulted the military and dedicated much space in the report to the military's need for Arabic speakers. No other body outside the Ministry of Education and the teaching force was consulted. The report formulators did not even feel the need to explain this preoccupation with the military at a time when academic departments and other stakeholders were not consulted and their interests in school education were not explicitly considered. The central position of the military in the area of Arabic instruction is taken for granted. See State Comptroller 1996.

is particularly acute since the generation of Jews who emigrated from Arabic-speaking countries is retiring or dying out and is not being replenished.

Military Intelligence is involved not only at the level of policymaking and implementation but also with the actual teaching of Arabic in Jewish schools. This involvement has taken various forms, including the creation in 1986 of *šifʿat*, a unit within the Ministry of Education that operated until 2001, was staffed by military personnel and headed by a senior intelligence officer, Nissim Atzmon, who had previously played a critical role in developing the military's in-house Arabic training apparatus. *Šifʿat* was charged with improving and broadening Arabic instruction, and also administered the national testing scheme of Arabic at Jewish schools. Military Intelligence also provides special educational camps and intelligence paramilitary training to young cadets, puts suitable high school pupils in touch with intelligence units that seek to target future conscripts, and provides a raft of speakers, teaching aids, and other material to support Arabic instruction at schools. Promising pupils are invited to summer camps and other activities of the *gadnaʿ mizraḥanīm* (literally, Youth Regiments of Orientalists). Arabic instruction at school also includes such activities as excursions to the National Memorial for the Commemoration of the Fallen Members of the Intelligence Community and motivational talks by intelligence officers.[7] Military Intelligence also funds educational development for teachers and endorses instructional material such as textbooks and dictionaries that are used at schools. Furthermore, the military reinforces the teaching staff of some schools, usually junior high schools in peripheral towns, with conscripts who are trained to teach Arabic (Military Intelligence, T.L.M.; State Comptroller 1996; Lustigman 2008, 170–171; Mendel 2014, chapter 4).

The very open involvement of Military Intelligence in Arabic instruction at Jewish schools in itself helps lift the status of the subject. Much of the informal curriculum, and a substantial part of the formal curriculum, revolve around preparing Jewish students for their impending military service. Building up the military significance of Arabic is thus a critical aspect of promoting a positive attitude among students towards the subject, lifting its prestige, and attracting academically successful students to it. Arabic teachers, for their part, actively seek military involvement in their classes as an effective means of increasing student motivation.

The formation of *šifʿat* under Minister of Education Yitzhak Navon marked the culmination of a takeover by Military Intelligence of Arabic instruction at

7 For example, see a report on one such visit in the *Journal of the Teachers of Arabic and Islam* 25 (2000):59.

the high school level (State Comptroller 1996, 374; Lustigman 2008, 174; Mendel 2014, 172 ff.). Arabic education in Jewish schools came under the effective direction of Military Intelligence in partnership with the Ministry of Education. The school and military Arabic curricula became coordinated into an integrated whole.

But with all the efforts that Military Intelligence puts into promoting Arabic, the results remain unsatisfactory from an intelligence perspective (State Comptroller 1996, 367–378; Lustigman 2008, 172). *Šif'at* was disbanded in 2001 as Zionist politics shifted further towards exclusivist nationalism.[8] While Military Intelligence continues to dominate Arabic instruction at schools, there is a general sense that the intelligence community cannot rely on schools and will be obliged to continue training its recruits to make up for the gap in their Arabic proficiency. The emergent symbiotic relationship is such that schools focus their teaching on the passive comprehension of Modern Standard Arabic. Military Intelligence then uses this knowledge base to further train its recruits in advanced Standard and colloquial Arabic.

The military thus becomes the major venue for post-secondary acquisition of communication skills through training, most effectively through active service, where Jews have the opportunity to use Arabic. With very few exceptions, Jews who have achieved any measure of command of Arabic within the Israeli education system are graduates of Military Intelligence Arabic training. But even this process leads to a circumscribed proficiency, one that is limited to "security" types of interactions.

Odd Coalitions

The Israeli security apparatus is not alone in promoting Arabic instruction. It is the autonomous nature of the field that allows for contradictory social forces to come together and, in this case, military efforts are reinforced by radical Israeli Arab political leaders who are concerned with improving the status of Arabic in Jewish schools. In the report of the Knesset (Parliament) Education Committee investigation into the teaching of Arabic, Arab Communist Member of Knesset Tawfiq Tubi outdid his colleagues by issuing a minor-

---

8   The decision was taken under the extremist duo of then Education Minister Limor Livnat and her Director General at the time, Ronit Tirosh. Tirosh was quoted as saying that the "Arabic language is identified in Israel with people who make our lives hard and damage our security ... This is a problem and therefore we suggest not forcing Arabic studies on pupils in schools as this would just not be beneficial" (Mendel 2014, 175). In her subsequent political career, MK Livnat has turned extinguishing the last vestiges of Arabic's formal status as an official state language into her *cause célèbre*.

ity recommendation to effectively make the teaching of Arabic compulsory throughout the education system (Knesset 1986). As of March 2017 there are five private member's bills before the Knesset Education, Culture and Sports Committee that would make Arabic instruction compulsory in Jewish schools. These have been submitted by members of Knesset ranging from staunch Arab activists like Joint Party's Jamal Zahalka and Hanin Zoabi (draft bill p/1104/20) all the way to right-wing Jewish settlers like Likud representative Oren Hazan (draft fill p/1637/20).[9] Similar educational initiatives come from liberal Jewish and radical Arab Jewish NGOs that seek to promote coexistence, such as the Abraham Fund's attempt to reinstate colloquial Arabic instruction in primary schools (an early practice that dwindled over the years and was finally abandoned in the late 1980s), or Hand in Hand's initiation of private bilingual schools.[10]

More remarkable than the constellation of forces that militates in favour of deepening and broadening the instruction of Arabic at schools is the fact that it has so far been singularly unsuccessful. Subversion from below restricts the breadth of Arabic instruction, while other players in the field, especially universities and teachers, restrict its depth.

Subversion from Below

Initiatives from above are thwarted from below by pupils, parents, and principals. The critical areas where decisions are subverted are the prioritisation of resource allocation at schools and, more significantly, the local action of teaching staff and students (cf. Mendel 2014, 148ff.). For their part, principals direct teaching resources (teaching time and budgets) to subjects that are tested at the matriculation level and away from marginal electives and non-examined subjects, even when this may involve contravention of explicit policy. This is sometimes achieved through highly irregular means. At least one principal has gone so far as to cancel the compulsory Arabic instruction at his school and hand out fictitious term grades to students. The supervisory staff at the Ministry of Education generally turn a blind eye to such practices, which, in fact, were revealed to me by one of the inspectors at the Ministry of Education. The State Comptroller reports on other techniques of reducing Arabic class sizes, including exempting weak students from Arabic classes so that they can focus on more central subjects (State Comptroller 1996, 372).

---

9 None of the bills stands any realistic chance of getting a hearing, let alone become law.

10 Abraham Fund. http://www.abrahamfund.org/ (accessed 7 June 2008); Hand in Hand, http://www.handinhandk12.org/ (accessed 14 December 2009).

The ministry's quiescence is recognition of two main facts. One is that a full implementation of all official curricular policies is unrealistic given the limitations on resources that are available at the local level. Official policy is seen, at best, as a wish list or, at worst, as a cynical, vacuous political statement that is made exclusively for the record or for public consumption. The other fact is the limit of the supervisory powers to confront a coalition of principals and parents. There is a common perception that in such situations being too dogmatic may end up in a political blow-out. Moreover, there is a split within the Ministry between those functionaries who are responsible for ensuring the smooth operation of schools—by making realistic compromises—and the subject inspectors who act as advocates for their own particular subjects. It is, in fact, the negotiations between these two sets of mid-level functionaries that shape many of the prevalent pragmatic compromises.

The inability to formulate coherent policy and to enforce existing policy is often camouflaged by intentional vagueness and ambiguity in policy statements, leaving much scope for mid-level machinations. In 2003, for example, internal correspondence from the ministry to principals stated that a policy decision had been made to reiterate Arabic's compulsory status at Hebrew schools from the seventh to the tenth grade, and to include a compulsory Arabic test in the matriculation examinations at the minimal level of one unit. These policies had been decided at the ministerial level but as it turns out, were progressively diluted down the rungs of the bureaucratic ladder all the way to the classroom. In most secular, public Hebrew schools Arabic continues to be generally offered as an optional second foreign language between seventh grade and ninth grade, and is often not offered at all in tenth grade (Hayam-Yonas and Malka 2006). There was never an enforcement of the compulsory inclusion of Arabic in the matriculation examinations. Indeed, it appears the policy decision that was mentioned in the correspondence I discussed above was never made public and was subsequently abandoned. In other words, effective policy—the policy of bureaucratic enforcement and resource allocation—failed to support the declared policy of Arabic instruction, reflecting a deep level of indecision and ambiguity at the top echelons of the Ministry of Education.

For their part, parents and pupils generally support the principals' concentration of resources on "important" subjects. In fact, many pupils resort to additional means to avoid wasting energy and scarce resources on subjects that are not examined at the matriculation level. In the last four decades, many students have been taking advantage of a mushrooming private market in educational psychology, where one can effectively buy certified exemptions from the study of a second foreign language on the grounds of a learning disability, allowing them to continue studying English, but freeing them from the compulsion of studying Arabic or French.

To further understand the motivations of parents and pupils we must consider the political economy of foreign language literacy, and especially the previously discussed devaluation of Arabic in contrast with the revaluation of English. The devaluation of Arabic and revaluation of English affect the way both are articulated to the personal and national interest. Learning English is motivated by personal interest, that is, by the benefits such knowledge bestows upon its bearer as an individual. It is taught in order to help pupils in their later years. A good mastery of English is a prerequisite for entry into university and is a highly valued skill in the labour market. It is deemed essential for professional, financial and personal success.

Learning Arabic is not of personal value as such, but rather of strategic, national (i.e. particularist Jewish) significance. Its benefit lies not in immediate palpable personal gain, but rather within the national interest, that is, the Zionist project. Maintaining a reservoir of Jews who can understand Arabic is deemed to serve this interest. While majoring in Arabic may lead one to a well-remunerated career with the security apparatus or diplomatic service, it makes little utilitarian sense to study Arabic for any other reason (cf. So'en and Debby 2006).

This explains how social agents who share ideological dispositions may come to adopt contradictory positions in the field. Official policymakers, as guardians of the national (that is, particularist Jewish) interest, are motivated by the demands of the perennial existential conflict with Arabs to strengthen Arabic instruction to Jews. Yet it is the refusal to accept Arabs as a permanent legitimate part of the Israeli collective that has led to the devaluation of Arabic. Moreover, the very same fear and loathing of Arabs leads parents, children, and principals who have little to gain from knowledge of Arabic to identify Arabic with Arabs, and to consequently adopt contradictory strategies and practices and resist Arabic instruction emotionally, aesthetically, and practically (see Brosh and Ben-Rafael 1994, 341–344; So'en and Debby 2006). One Jewish teacher of Arabic recounted how after a suicide attack in the centre of Israel, she came into her tenth grade classroom to find "Death to Arabs" written across the blackboard. This was not unusual. Several teachers and supervisors observed that the continuing conflict creates a mental block in some students towards Arabic in particular, and Middle East studies more generally.

These classroom hostilities towards Arabs and Arabic echo some broad contemporary political trends in Israel. Over the years there have been numerous attempts, motivated by a blend of chauvinism and populist opportunism, to eliminate or reduce Arabic's special status. These include legislative attempts to scrap the status of Arabic as an official language (Ilan 2008), government regulation to eliminate Arabic place names from road signs (Roffe-Offir 2009), and policy attempts to remove Arabic from the compulsory core of school instruction (Qashti 2008).

This clash between different interests—all motivated in various ways by a single, underlying particularist imperative—exemplifies that social and political practice is always mediated through fields of practice. The same particularist outlook thus produces mutually antagonistic positions towards Arabic instruction. It drives Military Intelligence to promote Arabic instruction, but motivates populist chauvinists to oppose it. By the same token, opposed imperatives that are embodied on the one hand by the security establishments and on the other hand by an Arab Communist Member of Knesset can produce a shared agenda of deepening and broadening Arabic instruction.

The Role of Universities

Along with the intelligence and security establishment, another major institutional framework that critically affects Arabic instruction at schools is the set of university departments of Arabic language and literature. Universities play a central role in cementing the status quo and preventing schools from emphasising generative language skills in Arabic instruction.

Academia influences school education in various ways. The Subject Committee in the Ministry of Education is charged with curricular development and determines such issues as textbook selection. It is dominated by academics, and is chaired by a professor, normally from the Hebrew University of Jerusalem. Moreover, the bulk of Arabic teachers—and especially the leading ones—are trained at universities (cf. Hayam-Yonas and Malka 2006, 46–81, 142–174). Even those who have been trained at teacher colleges will find themselves at universities once they rise through the ranks and require an advanced degree.

But it is not only that teachers are trained at universities. One of the major targets that shape curricular development at school is university entrance exams and curricula. Ideally, graduates of the school system should be able to perform well at universities. This imposes a requirement on both schools and universities to harmonise their curricula. The domination of the ministerial Subject Committee by academics ensures that this happens.

The intellectual and institutional orientation of academic teaching and research in Arabic is crucial. Israeli academia has always seen itself as part of the Western academic world. Arabic instruction in Israeli academia was initiated by European-trained scholars in the various fields of Orientalist scholarship, and has formed an organic and integrated part of European Orientalist scholarship ever since (Eyal 2005). The rejection of Israeli academia and scholarship by academia in the Arab world has reinforced this position.

The Orientalist heritage bequeathed Israel's academia an aloof philological approach to Arabic, one that positions itself as a non-participatory observer of Arabic usage. It emphasises passive decoding rather than creative mastery of the language, and treats its subject matter rather like Classics departments treat theirs. Legendary Professor Meir J. Kister of the Hebrew University is reputed to have advised a student who was concerned about the level of proficiency acquired at university, "If you wish to learn to speak Arabic, go to Berlitz."

Significantly, university departments of Arabic language and literature, like university departments of other major foreign languages and literature (e.g. English), are not strictly teacher-training programs, and the function of teacher training does not top their curricular priorities. Moreover, they nominally assume that students are proficient in the target language. What makes Arabic departments different, then, is not so much that they do not prioritise teaching proficiency in the various language skills (as that is not their avowed role), but rather that they tolerate the absence of proficiency among both students and instructors.

The philological approach was instrumental in fixing the language of instruction in departments of Arabic as Hebrew (in sharp contrast with departments of English where instruction is in English), and in devaluing Arabic proficiency in the implementation of instruction and in appointments. Consequently, university students complete their academic studies of Arabic without developing a balanced Arabic proficiency. By proficiency I mean the full set of linguistic skills, namely reading, writing, listening comprehension, and speaking, and ideally also appropriate paralinguistic performance and cultural proficiency. Many of these Jewish university graduates of Arabic subsequently become non-proficient teachers, who teach a school curriculum that does not produce proficient graduates. These non-proficient high school graduates then join the universities from which they graduate without proficiency to make up the next generation of non-proficient teachers (and academics). Thus emerges a sustained cycle of non-proficiency.

The majority of academics in Arabic language and literature departments—Jews who are non-native speakers of Arabic who have graduated from the Israeli education system—have an inevitable stake in the status quo regardless of whether they choose to support it or not. Changing the language of Arabic instruction at universities to Arabic will necessarily come up against the fact that a significant proportion of the lecturers are not sufficiently proficient to deliver instruction in Arabic, and may not be able to compete with academically trained Arabs. In chapter 1 I mentioned one such person—a tenured senior lecturer who specialised in medieval Arabic manuscripts. He readily conceded his limited proficiency, and claimed that my research inspired him to begin reading Arabic translations of European novels he had already read (e.g. by Dickens) in order to improve his mastery of contemporary Arabic. When I asked why he did not read novels by Arabs he replied that he was not interested in Arabic literature which he considered inferior. He did not pursue his reading of Arabic translations for long. Otherwise, he communicated with his Arab students and colleagues exclusively in Hebrew, and had no opportunity or reason to communicate in Arabic either verbally or in writing. In the period following my research trip he was further promoted eventually attaining full professorship. This particular academic is an extreme example, but demonstrates how unessential Arabic proficiency is for an academic career in Arabic.

The overlay of ethnic and personal politics, rarely explicit yet always present, accentuates the problem. This was brought home to me following the presentation I gave in Arabic at a departmental seminar. As mentioned earlier, mine was the only paper delivered in Arabic that semester. My forty-five minutes or so of presentation were followed by questions and answers in Arabic. Later that day, in a private conversation, one of the Arab adjunct instructors pointed out to me, in a gloating tone, that none of the Jews asked a question. He explained that they could not really speak Arabic, and were too scared to do so in such a public forum. I responded that I must have made a considerable number of mistakes myself, to which he laughed and responded "*ġalṭat al-ǧāhil basīṭa, wa-ġalṭat al-ʿālim faḍīḥa*" (roughly meaning that the mistake of the uneducated is not serious, but the mistake of the learned is scandalous). While the broad generalisation about the Jewish academics in the department was exaggerated—at least a few were fully proficient in Arabic—the quotidian performance of Arabic proficiency is clearly embroiled in intercommunal personal politics.

In addition to the communal-cum-personal politics of intellectual authority, the fact that Jewish schools produce non-proficient graduates would put these students at a disadvantage compared with Arab students if they had to undergo university instruction in Arabic. There is thus a pervasive concern that a shift to instruction in Arabic would reduce the interest of Jewish students in the subject, and result in Arabs dominating the ranks of both students and academic staff in Arabic departments (a process that may well be under way at Haifa University, where the relative value of Arabic proficiency in the curriculum is higher than it is at other universities and where Arabs are the overwhelming majority of students in Arabic). This concern was communicated to me by a senior Jewish academic. It was couched not in anti-Arab sentiments as such, but rather in a concern for the survival and administrative well-being of a department that would be stigmatised by the university and the public as composed of and catering exclusively to Arabs. In many ways, then, the fact of Arab superiority in Arabic proficiency retards the use of Arabic and the acquisition of Arabic proficiency by Jewish academics and university students.

The cycle of non-proficiency is particularly stable due to a lack of alternative sources of proficient teachers. Those Jews who have been trained by the security apparatus in Arabic are quite likely to have reached some level of proficiency, however they are unlikely to join the school teaching force because their career options within the security and bureaucratic apparatus are much more attractive. The generation of proficient Jewish immigrants, mostly from Iraq, which once accounted for a large number of Arabic teachers in Jewish schools and for leading Jewish scholars and writers of Arabic (e.g. Samir Naqash, Shimon Ballas, Sasson Somekh, Shmuel Moreh) is now largely retired. And Arab teachers, for reasons I will discuss below, are not integrated into the faculties of Jewish schools.

Segregation, Teacher Proficiency, and the Limits of Action in the Field

The scope of possible action within the field and the limits on it are themselves negotiated in practice as agents seek to influence and modify the conditions of Arabic instruction. Initiatives embarked upon by alarmed subject coordinators in the Ministry of Education to improve Arabic instruction by addressing the lack of proficient teachers demonstrate some limits on action. One seemingly straightforward way to overcome the paucity of proficient Arabic teachers would be to integrate Arab teachers of Arabic into Jewish schools. But the segregation of the teaching force persists in line with the communal-cum-ethnic segregation of Israeli society in general.

Officially, there is no policy of segregating the teaching force. Yet Arabs account for a meagre portion of Arabic teachers in the Jewish sector. The figure that is usually cited is "fewer than five percent" (roughly 50 of 1,200 teachers). However in a recent representative survey of Arabic instruction that was co-sponsored by the ministry, only 1.7 percent of responding teachers at the junior high schools were Arab, and not a single Arab teacher was found in the high school sample (Hayam-Yonas and Malka 2006, 46–81, 142–174).

When I questioned ministry administrators on the subject, they offered two kinds of explanation for the paucity of Arab teachers. One doubted the compatibility of Arab teachers with Arabic instruction in the Jewish sector. Such explanations highlight, for instance, difficulties that confront native speakers who teach their mother tongue as a second language.[11] Such difficulties may apply to individual teachers, but do not account for the broad phenomenon. Native speakers of English are the preferred teachers of English in the Jewish schools, and likewise, native French speakers are the preferred teachers of French. There is no inherent reason why the same should not apply to Arabic. Furthermore, the first few decades of Arabic instruction in the Jewish sector in the period following the proclamation of the State of Israel were marked by the integration of Arab Jews, mostly Iraqi Jews, into the teaching force. Evidently, the native mastery they enjoyed did not hinder their teaching of Arabic.

Moreover, Modern Standard Arabic—the core of Arabic instruction in the Jewish sector—is not quite a mother tongue. It is the colloquial Arabic dialects that are acquired the "natural" way by Arabs. Standard Arabic is acquired in part through formal instruction, although this acquisition is backed up by passive exposure in daily life and by the commonalities with colloquial Arabic. This further detracts from the credibility of ascribing the paucity of Arab teachers in the Jewish sector to some general difficulties in teaching one's mother tongue as a second language.

Another set of explanations, though, seems to account more directly for the lack of integration of Arab teachers into Jewish schools. These explanations revolve around the resistance of Jewish principals, parents, and teachers. This takes essentially two forms: one is a refusal on the part of principals to deploy Arab teachers; the other is the continued hostility and harassment of employed Arab teachers by students, parents, and staff. Such local interactions are critical in shaping, reproducing, and changing the field.

An experimental program seeking to train Arab teachers of Arabic for Hebrew schools was initiated and quickly abandoned in the 1990s after it became clear that none of its graduates was successfully integrated into Jewish schools.[12] A senior supervisor who is intimately familiar with this aborted initiative insists that Arabic is the toughest subject for an Arab teacher to teach in a Jewish school because the topic itself is emotionally charged and confounds attitudes towards Arabs with attitudes towards Arabic, profoundly straining the classroom interaction for Arab teachers of Arabic to Jews. The subject, in

---

11 Such rationalisations are by no means new. See the 1946 background briefing by the supervisor of Arabic in the Education Department of the Jewish Assembly in Palestine. Israel Ben Zeev, "*hora'at ha-ʿaravīt bi-shnat* 1946," in Yonai 1992, 36–38.

12 The program was administered at Givʿat Haviva College, and has yet to be studied by independent scholars. Givʿat Haviva archives contain the material and correspondence associated with this program. (For a general discussion of Givʿat Haviva College's Arabic program see Mendel 2014, Chapter 5).

fact, invites resistance and hostility from students and colleagues. By contrast, Arab teachers of "neutral" subjects such as mathematics integrate much more smoothly into Jewish schools.

Furthermore, Jewish resistance to Arab teachers of Arabic can be further aggravated by vested interests. When I raised with a Jewish teacher the question of integrating Arab teachers into the Jewish sector, her first response was that this would deprive the Jewish Arabic teachers of work. She then added that it may also not be a good idea "for security considerations". She could not specify what kind of security breach such a scenario would entail other than the general sense that it would be simpler, safer, and less worrisome if Arab teachers were kept away from Jewish children.

A related problem is that Military Intelligence's domination of Arabic instruction makes it hard to integrate Arab teachers, especially into high schools. Arabs—particularly educated ones—are public risks that Military Intelligence prefers to avoid, thereby potentially denying them much of the educational and curricular support that Military Intelligence normally provides to Arabic teachers in Jewish schools. Moreover, a significant role of high school instruction for Jews in Israel is preparation for military service. By virtue of their very being, Arabs cannot be part of this. They are integral elements of the perceived existential security threat and therefore excluded from military service. Ultimately, the entire security rationale of Arabic instruction would fall flat if delivered by Arabs.

The difficulty of integrating Arab teachers into the Jewish schools is further aggravated by a general incompatibility between the way grammar and syntax are taught in the Jewish sector, and the way they are taught in the Arab sector. I have examined some of the curricular documents that were drafted for the course that aimed to train Arabs to teach at Jewish schools, and there was little in the way of preparation for those teachers to handle the Jewish school curriculum. As I discuss in subsequent chapters, the approaches to grammar in Jewish and Arab schools are incommensurable, yet this incommensurability is overlooked by both Jews and Arabs, and experienced as individual incomprehension by those who need to negotiate their way through the alternative grammatical approach. Such incomprehension has likely been significant in thwarting the integration of Arab teachers of Arabic into Jewish schools.

Ultimately, the program failed. Arab teachers could not be successfully integrated into Jewish schools. With very few exceptions, Arab teachers of Arabic remain excluded from Jewish secondary schools. The ministerial administrators who ran the aborted training program to integrate Arab teachers into Jewish schools came crashing against the field's limits. They subsequently moved to redirect their efforts towards increasing Arabic proficiency among the Jewish teachers already in the system. They and others have turned to trying to ameliorate the poor level of Arabic proficiency among Jewish Arabic teachers through in-service training—with limited success. This sub-optimal option seemed more realistic than integrating fully proficient Arabs. Such pragmatic compromises are forced by the overarching segregation of Israeli society even as they reproduce and reinforce it.

Ongoing Contestation within the Field

There are ongoing struggles and negotiations that are actively playing themselves out, as it were, in the field, albeit with little change in practice. One of the most contentious issues has to do with the choice of register and level of Arabic to be taught in Jewish schools. Currently the concentration in instruction is on Modern Standard Arabic—and especially journalistic prose—with an emphasis on passive comprehension and the inculcation of formal rules of syntax and grammar. Students who specialise in Arabic may elect to undertake an additional unit of colloquial Arabic, but this is taught at a very rudimentary level and remains marginal to the Arabic major.

Two challenges to this Latinised approach are currently circulating in the field. One calls for the greater integration of colloquial Arabic, with the rationale of promoting verbal communication skills among students and enabling them to communicate with Arabs in the normal quotidian language. The other seeks to enhance the focus on Standard Arabic, but to move beyond decoding journalistic prose into the realm of aesthetics, generative writing, and personal expression in Modern Standard Arabic. The idea here is to enhance creative proficiencies along with cultural understanding and empathy among students, thereby enabling students to meaningfully engage with Arab culture.

The peculiarity of Arabic diglossia pits these two challenges against one another. Arabic poetry and the bulk of creative writing are expressed through Standard Arabic, which is removed from the colloquial variations. Thus, the promoters of cultural empathy and literary self-expression find themselves opposed to those seeking to promote verbal communication skills through refocusing the instruction on colloquial Arabic, even though both seek to replace the pedagogically alienating Latinisation of Arabic.

There is an underlying sociological and institutional logic to the different positions. The argument for shifting towards poetry and expressive literature emanates from elite circles of Arabic linguists and Arabic educators. The call for a shift to a focus on colloquial Arabic has a higher currency with sociologists and educationalists (not necessarily proficient in Arabic), and in the general public with support from students, parents, and principals who are frustrated by students' lack of effective Arabic communication skills in spite of years of Arabic education.[13] Proponents of colloquial Arabic suspect that Arabic communication skills elude students because of an excessive preoccupation with Standard Arabic, which they often (wrongly) perceive to be an essentially dead and irrelevant language, an impression sustained by the prevalent classroom practices they encounter. A common image of Arabs as essentially illiterate further detracts in the eyes of some Jewish parents and teachers from the value of Standard Arabic that is somewhat misleadingly dubbed in Hebrew "literary Arabic" (*ʿaravīt sifrutīt*—ערבית ספרותית).

By contrast, academics in university departments of Arabic who are involved in the classroom teaching of Arabic remain committed to an instructional concentration on Standard Arabic. Their position is sustained for reasons well beyond Eurocentric philological prejudice. Contrary to a common perception, the devaluation of colloquial Arabic is not itself a product of Western approaches, but rather an integral part of language ideology among educated Arabs. In fact, Western dialectology accords colloquial Arabic more academic respect than do most traditional and contemporary Arab scholars.

It is not only the ideological framing of Arabic diglossia that supports the contemporary concentration on Standard Arabic in instruction, but also the structure of the language. The morphology and syntax of Standard Arabic are more stable and regular than the colloquial variants, making the former easier to teach and learn, at least to Hebrew speakers. In fact, a good grounding in Standard Arabic facilitates the acquisition of a dialect, but not necessarily vice-versa (Weisblatt 2002; Levin 2002). Once a student has command of Standard Arabic, s/he requires relatively few rules of transformation to work through the bulk of the complications added by Palestinian dialects to the morphology and syntax of Standard Arabic.

Furthermore, the surrounding social context does not provide for exposure to colloquial Arabic and thus does not support its acquisition. The segregation of Israeli society is such that when Jews communicate with Arabs it is almost invariably in Hebrew, making it unlikely for ordinary Jews to find much opportunity to interact in Arabic. By contrast, print and electronic media are easily available to complement and support classroom instruction of Modern Standard Arabic on a continuous, long-term basis.

---

13 Much of the debate can be seen in contributions to the *Journal of the Teachers of Arabic and Islam*, and echoes of it can be gleaned from the open comments made by principals and students that are cited by Hayam-Yonas and Malka 2006, chapters 2–3.

Finally, Jewish Arabic teachers, the vast majority of whom have not been taught colloquial Arabic, are even less proficient in colloquial than in Modern Standard Arabic, so that when they do try to teach colloquial Arabic, they all too often create an unidiomatic variant that does not conform to any spoken dialect (cf. Brosh 1997, 121–123). It is therefore a combination of the position of prominent academics in Arabic, the structure of the language (the relative regularity of Modern Standard Arabic), the segregation of Israeli society, and the distribution of knowledge of Arabic among Jewish teachers that make it highly unlikely that the curricular focus on Standard Arabic will be displaced or substantially weakened.

Some of the same issues would impede the greater emphasis on creative literature, and none more so than the limits of the linguistic and cultural proficiency of teachers. The semi-official *Journal of the Teachers of Arabic and Islam* published a series of Arabic poems and short stories that were translated into Hebrew and analysed, but the limits on teachers' mastery of the language hinders any shifts in the curricular focus and, *ipso facto*, the effective instruction of the culturally appropriate integration of colloquial and Standard registers (cf. Ferguson 1963). Moreover, the militarist ethos of Arabic instruction is ideologically and emotionally discordant with attempts to turn Arabic instruction into an exercise of empathy with Arabs, or turn the acquisition of Arabic into an orchestrated enhancement of self-expression and self-exposure.

There is another conceivable curricular contestation, namely the emphasis on Arabic as a Jewish heritage language. This could be achieved by highlighting medieval Jewish-Arabic literature (texts written by Jews in Arabic, typically with Hebrew characters) and modern Jewish dialects. But this alternative construction of Arabic is irrelevant and gets no traction in Israel. The general irrelevance of this posture serves to further delineate the limits of the possible and probable within the field. Jewish dialects are not integrated into instruction, even in regions that have been dominated by Jewish immigrants from particular Arab countries. When colloquial Arabic is taught, it is invariably a Palestinian dialect (or a badly mutilated version thereof). Medieval Jewish Arabic is appended as a few brief snippets in selections from classical Arabic literature, without a systematic discussion of the linguistic reality in which they emerged. The practice of Arabic instruction continues to constitute Arabic as a non-Jewish language that is largely irrelevant to the historic Jewish experience (Brosh and Ben Rafael 1994, 339–341).

This is clearly not a deliberate imposition from academia. Medieval Jewish Arabic texts and Jewish dialects continue to be a major interest in Israeli academia. But efforts to raise teachers' awareness of the possible significance of these studies[14] have failed to trickle down the walls of the ivory tower of academia, and do not seem to have had a palpable effect in the classroom. The non-Arabness of Jews has become axiomatic in Israeli society. Thus, Shlomo Alon's historical review of the explicitly articulated goals that drive Arabic instruction in the Jewish sector shows that Arabic is always constituted as the language of the Arab, gentile other, and there is no mention of the Jewishness of Arabic or the aim of connecting to the cultural heritage of Arab Jews (Alon 1987). Not surprisingly, then, in a recent survey teachers thought the new curriculum must do more to improve student motivation to learn Arabic, yet they were disinclined to emphasise the link between Arabic on the one hand and Hebrew and Jewish heritage on the other (Hayam-Yonas and Malka 2006, 191).

The lack of interest in medieval Jewish Arabic and in recent Jewish Arab dialects further attests to the narrow security-oriented agenda that underlies Arabic instruction in Israel, and the successful de-Arabisation of Arab Jews.

Implications

The systemic logic of the field of Arabic instruction in Jewish schools raises themes that are relevant well beyond the narrow context of Arabic instruction in Israeli schools. First and foremost, it demonstrates the inherently political nature of technical choices. Pedagogical choices such as the language register that is taught, the language in which instruction is carried out, and the standards of teacher selection and training cannot be understood independently of their political context, even though they cannot be mechanistically reduced to particular political positions. The Zionist project of Jewish hegemony in Palestine conditions the field of Arabic instruction. But it is a measure of the autonomy of the field that the influence of Zionism is contradictory. We see how a single political imperative can inspire the adoption of contradictory positions, while conflicting imperatives may lead to practical overlap. The threat to the Zionist project that is imposed by the very Arab existence in Israel both motivates and retards Arabic instruction. Similarly, opposing agendas—those of the militarist and of the radical communist Palestinian—can motivate similar positions, in this case in favour of broadening Arabic instruction to Jews.

Arabic instruction forms a relatively autonomous field of social practice with unique dynamics. These dynamics are conditioned by other fields of practice

14 See, for example, *Journal of the Teachers of Arabic and Islam* 27 (2002):35ff.

and by powerful institutional agents whose positions regarding Arabic instruction are part of broader agendas. These include the critical influence of the political economy of linguistic proficiency (part of the process of anglophone globalisation), the strong involvement of Israeli Military Intelligence, and the profound influence of academia.

The field of Arabic language instruction remains dynamic, although its fundamental contours do not seem to be changing much. Rather, the *modus vivendi* that was reached at a very early stage seems stable. This is notwithstanding profound historical transformations in the country and the political economy, as well as in conditions of Arabic instruction, such as the availability of Arab Jews beginning in the 1950s and later the availability of Israeli Arab teachers.

No one professes to be satisfied with the current state of affairs, but most stakeholders seem to have learned to adapt to it. For the time being, Arabic proficiency seems set to remain elusive to most Jews in Israel, at least those who seek it through Israel's formal education system.

CHAPTER 3

The Tertiary Education System and the Double Alienation of Israeli Arabs from Arabic

Chapter 2 focused on the systemic dynamics that hinder Arabic instruction in the Jewish sector. It is time to shift the focus to the Arab sector in Israel, and discuss the alienation of Arabs from Arabic-grammar instruction.[1] The fact of alienation from Arabic grammar is not unique to Israeli Arabs. Arabic-grammar instruction in the Arab world in general has been in a state of crisis for generations, but the particular nature and the surrounding circumstances of Israeli Arabs' alienation from Arabic grammar instruction are quite unique. This specific alienation is accentuated by Israeli Arabs' double marginalisation—their marginalisation within Israel and from the Arab world.

Two integrated aspects of Arabic-grammar contribute to the alienation of Arabs from Arabic-grammar instruction. One is the institutional structure of Arabic education in Israel and its underlying power dynamics. This is the subject of this chapter. The other is the distinct ways Arabic grammar is conceptualised and organised for instruction in the Jewish and Arab educational systems. This is the subject of the next chapter. These two aspects are not independent. The difference between Jewish and Arab conceptualisations of grammar becomes significant because of the configuration of power in institutionalised education and the particular ways the educational trajectories of Jewish and Arab students intertwine.

A caveat is in order. My ethnographic research was not primarily focused on the Arab school system, and the literature on the subject is scant. This chapter is therefore by no means a definitive account of the issues confronting Arab Arabic instruction in Israel. It relies on interviews and discussions with Arab academics and Arab university students of Arabic, Arab school teachers of Arabic, educational administrators in the Arab school sector, and on curricular material.

Arabic instruction in Israel has been structured around the educational trajectories of the dominant Jewish population. Arab schooling was grafted, however unnaturally, onto the national—that is, Jewish-focussed—structures of

1 Earlier versions of some sections of this chapter were included in "Arabs and Arabic Grammar Instruction in Israeli Universities: Alterity, Alienation and Dislocation," *Middle East Critique*, 2012, 21(1):101–116, doi: 10.1080/19436149.2012.658499.

 | DOI: 10.1163/9789004349957_004

education. Consequently, there is a discontinuity in Arabic instruction between the schools that Arabs normally attend—Arabic speaking schools that conform to Arab curricular conventions of Arabic instruction—and the Hebrew-speaking, European orientated universities. Arab schools are Arab spaces, albeit under Jewish oversight, that are focused on Arab students. By contrast, universities are distinctly Jewish educational spaces that are structured around Jewish students and primarily support Jewish school educational systems, spaces into which Arabs are admitted as individuals but never quite integrated as a legitimate, distinct collective. The role of universities in shaping the effects of Arab schooling is no less critical than their role in influencing Jewish schooling, but the way that universities affect Arab schooling is fundamentally different from the way they affect Jewish education.

The tertiary level of Arabic-grammar instruction is one location where overarching communal power relations are negotiated in practice and translated into an instructional and linguistic reality. What makes universities a particularly critical site in the field of Arabic instruction is the fact that universities produce, control and hegemonise linguistic knowledge through their monopoly on its production, evaluation and circulation, and the fact that universities ultimately underwrite teacher training and curriculum design for schools.

The political reality of educational practice embodied in the contours of the field of Arabic instruction makes the Jewish knowledge dominant to the point that Arabs are compelled to engage with it not on their own terms, while Jews are not normally required to engage with Arab knowledge at all. Arabic grammar is a particularly acute area where the politics of knowledge overwhelms every aspect of teaching and learning. Jews and Arabs learn different grammatical systems at school. Jews experience grammar as coherent both across different languages that they learn, and throughout their educational career. It is essentially the same grammatical framework they learn in Hebrew grammar classes and in Arabic grammar classes, and it is the same framework that is taught at school and at university, often relying on the very same textbooks. Arabs, by contrast, experience grammar as incoherent and discontinuous across languages and along their educational careers. The grammar of Arabic that they learn at school is fundamentally different from the grammar of Hebrew that they learn at school, and from the grammar of Arabic they are exposed to at university, although the profundity of the difference evades notice by both Arabs and Jews, as the next chapter suggests. I will return to this issue below when discussing the role of universities.

This situation comes on top of a much broader crisis in Arabic instruction across the Arab world. The ongoing troubled relationship between Arabs and

Arabic, forms a baseline that is reinforced and complicated by the marginalisation of Israeli Arabs within the Arab world. These two combined aspects of Arabic instruction are critical to the alienation of Arabs from Arabic grammar. In fact, by the time Israeli Arab students arrive at university their relationship with the grammar of Arabic is already fraught with profound difficulties. And this fraught relationship in its turn is taken to a higher level of alienation by Arabic-grammar instruction at universities.

I gained an interesting insight into the problem when I received copies of an entrance exam for graduates of Arab schools, that was administered by one of the university departments of Arabic language and literature. (There are different entrance exams for graduates of the Jewish and Arab school systems. Jewish applicants would have sat for a different exam.)

At the time, I was trying to get aggregates of grades and other data to allow for a quantification of the ubiquitous phenomenon of Arab comparative underperformance at Arabic grammar. Concerns over privacy, both genuine and contrived, along with the general unease generated by the political sensitivity of the issues raised by my research prevented academic institutions from sharing the relevant data with me. While I was unable to get aggregate data, I obtained access to specific exams. These included the answer sheets to this entrance exam that was administered to applicants for admission to the Department of Arabic from the Arabic school streams. I was given copies of the material on condition that I did not identify the university where the exam was administered or the individual students who took it.

The structure of the exam and the relative performance of applicants in the different sections were revealing. The exam had two parts. The first presented the students with an uninflected paragraph in Arabic. The initial task required the applicant to mark the full desinential inflection[2] of all words in the paragraph. This was followed by three questions on the content of the paragraph. Section two included two exercises for verb conjugation. The first exercise provided conjugated verbs (and included pronominal suffixes) and asked for an analysis of radical, structure and person. The second provided a verb in the perfect tense and asked for it to be conjugated according to a given tense and person.

The relative significance accorded to each of the sections is interesting as it reveals much about the different value that the drafters of the exam ascribe to different aspects of language knowledge. The desinential inflection of the

2 Desinential inflection is the vocalisation at the end of the word that reflects its syntactical function or position.

whole paragraph amounted to 30 percent of the final grade, each of the three questions on the paragraph was worth 10 percent, and each of the two verb conjugation exercises was valued at 20 percent. In other words, verb conjugation accounted for 40 percent of the entrance exam score, while desinential inflection accounted for 30 percent. This is significant because verb conjugation is particularly highly valued compared with other aspects of grammar in Arabic grammar on the Jewish side, while desinential inflection is the central concern in the Arab stream Arabic instruction. The priorities in the entrance exam tend to reflect the Jewish rather than the Arab valuation of grammar. Also noteworthy is the complete absence from the exam of the stylised declamation of the desinential inflection, central to Arab Arabic-grammar instruction. The exam reflects a set of priorities that matches Western sensibilities much more than it does the traditional Arab preoccupation.

Nonetheless, this exam was specifically designed for graduates of Arab schools, and includes exercises which are similar to those that are included in the matriculation examinations in Arabic for students in the Arab sector. The first section of the exam—which required reading comprehension, response to open questions, and the desinential inflection of a paragraph—would have been entirely out of the range that graduates of Jewish schools could handle.

Twenty applicants sat for this specific exam. Eight of them were admitted. Two students' scores on the desinential inflection exercise, expressed in percentage, were over 80 percent. The rest of the grades, summarised in table 1 in the column entitled "Full inflection", were poor. The range of the grades, and the generally poor level of attainment are remarkable.

Turning to verb conjugation, the first of the two verb conjugation questions gave a conjugated verb and asked the students to indicate the paradigm (الوزن), the radical (الجذر), the tense (الزمن) and the person (الضمير). The verbs were يِنسى، تمادَّ، لم أحامِ، تَسِرنَ، يسرُّ، موسِرُ، إسْرِينَ، يَأسِرْنَ.

The second exercise gave a verb in the past tense and asked for it to be conjugated by tense and person. Here are the terms:

إحْتَجَّ—ماض، انا ؛ صلّى—امر، انتَ ؛ دعا—امر، انتِ ؛ خافَ—مضارع مجزوم، هو ؛
استقام—إسم فاعل، أنتما ؛ إنقضى—ماض، هم ؛ وأل—اسم مفعول، هم ؛ صَادَ—ماض
مجهول، هي.

The students' scores are given in the two columns under "Part 2: Verb Conjugation".

TABLE 1 *Entrance exam for graduates of the Arab school stream—summary of grades*

Student number	Part 1: Uninflected paragraph				Part 2: Verb conjugation	
	Full inflection (30% of final grade) In %	Content questions (3×10% of final grade) In %			Analysis of conjugated verb (20% of final grade) In %	Verb conjugation (20% of final grade) In %
Students who were admitted						
1	88	85	85	65	90	83
2	81	80	75	100	60	75
3	53	75	75	80	53	38
4	58	60	30	40	68	63
5	65	75	70	95	43	25
6	53	70	70	65	53	50
7	8	60	60	55	75	100
8	58	65	80	80	48	13
Students who were rejected						
9	43	65	70	5	58	63
10	27	70	65	75	70	38
11	12	60	70	75	58	63
12	0	100	65	65	43	38
13	0	75	70	0	53	68
14	0	65	55	65	58	43
15	13	70	50	70	45	30
16	0	55	50	45	58	50
17	7	60	50	70	50	25
18	3	60	40	40	53	30
19	0	65	70	0	58	25
20	0	40	10	40	43	18

The verb conjugation exercises were not particularly difficult and would be within the range of what Jewish students could be expected to handle. The poor performance of Arab students is remarkable.

On the grammatical front, the performance of these Arab applicants for admission into the Arabic undergraduate program is generally poor. By contrast, their performance on two open questions concerning the position of the author, and a task that included several multiple choice questions on the content of the paragraph, are substantially superior, although by no means impressive. The grades are given in three columns under "content questions" in Table 1.

Obviously, Arabic grammar is already a troubled domain of knowledge among Arab students even before they enrol in their undergraduate Arabic studies. Arab applicants to university Arabic programs come with an already strained relationship with Arabic grammar. Rather than mitigate this pre-existing alienation of Arabs from Arabic, Israeli academia accentuates and reinforces it. University Arabic-grammar instruction and the power dynamics that underpin Israel's tertiary education system serve to devalue Arab knowledge, disrupt its coherence, and undermine the autonomous Arab control over its production and reproduction. The consequent alienation of Arabs from Arabic grammar is expressed in Arab underperformance as students at university Arabic-grammar classes, and in relative self-exclusion as academics from Arabic grammar.

The Backdrop: Arabs and Arabic-Grammar Instruction

Arabs have had an uneasy relationship with Arabic grammar for centuries. Popular culture reflects this, for example, in satirical poems and other sharp complaints through the generations dating back as far as the third hijri century (about ninth century C.E.—Baalbaki 2008, 264–267). In modern times, a sense of existential crisis has come to pervade the discussion in the Arab world about the state of grammar and grammatical knowledge among contemporary Arabs (e.g. Al-Musa 1984). Much of the discourse is highly emotional. Some revisionist contributions, for example, such as recent calls to dethrone Sibawayhi, the iconic ancestor of Arabic grammar, are driven by a powerful emotive urgency (for an analysis and critique of such positions, see Suleiman 2006b and Baalbaki 2008, 268ff.).

Yasir Suleiman, a leading researcher and practitioner of Arabic instruction, insists only half-jokingly that Arabs are grammatically abused in childhood (personal communication, 22 June 2009). Arabic language instruction in general, and grammar instruction in particular, are experienced as punitive. The emphasis is on stamping out errors. Student learning is commonly driven by the correction of mistakes rather than the reward of skill acquisition. Indeed, speaking Standard Arabic in public involves a measure of performance anxiety.

A senior Arab scholar at Haifa University described to me how when he insists that students should use Standard Arabic in class, Arab students often resist him on the grounds that they do not feel competent enough in the language. I have heard similar accounts from other university instructors and from students.

This fraught relationship between Arabs and Arabic grammar is tied to the historical development of the Arab science of grammar and its pedagogy (Baalbaki 1995). The Arabic Linguistic Tradition or, more narrowly, the Arabic Grammatical Tradition, crystallised as a field of scholarship around the 8th century C.E. as the Islamic imperial structures consolidated and the first wave of Arabisation was in full swing throughout the lands that had been incorporated into the Islamic polity. Linguistic scholarship in the Islamic World emerged in response to two imperatives. One was the increasing need in judicial, administrative and theological circles for an auxiliary field of knowledge that would help in the interpretation and reinterpretation of Qur'anic script. The other was the need to define correct usage in order to defend the purity and perfection of the language of the revelation from corruption at the hands of the massive number of non-Arabs who began to use the language and participate in public life (cf. Owens 1997, 46–47).

The target language of the Arabic Linguistic Tradition was that which was manifest in the Qur'an, the Hadith and Arabian poetry and folk wisdom of the time of the revelations, and still extant in common Bedouin usage at the time of the early grammarians. Grammarians set out to discover the genius of the language, which they found in the patterns and regularities of this corpus. These regularities demonstrated the divine perfection of the revelation, and seeming exceptions needed to be accounted for within the terms of these regularities (Bohas, Guillaume and Kouloughli [1990] 2006, 17 ff.).

The linguistic scholarship that ensued was not primarily concerned with language instruction. Linguistics was not intended to support a deliberate inculcation of language through formal schooling. The Bedouin were thought to acquire proper Arabic either instinctively or through immersion in the Bedouin world. It was, in fact, Bedouin intuition that early grammarians took as the ultimate yardstick for correctness and propriety, not formally articulated rules of grammar. Non-Bedouin were expected to learn the language through memorisation and imitation, but their intuitive mastery would never assume the authority of the Bedouin—the authentic native speakers of the language. The study of grammar, then, was not pedagogical, but rather defensive in nature. Grammarians set out to discover and defend the divine order as manifest in the language of the revelation. They addressed the general public in order to defend the language from linguistic mutilation by alerting the community to common mistakes and failings that were spreading and threatening the divine linguistic order of Arabic. Furthermore, the science of linguistics did not seek to produce a fully descriptive framework of the language. This is in part because the language, as constructed in the scholarship of the time, did not exist independently of the canonical corpus, so that pure description would collapse into citation of texts. Rather, linguistics became a science of making sense of the language in a way that resembled theology. It sought to discover how the behaviour of language conformed to a presumed inherent divine perfection of logic (Versteegh 1978).

Being the vehicle of the revelation to end all revelations, Arabic exhibited, in the eyes of early Islamic grammarians, a perfection unparalleled by any other language. Language was deemed neither arbitrary nor a distinct domain that is set apart from the physical world or from the realm of aesthetics, all of which stood in testament to divine order. Indeed, the phenomenon of language was seen as part of a natural whole that included the physical world, the cognitive processes of humans, and the sensory aspects of language. This approach was predicated on the notion of an automatic, intuitive and unmediated acquisition of a mother tongue. The perfection of Arabic placed it, more than any other language, in harmony with the physical world. Arabic's perfection was mediated through the natural perception and aesthetics of the ancient Arabs. One paradigmatic manifestation of this harmonious place of Arabic within the physical world is the doctrine of a natural tendency towards lightness (*ḫiffa*—Bohas, Guillaume and Kouloughli [1990] 2006, 80ff.). When Sibawayhi and his followers accounted for morphological and phonological phenomena, one important criterion they used was relative weight, *a* being lighter than *i*, which was in turn lighter than *u*. The Bedouin were understood to be instinctually inclined towards lightness, which was associated with harmony and aesthetics, and this conditioned their linguistic choices. So, returning to the issue of phonology, the relative weight of different sound combinations affected the resolutions of unacceptable diphthongs in favour of the lighter variants.

The perfection of Arabic manifested itself not only in its regularities and harmony with nature, but also in the stylistic perfection of the Qur'anic revelations. Scholars thus sought to systematise the regularities of Arabic, define and clarify the perfection of Arabic as demonstrated in the stylistic perfection of the Qur'an. Unusual and difficult characteristics that seemed to violate the orderly harmony won disproportional analytic treatment and were reformulated in ways that could adhere to the perfection of Arabic. This kind of intellectual gymnastics became one of the hallmarks of the Arabic Linguistic Tradition. In fact, one of the most significant characteristics that would mark off true virtuosity in linguistic scholarship was the capacity to systematise and account for the most seemingly inexplicable phenomena in terms of the logic that underlies the language's regularities.

These foundational characteristics of the intellectual projects of the Arabic Linguistic Tradition set in motion much of its subsequent intellectual trajectory. The differences between these characteristics and the fundamental goals that defined European grammar are responsible for much of the difference between the contemporary educational manifestations of both traditions.

The Educational Legacy of the Arabic Linguistic Tradition

Some aspects of the Arabic Linguistic Tradition that emerged from an early stage continued to affect the pedagogical dynamics of Arabic grammar instruction up to modern times. One of the most crucial of these was an escalating intellectual conservatism.

The Arabic Linguistic Tradition developed in what Jonathan Owens calls an "accretionary rather than substitution-like fashion" (Owens 1997, 52). New developments were construed as extending and fitting into the older achievements of earlier scholars. There was not much value placed on novelty, innovation, or intellectual radicalism. Over the generations the Arab Linguistic Tradition evolved a progressively diminishing scope for debate, and eventually intellectual innovation in the field petered out. The linguistic body of knowledge that reached modernity and underlay modern curricular development was largely fixed. (For a general overview of the history of the Arabic Linguistic Tradition see Bohas, Guillaume and Kouloughli [1990] 2006, 1–17).

Over the centuries, along with intellectual closure came pedantry. Baalbaki sees this as ongoing "degeneration" (Baalbaki 2008, 250–262). Specifically, Baalbaki laments the shift to a formalistic, prescriptive stance that supplanted the empirical, cognitive-centred approach of early grammarians, most notably Sibawayhi.

The pedantry and closure in the science and pedagogy of Arabic grammar have evolved over the generations into what is essentially a strict behaviourist orientation, as it were, whereby the focus centres exclusively on correct observable performance and correct response to given stimuli, while paying little heed to comprehension and other non-observable "innate" cognitive processes. Moreover, this approach seeks to inculcate not simply the facts of grammar but rather primarily a formulaic, stylised, declamatory method of analysis of desinential inflection. Correct conventionalised recitation of grammatical analysis is the measure of educational success in this approach. Comprehension of the concepts of grammar is relegated to secondary importance as is the understanding of the given text or of the semantic effects of grammatical manipulation.

It is this behaviourism *avant la lettre* that is responsible for the fact that Arab textbooks of grammar do not expand on the underlying grammatical theory upon which they are predicated. Typically, the core theoretical term *ʿamal* (often rendered in English as governance—see Chapter 4) is mentioned sparingly in the textbooks or in references that are used by teachers in Arab schools inside Israel. For example, volume 4 of Rashid al-Shartuni's *mabādiʾ al-ʿArabīya* (Shartuni 1986), which Arab teachers use extensively as a reference, confines itself to a laconic account of the concept of *ʿāmil* (the "governor") in one paragraph only. The theory of *ʿamal* is not expounded in school grammar curricula either. Students are expected to internalise the rules of grammar blindly without being burdened with the rationale behind them. Indeed, grammar is often referred to as "the rules" (*al-qawāʿid*) in common speech.

Critics charge that rather than inviting learners to seek the logic of such phenomena as the inflectional system of Arabic, and rather than teaching grammar as a means of expressive power, Arab grammar instruction has become vindictive, with little practical relevance (see e.g. Baalbaki 2004; 2008).

Another enduring legacy of Arabic linguistics is its association with the religious field of knowledge. Being part of the broad field of religious Islamic scholarship, its transmission and inculcation in pre-modern times had been achieved through the institutions of religious instruction, and it became subject to the pedagogical approaches that typified religious teaching, in contrast with secular fields of knowledge.

In line with the accretionary nature of its underlying scholarship, the Arab field of Arabic linguistics generated another conservative imperative—the need to adhere to some fundamental level of consensus in the absence of a recognised centre of legitimate wilful oversight. In this, too, Arabic Linguistics follows Islamic religious scholarship. Only widely accepted changes to the status quo could gain legitimacy. This pressure towards consensus has had a remarkably enduring hold and a progressively stifling effect on modern theorists, bureaucrats and educators that have undertaken the development of Arabic instruction in the emerging schools in the Arab world, beginning in the nineteenth century. National academies of Arabic Language that have emerged in the twentieth century in the newly invented Arab nation states have been reluctant to go their own way notwithstanding their institutional independence from one another. Even at times of major disunity in the Arab world, these academies maintained a common bond and exhibited an extreme reluctance to break rank with one another or transgress prevalent practices and the perceived consensus. This imperative of adherence to a consensus, coupled with the fact that no institution "owned" the language or had authority to revise it, has hamstrung linguistic radicalism and stifled pedagogical reform in grammar instruction.

The very association of Arabic with Islam has further complicated pedagogical development, as debates over Arabic came to be embroiled in broader debates over regionalism, nationalism, and the place of religion within it.[3]

Formal grammatical analysis, bundled with religious knowledge, came to acquire moral significance in its own right, something that continues to dog instructors, students and reformers to date. Purists often feel that changes to the modes of grammatical instruction and to conventionalised performances of grammatical knowledge—especially the stylised declamation of syntactic analysis—are tantamount to interfering with the very grammar of the language, or at least that they are the very first step on the slippery slope towards simplification and mutilation of the language and towards undermining the linguistic unity of Arabs and the linguistic integrity of Islamic textuality. This raises the stakes quite considerably in debates over reform of grammatical instruction in the modern Arab world.

Another relevant characteristic of the Islamic nature of the Arabic Linguistic Tradition is its exclusive focus on the Arabic language, and its classical variety at that. Though some Islamic scholars have been interested in other languages, the corpus of Arabic linguistics is centred on Classical Arabic alone with minimal interest in other Semitic languages, or in the phenomenon of language in general. This attitude has been coupled with a vigilant disdainful disinterest in colloquial Arabic (other than that of the Bedouin of the time of the prophet, of course).

The social function of Arabic grammatical scholarship should also be seen in its historical context. Much of the seeming sophism in the scholarship, including the preoccupation with exceptions and elaborations on such seemingly

3 In fact, the very association of Arabic and Islam in the modern era was a product of this ideological field and was by no means inevitable. It was, surprisingly perhaps, Christian schools and institutions that initially played a critical role in the revival of the Arabic language along with the emergence of secular Arab nationalism in the 19th century, at the same time as the educated Muslim elites clung to other languages, namely Turkish and Persian, in the political, administrative and high cultural spheres in the Islamic world. There is an interesting parallel here with Hebrew revival, a movement that was led by secular nationalists in opposition to the religious establishment that confined Hebrew to a circumscribed sanctified status and relied on other vernaculars for mundane usage. In both instances of language revival, a language-focused secular nationalism formed a radical divergence from a traditional, religiously inspired political order. Religious attempts to reclaim "sovereignty" over the language only came later.

impractical areas like positional desinential inflection (*ʾiʿrāb maḥallīy*—إعراب محلي) can be attributed to the elitist nature of grammar. Within the culture of *ʾadab*—the classical literary high culture in the courts of Islam's heartland—grammar was one of those fields of knowledge, mastery of which distinguished the refinement of the cultivated elite (Bohas, Guillaume and Kouloughli [1990] 2006, 49). Neither the elaborate treatises nor the more condensed "textbooks" were aimed at educating the masses or the semiliterate (Peled 2010, 168–171, 185). The discursive aesthetics and sensibilities that developed in this elitist context are responsible for some of the alienating aspects of the grammar as taught in contemporary Arab schools, structured as these schools are to provide universal education to the general public.

For reasons that can be traced back to the shifting social and cultural context of Islamic scholarship and to the internal dynamics of the discursive tradition of Arabic grammar, the field has undergone substantial transformations. The 11th to 15th centuries CE saw a general culmination in conservatism and a move towards closure throughout scholarship in the Islamic world, and the Arabic Linguistic Tradition was no exception. Arabic linguistic scholarship seems to have reached a climax of sorts and scholars moved away from further investigation towards systematising knowledge. Al-Suyūṭī (d. 911 hijri /1505 CE) is commonly regarded as the last Arabic grammarian of note in this tradition. Although his works are characterised by a pervasively conservative spirit, he still preserves the basic theoretical insights that informed the classical theory. After him, the historiography of grammatical theory recounts a story of gradual degeneration into a set of prescriptive recipes to which some dry strips of dead theory still adhere. Texts written in that period form the basis of understanding of contemporary scholars of grammar in the Arab world and are still used in advanced university instruction in Arab and Muslim countries (Bohas, Guillaume and Kouloughli [1990] 2006, 14–17).

The stagnation that historians describe in the study of Arabic coincided with the relative decline of the significance of Arabic in the secular domains of politics and administration as Turkish and Persian came to displace Arabic. Modern Arab nationalist narratives reconstruct this period as the Period of Degeneration (انحطاط) that immediately precedes the awakening of Arab national consciousness and the revival of the Arabic language and spirit.

Modernity saw the emergence of a collective project of Arabic revival—the *nahḍa* (نهضة) as it became known—which grew out of the cultural dynamics of the nineteenth century and gave rise to an enduring debate over the control and deliberate development of Arabic grammar, a debate that remains unresolved. If Standard Arabic is to be the standard language in Arab countries, it must be made to fit the needs of the time. It must also be made easily accessible to the masses whose mother tongue is the local dialect rather than Standard Arabic. While the vocabulary of Arabic proved sufficiently malleable to be stretched to meet the challenges of modernity, the challenge of making the language in its entirety accessible was much harder to meet. Arabic grammar is commonly singled out as the major obstacle, yet no consensus has emerged as to what could or should be done about it.

Reformers have come to direct their calls for reform in two directions. One direction is that of simplifying Standard Arabic. The other is to modernise the science and pedagogy of grammar, without modifying the actual grammar of the language. Sometimes it is not clear which of the two positions is advocated in a given call for grammar simplification. In any event, under the pressure of inertia and conservatism neither direction achieved general support, and the Arabic classroom has not seen much sustained transformation one way or the other (Suleiman 1999a, 111–112).

Prototypical Pre-Modern Formal Arabic Instruction in the Arab World

Historians of the Arabic Grammatical Tradition, and more broadly the Arabic Linguistic Tradition, focus on ideas, theories and inter-textual relations. The evolution of the distinctive tradition of Arabic grammatical instruction is relegated to the background of the historiography. Arabic grammatical instruction obviously varied considerably from time to time, from place to place, and among different social classes.

Keeping this variability in mind, and acknowledging the paucity of definitive accounts of the evolution of formal instruction in Arabic grammar, I sketch an ahistorical ideal type of pre-modern Arabic-grammar instruction. This artificial analytic construct is intended to serve as a heuristic basis that captures some common dynamics of the many and varied local conditions on the eve of modernity. This baseline will facilitate the consideration of the effects—especially the unintended ones—of modern reforms that were imposed on pre-modern systems.[4]

Classical grammar instruction was aimed at males. It was further an elitist pursuit, not intended for universal access. It was rather the rote memorisation of the Qur'an, free of grammatical elaboration, that formed the lowest common educational denominator, at least for sedentary Muslims.

4 While there have been several works summarising the history of Islamic education in general, I am not aware of an authoritative historical overview of Arabic grammar instruction in the Islamic world. For a review of traditional educational practices and education, along with annotated bibliographies, see Barazangi et al. [2014].

Prototypically, education beyond the basics of Qur'anic instruction was a mark of social privilege and a means of social reproduction and mobility. To enable the continued education of their sons, families would need to forego the sons' productive capacity for the duration of their study, and pay out whatever sums were needed to support them through their education.

The methods of teaching at the preliminary stages of grammar instruction followed quite closely those that prevailed in the broader initial Qur'anic instruction, and would commonly be conducted by the same instructor at the same mosque at the local level. An emphasis would be placed on memorisation of rules, often in verse. Ibn Malik's *ʾalfīya* is probably the most famous versed grammar of Arabic.

The emphasis on rote learning is often singled out in modern discussion of Arabic instruction, and has attracted a great deal of attention from both scholars and reformers. It is commonly presented as a mindless, punitive and pointless exercise that produces little in the way of comprehension.[5]

One must see past the anachronistic modernist reinterpretation of the significance of rote learning. Rote learning is often taken to be a mark of pedagogically inferior, teacher-centred education that is preoccupied with superficial displays of knowledge at the expense of genuine internalisation by students of the subject matter. This view is not helpful in reconstructing the logic of pedagogical practice in the pre-modern and early modern Middle East. An emphasis on memorisation was practically inevitable given the status of educational technology in pre-modern times. Mass production of textbooks was not available and therefore students did not have quick access to printed expositions of the subject matter. Under such conditions memorisation was an ideal way of making the knowledge available and accessible to students for further elaboration.

Moreover, the use to which knowledge was put was also significant in adding to the value of memorisation. The modernist, logocentric common sense of

5 The emphasis on the memorisation of rules is significant, although it is easy to overstate its significance in the curriculum or its deleterious effects on students' learning and comprehension. Rote is foundational to other fields of instruction even in contemporary, Western, student-centred instruction. The rules of arithmetic, for example, are normally taught precisely as such—rules—with little elaboration of their underlying rationale. But while the rules of arithmetic are intuitively meaningful because they are continuously borne out in daily practice (a child with three marbles who wins two marbles will have five marbles regardless of the underlying theory of arithmetic), there is not much that is self-evident in the desinential inflection, an obsolescent syntactic device that is not normally used in normal prose writing or in speech, and is not produced unselfconsciously by Arabic speakers.

instruction is that the instructional material, in a textbook for example, conveys some basic truths or insights, and a student must somehow comprehend the meaning that the text conveys, internalise it, and preferably make sense of it. A mark of successful learning would be a student's ability to paraphrase the main points and reconstruct the argument of the text in his or her own words. In fact, the essence that education tries to convey is that of paraphrased meaning. The exact words of one textbook or another are simply ephemeral artefacts to be judged pragmatically on utilitarian grounds. Some textbooks convey the material better than others. What is essential is the truths or observations that are conveyed through these textbooks.

In contrast with the educational ideology of modernity, the meaning of the material taught in pre-modern Islamic schooling was not fixed, but open to interpretation and reinterpretation within a given range. The exact meaning of a Qur'anic verse is never finite and may always be called into question and challenged. The Qur'an is not a treatise whose comprehension can be demonstrated through successful paraphrasing. Quite to the contrary. The actual words are the immutable truth. Their interpretation and meaning are ephemeral and contestable.

As Eickelman observed about such classical education, the true mark of a virtuoso and the ultimate indication of proper mastery of the Qur'an is the capacity to mobilise the right verse in the right context to the right rhetorical effect (Eickelman, 1978; 1985 chapter 3). So learning the one, decontextual, "correct" meaning of a verse is impossible. Rather the aim is to learn how to deploy the verse with virtuosity and panache, and this requires memorisation.

Hence the preponderance of rote memorisation in the pre-modern pedagogical technological toolkit is motivated by the very aims of education and the nature of the material conveyed. In fact, this approach is close to the educational approach that is used in contemporary European poetry instruction where, indeed, rote memorisation is commonly seen as an ideal first step in the process of comprehending the multi-layered and ever-shifting significance of poems. Another pertinent parallel may be the practice of memorising the words of a constitution with the knowledge that the judicial interpretation of the constitution changes, yet its words remain fixed.

Returning to the pre-modern educational trajectory—following the grammatical instruction at the local level, some select few students would continue their studies at the centres of knowledge—prototypically mosque universities—where they would read advanced treatises, participate in study circles, pore over texts with peers, and eventually win an authorisation by teachers to pass on the knowledge that they acquired. In this very phonocentric approach the instruction resides in the interaction with the teacher, the text being an aid to the process. Here, too, meaning is not as fixed in words and decontextualised as it is in modernist logocentric instruction, complete with its textbooks and essay exams.

In essence, then, the prototypical pre-modern Arabic-grammar instruction takes for granted a prior knowledge of the Qur'an, along with a high level of motivation backed by family investment in education, a continuing successful experience among students in learning through memorisation, a fluidity in meaning in the subject matter, and the embeddedness of the transmission of knowledge in a master-pupil relationship.

An Outline of the Crisis in Modern Grammar Instruction

The contemporary crisis in Arabic instruction in the Arab world was probably inevitable given that Arabic instruction relied on the application to a modern educational context of pre-modern knowledge and teaching designs (cf. Baalbaki 1995). And if the perennial state of crisis in Arabic and the modern shift from phonocentric to logocentric instruction were not enough, the universalisation of formal education across all socioeconomic segments ensured the crisis would deepen.

The emergence of modern state control of public schooling intensified the crisis in grammar instruction. Bureaucratic control requires some form of standardisation of the curriculum and instruction across schools and social sectors. This imperative forced differences in approach into view, and forced differences to be resolved one way or another. The scope for differences to coexist was reduced.

The intense ensuing crisis in modern language education demanded some form of radical reform. This newly heightened urgency of reform exacerbated an already fractious intellectual sphere. The literati's concern over the poor proficiency of the masses is, in fact, as old as the Arabic Linguistic Tradition, and so is the preoccupation with the colloquially obsolescent desinential inflection. Concerns with the pedagogical implications of grammar, and suggestions to simplify it, are not a contemporary invention either, as Suleiman points out when noting the influence of 12th century scholar, al-Qurṭubī, on modern reformers such as Ibrahim Mustafa (Suleiman 1999a 111–112).

Nonetheless, the modern scene forced an escalation of the debates. Some reformers attempted to remain loyal to the Arabic Linguistic Tradition, yet to produce an easily accessible knowledge framework. Critics charged that these attempts failed on both counts, diverging from the traditional approach to grammar, while not providing a sustainable contemporary alternative. Traditionalists and reformers entered into an often acrimonious debate that became fixed in a stalemate. Given the required consensus for any legitimate change in the field, paralysis ensued.

Contemporary schooling creates new points of crisis in the trajectory of grammar instruction. These might artificially reinforce the sense of a recent cataclysmic decline in grammatical knowledge. The extension of schooling and literacy throughout society forces to the surface some problems that in the past might not have arisen. Widespread failure to internalise grammar becomes apparent through systematic examinations that cover increasing sectors of the population. Social classes that in the past would have been excluded from extended formal schooling are now processed through the system, and their failure becomes an observable fact. The contemporary significance of educational qualifications for employment makes such failure consequential.

In other words, the contemporary democratisation and standardisation of education forces such failure to the surface and recasts it as a paramount, quintessential, political and administrative challenge. But this seeming increase in the failure rate may have more to do with the shifting contexts of grammatical instruction and the demographic changes in the student body, than with any emerging, novel crisis in grammar instruction as such.

The changes in the demographics of the student body are only part of the transition that has occurred between pre-modern times and modernity. The techniques and facilities of teaching and learning have also changed. Memorisation is no longer central in modern schooling. Pupils consequently are not as skilled in the art of memorisation or learning by rote. The material is now reworked to presentation in textbooks in self-contained units that move progressively from simple to complex—a completely different medium from the compilation of rules in verse that were designed to be initially memorised, and only subsequently applied and understood.

The fact that memorisation of the Qur'an is no longer the essence of primary schooling nor a precondition for advancing to learning grammar means that contemporary Arab students reach grammar instruction with a relative lack of knowledge of the register whose grammar they learn. Students begin to study grammar with a reduced mastery of the corpus of Standard Arabic compared with the prototypical student of grammar in the classical age of the culture of *ʾadab*. This is particularly detrimental to students' acquisition of the morphosyntactic system of desinential inflection which is all but absent from dialectal usage or media language. Yet it is precisely this system, appropriately entitled *ʾiʿrāb* (إعراب)—Arabisation—that has come in the Arab tradition to symbolise grammatical mastery on the whole, and is consequently greatly emphasised in grammar instruction.

Furthermore, the demands that are placed on grammar instruction have shifted along with the expected effects it should have on students. Modern grammar instruction is supposed to be focused primarily on enabling students to produce correct Arabic. It is supposed to integrate with other aspects of language instruction to support correct, creative language usage. By contrast, pre-modern formal grammar instruction of Arabic was preoccupied with empowering students to explain and interpret scriptural writing, and not as much to facilitate creative writing.

For example, as Yishai Peled (2010) points out, students in Arab schools are commonly expected to read a sentence, while fully vocalising it, and are then taught how to recite the analysis of its desinential inflection in a stylised declamatory way. This runs counter to the contemporary logic of language instruction, according to which students need to first understand the sentence and its syntactical structure as a precondition to vocalising the sentence with correct desinential inflection. The syntactic approach that seeks to account for the way meaning is folded into the sentence was not the primary concern of pre-modern grammar instruction. The instruction of *ʾiʿrāb* is consequently of limited use in facilitating student comprehension of the syntactic logic of the vocalisation of sentences.

Arabic-grammar instruction is thus left mired in historic incompatibility between, on the one hand, pre-modern approaches to grammar instruction and the cognitive habits it presupposes, characteristics which still inhere in contemporary Arab Arabic grammar instruction by force of inertia, and on the other hand, the realities of contemporary schooling. This incompatibility has animated much of the debates over reform in grammar instruction in the Arab world and infused the perennial crisis in Arabic instruction with unprecedented force.

The debate over grammar instruction in the Arab world, then, was framed within a pervasive sense of crisis—an endemic aspect of the grammatically educated class since the inception of the Arabic Linguistic Tradition—and against the background of the emergence of state administered schooling and the public politics of education. This is how debates about language instruction and language reform became focused on ideological discourse that had all to do with competing visions of nationalism, religion and history, and very little to do with educational linguistics and pedagogy.

Commenting on corpus planning in the Arab world in the twentieth century, Suleiman acutely observed that "Corpus planning initiatives in the Arabic speaking countries share two major properties with similar plans elsewhere. On the one hand, they tend to be based on no more than an impressionistic assessment of the problems they are designed to solve. On the other hand, they cannot be divorced from the ideologically motivated non-linguistic ends which constitute their ultimate, albeit often undeclared goals" (1999a, 111).[6]

The difficulties of reconciling Arabic-grammar instruction with contemporary schooling throughout the Arab world are made all the more critical by the competition with the powerful languages, or rather, the languages of the powerful, most notably English (Fishman, Cooper and Conrad 1977). This applies to both actual language usage in society, and to the consequent emerging demand for more educational resources to be dedicated to these foreign, menacing languages. The increasing value of proficiency in foreign languages which has accompanied the rising power of the globalising Arab corporate sector and Western orientated professions is often perceived as a threat to Arabic and to the position of the inward-looking segments of the cultural elites that have set themselves up as the guardians of Arabic. The conflation of anxieties over the future of Arabic, of Arab culture, of Islam, of Islamic civilisation and the moral order has raised the stakes when it comes to the science of grammar. Conservatives often construct the battle over the traditional form of grammar instruction as a battle over the very language itself and an integral part of a defensive war against the onslaught of the West. For their part, reformers may present their calls for change as a step in the struggle to modernise the supposedly stagnant Middle East (cf. Suleiman 2004, chapter 3, pp. 58ff.). Whatever the case, Arabic grammar and its instruction have become burdened with enormous moral weight. Students' grammatical mistakes and failures have come to carry an existential significance far greater than mere mistakes in an academic subject.[7]

Both the sense of crisis and decay in the linguistic capacity of Arabs and the problematic relationship between Arabs and Arabic grammar are further aggravated by the way pedagogues have responded to the challenges and opportunities provided by Arabic's diglossia. Standard Arabic is nobody's mother tongue. Rather, Arabs' mother tongues are specific dialects of colloquial Arabic. Yet the canonical ideological illegitimacy of the dialects means that the grammar of dialects is not taught, not even as a contrastive background for the grammar of Standard Arabic. This may deprive Arab students of a measure of intuitive understanding of grammar. Instead of having their intuitive language—colloquial Arabic—as a system of conceptual pegs for

6 This, of course, is by no means unique to the debates over language education and language reform in the Arab world. Contemporary educational policy debates throughout the world often become an arena marked by moralistic posturing with little regard for the way educational processes actually unfold.

7 Note, for example, the moral urgency in Al-Musa 1984.

grammar, they have to master a grammar of a second albeit not vastly different language, namely Standard Arabic. In fact, the very focus on desinential inflection—absent as it largely is from colloquial Arabic—accentuates the difference between the colloquial and Standard varieties. Here, too, we see how the pre-modern pedagogical agenda with its contempt for colloquial varieties weighs heavily on contemporary Arab students.

The troubled relationship between Arabs and Arabic grammar is thus an ongoing social process with profound implications for the way grammar and its instruction are constructed and experienced in the Arab world. The study of grammar is popularly perceived as an unpleasant chore one must endure in the course of schooling. While such dampened enthusiasm for the subject is not a new phenomenon, as demonstrated by Baalbaki's discussion of attitudes towards grammarians and grammar instruction in the 9th and 10th centuries (Baalbaki 2008, 264–267), the contemporary Arab student seems particularly alienated from Arabic grammar by the very circumstances of its instruction, hence Suleiman's pithy quip on "grammatical abuse". This alienation of Arabs from Arabic grammar forms an already troubled precondition that is further disturbed by the conditions of Arabic instruction in Israel which are an integral aspect of the realities of Israeli Arab political, social and cultural dislocation, containment and marginalisation.

If the grammatical and linguistic debates throughout the Arab world have little practical relevance to the classroom in general, they are even less relevant to the particular realities of the Arabs within Israel. Israeli Arabs, arguably the only Arabs to still face direct colonisation, were generally on the margins of the debates, lacking as they do educational autonomy or control. This disempowerment has rendered debates among Israeli Arabs on how to lead reform of Arabic-grammar instruction rather pointless. Moreover, the linguistic challenges facing Israeli Arabs are different from those facing Arabs elsewhere. The fate of Palestinian dialects is a case in point. Throughout the Arab world there have been different approaches to colloquial Arabic. Some see it as the "real thing" as did for example Egyptian nationalists in the early twentieth century. Others see it as an inferior vulgar nuisance that hinders the acquisition of the "real thing", namely Classical Arabic. All of these positions presuppose that colloquial Arabic has a secure grip over Arabic speakers, in a way that Israeli Arabs cannot take for granted.

Israeli Arabs often identify the current existential threat to Arabic with a flood of Hebrew that is overwhelming common usage (e.g. Amara 2015). There is a pervasive sense that Arabs' very mother tongue—colloquial Arabic—is being eroded under the pressure of Hebrew, and that young Arabs speak a corrupted colloquial Arabic. While the defence of colloquial Arabic may not resonate with the intellectual elites in the Arab world at large, it is a substantial concern among Israeli Arabs ranging from language professionals all the way to non-grammatically inclined people (cf. Bawardi 2012a, 2012b).[8]

Israel's political economy of languages plays a critical role in facilitating Hebrew's creeping displacement of Arabic in the Arab linguistic space, and further reduces the motivation of both Arab students and educators to invest emotionally and materially in Arabic. As I mentioned in Chapter 2, the Israeli market in linguistic proficiency is segmented. The value of a speaker's linguistic proficiency is determined by whether s/he is Arab or Jewish. Jews who acquire a high proficiency in Arabic can look forward to well-remunerated careers in the security and Arab-management apparatus with its insatiable demand for Arabic-speaking Jews and from which Arabs are excluded. More generally, knowledge of Arabic is more readily converted by Jews than Arabs into material capital through access to prime employment (Uhlmann 2008, 106–110).

By contrast, high-achieving Arab students can expect none of these benefits from Arabic, and are consequently not drawn to major in Arabic. Indeed, for Arab students a major in Arabic is the natural entry point into Arabic teaching in the Arab school sector—a poorly paying professional choice with an oversupply of qualified teachers and where conditions and security of tenure are particularly compromised and subject to such added irritants as the heavy-handed attempts at political control of Arab education by Israel's security apparatus.

In fact, Arab private schools, which are major producers of the Arab intellectual elite in Israel, often restrict Arabic instruction to a minimal level at the matriculation examination (an extension of three units), and numerous Arab high school and university students with whom I spoke were quite explicit about the uselessness of Arabic, and the comparative pragmatic advantages of Hebrew and English, the two languages that are tested at a high extension in the matriculation examinations, and are prerequisites for university studies and for access to sought-after careers. Ironically, it is Hebrew proficiency that is of great value within the Arab sector where Hebrew proficiency is unevenly distributed, thereby giving highly proficient professionals a competitive edge, especially in such areas as medicine and law.[9]

---

8 This is a different concern from the drive towards (re)Arabisation in places like Morocco. Arabisation initiatives have focused on the reintroduction of Standard Arabic to public spaces. The place of colloquial Arabic in private spaces did not excite much concern, and seems to be taken for granted.

9 The high motivation to excel in Hebrew has led over the years to an increase in the numbers of Arab students in Hebrew language programs at Israeli universities, culminating in a

Tertiary Education and the Alienation of Arabs from Arabic Grammar

The depressed value of Arabic in Israel—especially to Arabs—along with the longstanding unpopularity of grammar in Arab history and the crisis in Arabic instruction throughout the Arab world, all serve to detract from the motivation of Arab undergraduate students to engage in Arabic. But it is ultimately the structure and function of Israel's formal education system that in the final analysis plays a decisive role in alienating Arabs from Arabic grammar. Not only does the formal education system not act so as to mitigate these difficulties, but it greatly accentuates the alienation of Arabs with its own unique contribution to the situation.

A critical element in bringing about this alienation is the asymmetrical bifurcation of the school system in Israel into a Hebrew-language stream that caters predominantly to Jewish students and an Arabic-language stream that caters to Arabs. Arabic-grammar instruction in the Arab stream follows the conventions and methods that are common in the Arab world and derive from centuries of the Arabic Linguistic Tradition. The way this approach materialises in instruction is fundamentally different from the approach that predominates in the Jewish sector.

The different ways grammar instruction coheres, or not, across the curriculum have been mentioned above. To briefly recapitulate, Jewish schools teach Arabic as a second foreign language, typically beginning in junior high school. These schools follow Western, Orientalist conventions of Arabic grammar and its instruction. It is the same mode of grammatical analysis and the same conceptual framework that is used in Hebrew grammar instruction, and it is this grammar that is generally taught at universities, too. In this, Jewish schools differ from Arab schools. In contrast with the single, coherent conceptual framework that undergirds the instruction of grammar in Jewish classes of Hebrew and Arabic, Arab schools have a fractured curriculum. They draw on the Arabic Linguistic Tradition to teach Arabic, yet rely on the Western approach to teach the grammar of Hebrew, thereby teaching two discontinuous grammatical systems across the two main languages that their students learn. The fact that universities teach Arabic grammar in line with the Israeli-Jewish approach further creates, for Arab students, discontinuities between secondary and tertiary-level Arabic-grammar instruction.

---

nationalist moral panic among Jewish academics in Hebrew who found themselves faced with the Arabisation of their student body (see e.g. Lori 2008).

This is a particularly acute instance where the asymmetry of political relations affects the construction of knowledge. It is a Western grammar that is forced upon the instruction of Hebrew in Arab schools, and on Arabic instruction in the joint Jewish-Arab context of university instruction. This produces a significant divergence in the quality of educational experience.

Jews experience university Arabic-grammar instruction as an extension of their Arabic-grammar instruction at school. Moreover, even at school, there is a clear convergence and reinforcement between the grammar of Hebrew and grammar of Arabic that are taught because the grammar of Hebrew that is taught is the same Westernised grammatical approach.[10] Students commonly transfer what they learn in grammar from one context to the other. Teachers of Arabic in the Jewish sector regularly invoke students' grammatical knowledge of Hebrew to clarify and reinforce points of Arabic grammar and employ what is essentially an identical conceptual framework in both grammars. Consequently, Jews learn a comparative, relatively coherent grammatical system in Hebrew and Arabic classes at school, and later at university.

Arab students do not experience the various contexts of grammar instruction as a coherent whole. While the Hebrew grammar they learn at school is the same conceptual framework that prevails at university grammar of Arabic, the grammar of Arabic that they learn at school is profoundly different in its approach and intellectual framework. Consequently, Arab students do not seem to spontaneously transfer their comprehension of grammatical analysis from Hebrew to Arabic, at least not to the same extent that Jews do.

This reduced inclination to transfer knowledge across domains may reflect any number of aggravating factors. Possibly the common practice of school teachers of Arabic in the Jewish sector to rely on prior knowledge of Hebrew grammar establishes and reinforces for Jewish students the comparability of the two methods in a way that Arab students do not experience. Another possible factor may be that it is easier to transfer knowledge from one's first language to one's second language rather than vice versa. This could be because the formal grammar of one's first language is internalised more intuitively and lends itself to extension more easily.

Furthermore, it is not only the choice of grammatical approach that is significant to the asymmetrical experience of Jewish and Arab students, but also

---

10 There is also an Arabic tradition of Hebrew grammar—which includes, for example, the medieval Qara'ite grammar of Hebrew—that differs markedly from the contemporary grammar of Hebrew in ways that parallel the difference between the Arabic Linguistic Tradition and contemporary European grammar. But this long obsolete tradition is all but forgotten, and plays no role in contemporary instruction in Israel.

the choice of language of instruction. With the exception of Haifa University's preliminary classes for Arab students, Arabic grammar is taught at universities in Hebrew using a European conceptual apparatus that has been translated into Hebrew. This further reinforces the sense of alienation of Arab students. A symmetrical situation that improbably emerged at Haifa University left Jewish students stranded in Arabic-speaking classes of Arabic grammar delivered in Arabic, completely disorientating these students (see chapter 4 for more details).

At any rate, even for those Arab students who aspire to become Arabic school teachers, the Arabic grammar curriculum at universities is largely irrelevant. The European approach to Arabic grammar is a topic they had not encountered at school as students and a topic they will not teach when they return to school as teachers. Rather, they will be teaching the Arab grammar of Arabic. By contrast, Jewish student teachers who end up teaching Arabic at schools will teach the very Westernised grammar of Arabic that they are taught at university. Not surprisingly, Arabs who break into the academic ranks of Arabic departments at universities tend to specialise in areas other than grammar and syntax, areas such as literature or religion. It is Jews who dominate grammar which is usually bundled with dialectology.

The fact that university Arabic grammar is orientated towards the Israeli-Jewish grammar of Arabic and is conducted in Hebrew is a reflection of two related factors. One is the fact that Israeli academia is integrated into the Western/European academic world. The other is that Arabic instruction in general at Israeli universities is geared first and foremost towards Jewish students. In overvaluing the Arabic linguistic skills of Jews, Arabic instruction disadvantages Arab students (Uhlmann 2008, 102 ff.).

These circumstances strongly condition the very pedagogical encounter at universities, and create a very alienating experience that further strains the already fraught relationship between Arab students and Arabic grammar. Arab university students of Arabic grammar find themselves in courses where material that is presented to them is unexpectedly and inexplicably alien, replete with a strange conceptual framework, and delivered in what is essentially a foreign language (at least for grammar), by mostly Hebrew-speaking Jewish teachers whose teaching anyhow is directed primarily at Jewish, Hebrew-speaking students, many of whom are on a career track in various intelligence and bureaucratic agencies that target precisely those very Arab students and others like them.

To this alienating set of circumstances one might add the observation that many of the Arabic teaching academic staff are themselves reservists in or collaborators with various elements of Israel's intelligence community. This adds to the undercurrent of tension that already exists between Arabs and Jews in an educational context where the latter predominate.

This undercurrent expresses itself in numerous ways, including a perennial suspicion on the part of some students and an instinctive resistance to the material that is taught. Academics from different universities have recounted to me instances in which Arab students had difficulties accepting the professional authority of Jewish grammar teachers, especially when the latter would convey material that contradicted some commonly held beliefs among Arab students, or some entrenched practices in Arab grammar instruction. One academic related how a seemingly trivial matter assumed exaggerated significance when Arab students found it exceedingly difficult to accept that some other languages have a consonant identical to the common standard ways Arabs actualise *ḍād* (ض), a consonant that had traditionally been thought of by Arab linguists as unique to Arabic and has come to designate the very language in the term *luġat al-ḍād*—the language of the *ḍād*. Arab students also found it hard to accept that the full range of the ways that populations of Arabic speakers actualise the consonant is much wider than is traditionally thought.

More significantly, however, some Arab students respond to the academic reliance on Western grammatical analysis with hostility and suspicion, seeing it as an attempt to supplant their indigenous traditional grammar with an alien science of Arabic. This hostility usually simmers below the surface and is rarely overt.

Classroom interactions are by no means the sole, or even primary, site where universities accentuate the alienation of Arabs from Arabic. Rather, through their very structure and function, universities play an additional, decisive role in alienating Arabs from Arabic grammar, and disturbing Arabs' control of their own linguistic destiny. Beyond the effects on individual students, the communal power relations that are embodied in the tertiary education system are critical. As described above, the tertiary education system in Israel is tiered. The top tier is composed of eight universities, all of which are Hebrew-language institutions. Four of these have departments dedicated to advanced instruction in Arabic language and culture—that is, departments where instruction builds upon a presumed prior student knowledge of Arabic (in contrast with programs of teaching Arabic as a foreign language). The second tier in Israel's tertiary education is composed of colleges, typically teachers' colleges. Some of these are Arabic-language institutions. The four university departments of Arabic set the tone in research, monopolise postgraduate Arabic instruction, teach the majority of Arabic school teachers, and are the most prestigious Arabic programs in the country. University research on Arabic grammar falls within the scope of the European tradition of Arabic linguistics. Consequently, the relative value of the Arab grammar of Arabic is decreased compared with the European grammar of Arabic. It is the latter that one needs to master in order to attain advanced academic degrees and succeed in Israel's academic world.

The top tier universities adhere to the European Arabic grammatical approach not only in research but also in teaching. With one partial exception, all universities teach an Israeli-Jewish approach to the grammar of Arabic. The partial exception is Haifa University, where the first two years of grammar classes for graduates of the Arab school stream follow a curriculum of Arab grammar of Arabic, while graduates of the Hebrew schools follow the normal trajectory of Westernised grammar. Third-year grammar classes are unified and follow the Westernised grammatical approach. Other than this partial exception at Haifa University, it is Arab teacher colleges or autonomous Arab units within teachers' colleges that teach the Arab grammar of Arabic. The Hebrew-language college programs teach prospective Arabic teachers the Israeli-Jewish grammar of Arabic.

We see here at the tertiary level of Arabic instruction and research a clear institutional hierarchy. Westernised Arabic grammar predominates in the top tier. Arab grammar of Arabic is relegated to the second tier. In the one partial exception—Haifa University's courses in Arab grammar of Arabic for Arab students—the instructors are generally Arab adjuncts, thereby extending the general institutional hierarchy in Arabic-grammar instruction.

This hierarchy is significant in its own right but has further ramifications as well. Academia plays a crucial role in shaping school instruction in Arabic, not least through academic domination of school curricular policy and design. This has the effect of further devaluing the Arab grammar of Arabic and of disrupting possible integration, or even adjustment, of grammar instruction at Arab schools to Arabic-grammar instruction at universities. All this stands in sharp contrast with academia's role in shaping Arabic instruction in the Jewish sector and harmonising Arabic-grammar instruction at schools and universities.

Those scholars who oversee Arabic instruction at the Jewish schools tend to come from the ranks of senior top-tier academics, the Hebrew University of Jerusalem being particularly important in this regard. By contrast, the intellectual elite that guides Arabic instruction in Arab schools is confined to colleges and to adjunct positions at the top universities. In other words, the intellectual leadership of Arab Arabic grammar is situated in the relatively poorly paid segment of the academic labour market, with no capacity to question or transform the academic agenda at the top tier, and with a substantially reduced security of tenure and profoundly fewer opportunities to develop research and shape knowledge more generally. This contrasts with the intellectual leadership of the Westernised grammar of Arabic that enjoys the relatively superior conditions in the primary academic labour market.

The marginalised position of Arab linguists and Arab Arabic linguistics means that most Arab university students will not receive a comprehensive academic instruction in the grammar they will teach at school (with the partial exception of Haifa University's separate grammar instruction in the first two undergraduate years). This situation in which teachers-to-be are deprived of advanced training in the subject they will be teaching at school cannot be beneficial for Arabic instruction at Arab schools. Arabic teachers in the Arab sector who have not received advanced training in the grammar they teach at school must fall back on their own experience as secondary school students for instruction. They are thereby deprived of a deeper understanding of Arabic grammatical theory and pedagogy and of an opportunity to participate in any orchestrated reform of the curricular approach. This partly explains the great difficulty that those intellectual leaders of Arab Arabic-grammar instruction have in controlling and reforming Arabic-grammar instruction in the Arab classroom. Those who seek to transform the curriculum to address the troubled relationship between Arabs and Arabic grammar may have very limited access to Arabic teachers—one limited to the occasional in-service training.

Thus in the 1990s a new curriculum was introduced into government schools to replace the one that was based on the Egyptian textbook written in the 1930s by al-Jarim and Amin, *al-naḥw al-wāḍiḥ*. The new program, organised around a series of textbooks called *al-ǧadīd fī al-luġa*, made some substantive and procedural changes such as postponing the much maligned systematic discussion of desinential inflection and its stylised declamation till tenth grade. But the developers of the program as well as teachers with whom I spoke have concurred that adherence to the curriculum is patchy at most, as teachers continue to rely on the materials and methods they experienced as students. Perhaps if the Arab grammar of Arabic had been taught at universities to the bulk of the Arabic teachers-to-be by those academics who ultimately design school curricula, as is currently the case with Jewish teachers-to-be, it would have been easier to develop and effect reforms in grammar instruction in the Arab sector.

Implications

In essence, then, from the perspective of Arabs who are going through the system of academic instruction as students and even as instructors, Israel's tertiary education system has effectively colonised Arabic grammar, and restricted Arab control to marginal, circumscribed enclaves.

The academic structure of Arabic-grammar instruction within Israel combines the effects of the fraught relationship between Arabs and Arabic grammar along with the power relations between Jews and non-Jews. But this academic structure is not alone in aggravating the alienation of Arabs from Arabic grammar. The position of Israeli Arabs within the Arab world further amplifies the alienating effect of Israel's intellectual structure and further aggravates the situation. The intellectual leadership of Arab Arabic grammar is not only marginalised within the Western orientated academic structure in Israel, but is also marginalised within the Arab world. In separate conversations, three of the leading scholars who developed the program of *al-ǧadīd* recounted the constant internalised pressure to defer to linguistic conventions in the rest of the Arab world and to prove to their colleagues in the Arab world that they were neither breaking with Arab unity, nor were they intellectual collaborators with Zionism. One of them confided that he and his colleagues felt constrained in what they could do with the curriculum, because any substantial departure from common practices in the Arab world would have been viewed with suspicion by fellow Arab intellectuals. In other words, Israeli Arabs' marginalisation within the Arab world further limits the intellectual autonomy and space for manoeuvre for those who are charged with steering Arabic-grammar instruction in Israel's Arab sector. And this is on top of the paucity of resources and the lack of institutional and educational frameworks that would facilitate the introduction of such reforms, such as university programs that teach the Arabic grammar that is taught at Arab schools.

While Israel's Western academic orientation restricts research and scholarship in the Arabic Linguistic Tradition, the suspicion with which Israeli Arab scholars are viewed in the Arab world further curtails their avenues for scholarship and publication. I have learned from a few such scholars that they have faced great difficulties getting published in Arab intellectual journals or participating in conferences, although this is not a universal complaint and others do get published in the Arab world and are often invited to conferences.

In any event, the double marginalisation of Israeli Arabs—both within Israel and throughout the Arab world—constrains the development of Arabic grammar in the Arab sector in Israel. Arab intellectuals have a limited capacity to adjust grammar and its instruction to contemporary educational requirements of Arab students. They are greatly limited in their capacity to make tertiary Arabic education relevant to Arab students. Their capacity to carry out and implement educational reform in school classrooms is further limited by the limited capacity they have to access and influence Arabic teachers in the Arab sector. For their part, Arab students face a harrowing task trying to learn Arabic grammar, first with an outmoded approach at school, then confronted with an alienating instruction at university, and ultimately, having to endure substantial opportunity costs in whatever investment they make in Arabic owing to the depressed value of Arabs' Arabic in the highly segmented Israeli linguistic market.

The Arab experience of alienation from Arabic grammar takes a particularly personal turn in university grammar classes, where the communal power relations and the political economy of education are translated into differences in student educational experience. This is a paradigmatic example of how power relations, structures of knowledge and cognitive practices interact to personalise social relations, without any purposeful design or conscious intention to produce these effects. The next chapter will delve into the details of grammar to explore the intellectual structure that, in conjunction with the political context of education, produces this alienating effect.

CHAPTER 4

A Cognitive Clash in the Classroom: The Incommensurability of Jewish and Arab Grammars of Arabic

University departments of Arabic language and literature bring Jews and Arabs together as students in mixed classrooms.[1] These departments are intended, nominally at least, to teach advanced Arabic linguistics and literature to students who are already proficient in the target language. These departments are distinct from language-instruction programs that are aimed at non-proficient students and teach Arabic as a foreign language. One might have expected that these departments should have been a particularly useful academic avenue for Arab students, enabling them to translate their superior mastery of Arabic into academic advantage. Furthermore, the mix of Arab and Jewish students might have been another useful means to support a more profound acquisition of Arabic proficiency, both linguistic and cultural, by Jewish students.

Both these goals would be welcomed, or so it would seem, by those who are involved in academic Arabic instruction. Yet neither seems to fully eventuate in practice. Jewish students' lack of proficiency is accepted, legitimised and reinforced through their academic success, while Arabs' superior knowledge becomes devalued by the institutions of Arabic instruction, and fails to translate into superior attainment in areas such as Arabic grammar.

Earlier chapters describe the ongoing alienation of Arabs from Arabic grammar in general, and the unique, aggravating circumstances of Israeli Arabs. This alienation is further accentuated by the very educational encounter at the tertiary level of Israel's education system. This alienating effect of tertiary Arabic instruction stems from the interplay between, on the one hand, the differences between the grammatical approaches in the Jewish and Arab sectors, and, on the other hand, the power inequality that underlies the tertiary educational encounter.

The Jewish and Arab grammars of Arabic are two distinct, incommensurable, bodies of knowledge. One is used in Arab schools and the other is used

1 Earlier versions of some sections in this chapter have appeared in "The Failures of Translation across Incommensurable Knowledge Systems: A case study of Arabic grammar instruction," in Peter G. Toner (ed) *Strings of Connectedness: Essays in Honour of Ian Keen*. Canberra: ANU Press, 2015, 143–159, URL: http://press.anu.edu.au?p=325141.

 | DOI: 10.1163/9789004349957_005

in Jewish schools. I refer to the two approaches as Israeli-Arab and Israeli-Jewish grammar of Arabic respectively. The Israeli-Jewish approach to grammar draws on the European Orientalist tradition and differs fundamentally from the Israeli-Arab grammar of Arabic which derives from the Arabic Linguistic Tradition. The differences between the two approaches to grammar instruction are systemic and comprehensive.

Israeli universities are dedicated to satisfying the educational interests of the dominant Jewish population. As a result, the tertiary Arabic grammar classroom pits the Israeli-Jewish grammar of Arabic against the Israeli-Arab grammar of Arabic in an asymmetrical cultural clash. The effects of this cultural clash are decisive and fateful, even as they are misrecognised and poorly understood by participants in the educational process.

Chapter 2 explains how the educational system in the Jewish sector produces graduates with an impaired command of Arabic cultural and linguistic literacy. The power relations that structure the educational exchange support and enhance this impaired cultural literacy. Jews do not need to understand the extent of their misunderstanding of Arab knowledge constructs, or the specific differences between the way they themselves conceptualise grammar and the ways Arabs think grammar. In fact, from their elevated position Jewish students and teachers of Arabic remain generally oblivious to the very possibility of radically different grammatical approaches. Their Arabic grammar is *the* Arabic grammar in the domain of education and scholarship.

Arabs, for their part, are locked into these very power relations to no lesser extent than are Jews. Arabs, as a collective, cannot avoid Israel's tertiary education system with its inherent power differential whereupon the Israeli-Jewish approach to Arabic grammar predominates. The pervasive inability to see the systemic differences between the two grammars of Arabic for what they are means that even Arabs do not account for their difficulties in grammar in systemic ways, and consequently they are less likely to confront the problem with systemic solutions such as the radical reform of the Arabic curriculum or, even more comprehensively, the formation of an alternative tertiary Arabic program for Arabs in Israel.

This chapter gauges the systemic incommensurability between Israeli-Arab and Israeli-Jewish grammars of Arabic. It highlights its effects on Arab students, and suggests ways through which it escapes the notice of both students and scholars involved in Arabic instruction. Unlike previous chapters, this chapter engages directly with Arabic grammar, its conceptualisation, and the organisation of the material for instruction.[2] Some schematic charts that are

2 Readers who are not conversant with Arabic grammar might find it easier to skim the text

provided in the course of the discussion may help visualise some of the points that are made in the chapter.

A Lévy-Bruhlian Moment

To set up the discussion of cultural incommensurability in knowledge I briefly digress and revisit one of the originary moments in the development of the modern inquiry into the cultural and historical constitution of reasoning and cognition. Specifically, I would like to define a "Lévy-Bruhlian" moment.

Philosopher Lucien Lévy-Bruhl (1857–1939) is best remembered today for arguing that members of different cultural configurations have different mentalities, that is, different modes of thought, that are potentially incommensurable and mutually incomprehensible. His insights, ingenious and revolutionary though they were, were doomed. They were set in the very flawed common sense of the Victorian anthropology of his time. I do not want to elaborate on Lévy-Bruhl's theoretical edifice here, but invoke the moment of inspiration that led to the development of his thesis.

By Lévy-Bruhl's own account, his eureka moment came after reading a French translation of three books written by a Chinese historian. The translation was irreproachable and closely conveyed the original text. Yet upon reading and rereading the text, Lévy-Bruhl could still not figure out how the ideas cohered, nor could he follow the author's argument. Having grappled with this issue, and having read more about Chinese scholarship, yet still struggling unsuccessfully to grasp the logic of the text, Lévy-Bruhl became convinced that a cultural gap existed between the mode of thought and reasoning—the mentality—of the Chinese author and his. This is what propelled him to hypothesise that culture conditions peoples' mentalities to the point that where cultures diverged to a great extent, the mentalities they engender would equally greatly diverge, preventing mutual understanding (Lévy-Bruhl et al 1923, 634).

It is this moment—the moment when one realises that one understands the words, the sentences and the syntax, yet fails to apprehend the progression of ideas and the underlying logic of a given argument or narrative—that I call the Lévy-Bruhlian moment. It is the moment of transition from trying to

---

when specific points of grammar are explicitly discussed. They should still be able to follow the general argument, although may need to take on trust some of the propositions that are derived from the specific examples.

understand alien concepts or ideas in isolation, to a strategy of trying to understand the incomprehension itself by evaluating the differences between one's own axiomatic conceptual framework and that in which the alien concepts are embedded. In a way, it is an instance of a shift to metacognitive strategies. Many anthropologists and migrants would have experienced moments like this.

Well over a century after Lévy-Bruhl had his moment of productive incomprehension, I underwent a similarly disorientating experience. I embarked on the research project that led to this book, wondering whether there was something in the way the material was organised in university classes of Arabic grammar that alienated Arab students. I could not otherwise explain how it was that Arab students who had taken Arabic grammar along with me at university, who were immeasurably more proficient than any of the Jewish students in class, struggled so valiantly yet ineffectually with what to me and my Jewish peers seemed trivial points of grammar.

Having enquired about the textbooks that were used to teach Arabic in Arab schools, I made my way to the National Library in Jerusalem to consult a copy of the classic of contemporary Arabic-grammar instruction in the Arab world—al-Jarim and Amin's textbook *al-naḥw al-wāḍiḥ* (النحو الواضح—[1938] 2005). I began reading the first chapters in Volume 2—the volume that was aimed at secondary schools. These chapters dealt with verbs and their conjugation—the material I knew so well from my own schooling. Or so I had thought. Within a page I discovered that while I seemed to understand the vocabulary of the explanations and discussion, I was completely lost as to the progression of ideas and had no intuitive sense of what the purpose of a given point was or what was to come next. It simply did not make sense. Clearly, I was lost. And that was in the area of Arabic grammar I knew best of all.

There was my Lévy-Bruhlian moment, along with the realisation that, coming at the material from the other direction, my former Arab peers had experienced a very similar comprehensive incomprehension when they were made to struggle with the grammar with which I was familiar. Unlike Lévy-Bruhl, or me for that matter, they were not disposed to explain the incomprehension in systemic terms. Rather, the incomprehension was experienced as a personal failure. This construction was, of course, motivated by the fact that their incomprehension translated into poor grades awarded to the students as individuals, while Lévy-Bruhl's, and mine, led to academic publications.

When reading al-Jarim and Amin's chapters on verbs I was particularly baffled by the elaborate classificatory edifice that distinguished the simple from the augmented verbs, and then proceeded to subdivide the augmented verbs to verbs augmented by one letter; by two letters and by three letters (see below). This stood in sharp contrast with the way I thought about verbs, namely in terms of the basic distinction between radical and paradigm and the subsequent systematic morphological analysis of specific paradigms.

It did not make much sense to me to make the qualitative distinction between what in my scheme was the first paradigm and all other paradigms. It made even less sense to group what I had hitherto known as the second, third and fourth paradigms in one category (augmented by one letter), the fifth, sixth, seventh, eighth and ninth in another (augmented by two); and the tenth along with various others in a third category (augmented by three). I had no sense of why this was being done or where the discussion was going. What is more, in trying to make sense of the very statements I was reading I found myself constantly straddling the conceptual gulf between al-Jarim and Amin's scheme of things and the one with which I was familiar.

The other thing that struck me was the extent to which the presentation in these textbooks did not rely on mindless memorisation. The sense I had had before embarking on the project, the commonsensical view in the Jewish sector at least, was that Arab Arabic instruction was primarily based on rote memorisation. Yet this was not what I found in the textbooks I was reading.

Al-Jarim and Amin's textbook, *al-naḥw al-wāḍiḥ*, proved rather typical of the Arab Arabic textbooks that I encountered later as my research project unfolded. These books would normally begin a chapter with either some sample sentences or a brief paragraph of language in use, and then proceed to guide students through the inductive derivation of rules which are then formally defined and exemplified.

This is not to say that rote memorisation is not an important aspect of Arab grammar instruction as envisaged in Arab textbooks. It is, especially in the formal, stylised declamation of syntactical analysis. But for the purposes of the mundane instruction in morphology and basic syntax it was not memorisation as much as inductive presentation that marked the textbook approach in Arabic. Students were typically invited to discover the rules from specific examples that were presented, and then instruction proceeded to refine and define the discovered rules.

I found this rather ironic, because it was in fact the instruction in the Jewish sector that relied more heavily on memorisation along with deduction. Thus, for example, the book *madrīḵ bi-šviley ha-poʿal ha-ʿaravī* (מדריך בשבילי הפועל הערבי—Landau n.d.) begins by defining morphological rules which are construed as the essentially arbitrary way the language functions, and then proceeds to give examples, followed by drills that aim to inculcate the application of these rules.

As I found out later, and as I explain below, these methodological differences in instruction are underlain by differences in the implicit notion of what a language is. This adds further weight to the profoundly disorientating difference in the conceptual structure of the material which makes the two approaches of teaching grammar—the Israeli-Jewish and Israeli-Arab ones—incommensurable.

The bulk of this chapter conveys the bewildering differences in the approaches to Arabic grammar in the two educational systems. It is these differences that ultimately precondition the cultural clash in the university Arabic grammar classroom, and which disguise it as a problem in individual educational attainment rather than a politically situated, systemic difference in the construction of knowledge.

The Sources

Much of the research for this chapter revolves around an analysis of curricular documents and textbooks. I draw on several textbooks to illustrate my points. For instruction on the Arab side I use three main texts. The first is the two-volume classic, *al-naḥw al-wāḍiḥ fī qawāʿid al-luġa al-ʿarabīya* (al-Jarim and Amin [1938] 2005). This textbook was originally published in Egypt in the early twentieth century and has been reprinted and reissued over the years in Egypt and later in Lebanon, and is still in print. It was the main text used in Arab schools in Israel up until the 1990s, and is still used in some Arab schools, including Druze schools (which have been separated administratively and pedagogically from other Arab schools as part of Israel's policy of dividing its non-Jewish Arab population into different, artificial, quasi-ethnicities). The second textbook source is the series of *al-ǧadīd fī al-luġa*—the textbooks that are part of the Ministry of Education's new curriculum for Arab schools (Abu Khadra et al 2000). This series was introduced in the 1990s to replace the outmoded books by al-Jarim and Amin. Thus, the series postpones desinential inflection till high school (tenth grade), and places a greater emphasis on syntax and its link to meaning. This book series is supposedly used throughout Arab schools in Israel, although the extent to which it has transformed instruction in practice is not very clear. Teachers often fall back on their own experience in teaching, for example by introducing aspects of the desinential inflection at much earlier stages than the designers of the new curriculum intend. Many teachers insist that it is not practicable to adhere to the program advocated by the developers of *al-ǧadīd*, and chart their own way through the material. One visible innovation in *al-ǧadīd* that readily resonates with current teachers is the type of sample material used to derive rules of grammar. The books rely on themes that are linked to contemporary youth experience and youth literature, reflecting perhaps a shift from a focus on Classical Arabic which typifies the work of al-Jarim and Amin, to a broader conceptualisation of the target language as, literally, the standard language (*al-luġa al-miʿyarīya*—اللغة المعيارية). The third textbook I use to analyse Israeli-Arab instruction is volume 4 of *mabādiʾ al-ʿarabīya* by Rashid al-Shartuni (Shartuni 1986), which is universally used as a reference book by teachers and often inspires class preparation, although I have not heard of it actually being used as a textbook in class. I also draw on segments from the textbook by Walīd ʿAṭif al-ʾAnṣārī, *Naẓarīyat ʾal-ʿāmil fī al-naḥw al-ʿarabīy* (al-Ansari 2003) that were used in one of the advanced courses designed for Arab students at Haifa University. While clearly each of the textbooks exhibits a unique approach, the commonalities among them are profound when contrasted with the textbooks that are used in the Jewish sector.

For Jewish instruction I use primarily the following books. Yaakov Landau, *Madriḫ bi-šviley ha-poʿal ha-ʿaravī* (Landau n.d.) is the standard textbook for verb conjugation instruction beyond the very basic forms. It is used at both schools and universities. Dov Iron, *taḥbir ha-lašōn ha-ʿaravīt* (Iron n.d.) remains a standard of Arabic syntax which is used at universities, and is relied on by school teachers in the Jewish sector for specialised exercises and for explanations more generally. Peled's *Written Arabic Syntax: In Theory and Practice* [in Hebrew] is a university level textbook that is used at Tel Aviv University (Peled 1998). I also occasionally refer to other textbooks that are used or have been used in Jewish schools.

As a whole, the two sets of textbooks differ fundamentally in their organisation of the material and the educational encounter, attesting to the systemic difference between Arabic-grammar instruction in the Jewish sector and Arabic-grammar instruction in the Arab sector.

These differences pervade the entire educational encounter including instructional strategies and student classroom experience. The effect of these differences is uneven. Educational choices are motivated by the fact that academic instruction is geared towards Jews, and that Arab Arabic instruction occupies a liminal position in a no-man's land between mainstream Israeli schooling and instruction in the Arab world.

The discussion that follows begins with examples where instructors misconstrue Arabic grammar to fit the grammatic common sense of Jewish students. These examples include the presentation of the Arabic hamza (ء) and the explanation of the present participle. Forcing the material to be intuitive to Jewish students puts them at risk of error and miscomprehension, and obscures things for Arabs. These effects are much starker when Arabic grammatical terms rooted in the Arab theory of *ʿamal* are misconstrued as elements of a European syntactical typology. Jewish Arabic teachers and university instructors unwittingly use Arab terms to mean something different from what they mean in their Arab context. I will be canvassing the consequences of misconstruing nominal sentences, topicalisation, and the relationships between subject and predicate. Such misconstructions cover up the difference between the Arab-Israeli and Jewish-Israeli grammars, and leave Arabs in a state of inexplicable incomprehension. To convey the radical alterity between the two systems I will first present Jewish appropriations of Arab terms and the theoretical edifice that is constructed over these appropriations, and then cover the same grounds from the Arab perspective ending up with a completely different construct.

Another dimension of difference between the two grammatical approaches is the way grammar is carved up. I look at the different positions of pronominal affixes in the two grammatical approaches. They are primarily elements of morphology in Jewish instruction, and elements of syntax in Arab instruction. The adoption of the Jewish scheme overvalues areas of grammar—typically the decontextualised conjugation of verbs along dimensions that include person and number—that Arab students had not been drilled at to the same extent as Jews. I then move to broaden the discussion into language ideology showing how the Arab and Jewish approaches differ in the way they understand language, in where they locate agency, in the metaphors that animate the grammatic imagination, in the status they ascribe to their linguistic rules, and in the aims of their pedagogical endeavour. These elements can be seen in the mutually counterintuitive approaches to verb classification and to desinential inflection. I contrast the Jewish and Arab approaches in some detail. I then highlight how the difference in linguistic ideology extends to differences in affective tonality, humour and so forth.

The two systems of grammar emerge as incommensurable. By incommensurable I mean that one cannot translate concepts or turns of phrase between the two systems; that it is impossible to graft areas of analysis from one to the other; and that one cannot base a singular analysis upon both approaches. Rather, the two approaches are mutually exclusive. They differ in their purpose and in how they understand knowledge, language and instruction. They differ in the mix of cognitive operations that they require of students. They differ in their ultimate measure of success and failure, and the significance they accord both outcomes.

The chapter concludes with a discussion of the alienating effects of this grammatic incommensurability, including a rare, yet highly instructive, role reversal whereby Jews were placed on the receiving end of this clash in the construction of knowledge.

Lost in Simplification: The Light Hamza and the Meaning of Tenses

The fact that Arabic-grammar instruction at universities is geared towards non-proficient Jews motivates university course designers to integrate some of the unsubtle shortcuts that typify the instruction of Arabic grammar at Jewish schools. University Arabic instruction in Israel builds on the curriculum and approaches of Jewish secondary schools. Because Arabic instruction in Jewish schools teaches Arabic as a foreign language, Arabic grammar instruction aims to inculcate correct, as opposed to incorrect, usage. Using this dichotomy of judgement often compels instruction to refrain from canvassing the full gamut of subtleties and alternative practices. Liminal usage is suppressed in favour of a stark, right/wrong dichotomy. In other words, in Jewish schools Arabic grammar is standardised and simplified, and the instruction is essentially prescriptive. Consequently, when university instruction follows the approach of Jewish schools, the fluidity of Arabic usage—an integral aspect of Arabic as a living language—is very often downplayed. Furthermore, whenever possible teachers draw analogies to Hebrew grammar even when such an analogy violates some of the subtle differences between the two languages.

While this approach may be inevitable in Jewish schools where Arabic is the second foreign language taught, it is not inevitable at universities, where many students are Arab, and all students should presumably be substantially proficient. Instructional choices are clearly not motivated by pure considerations of pedagogical effectiveness.

The harmonisation of educational approaches at the secondary and tertiary levels may be motivated, at least in part, by the fact that the market is small, forcing textbook writers (with rare exceptions such as Peled's Hebrew textbook *Written Arabic Syntax in Theory and Practice*) to compose what is essentially a high school level textbook, to which they add some advanced exercises to make it relevant to university-level instruction. A case in point is Landau's Hebrew textbook that is dedicated to the Arabic verb (Landau n.d.). The universities' pervasive use of secondary-school textbooks has the effect of reducing the extent to which university instructors can diverge from the curricular priorities that prevail at the secondary educational level.

Some of the simplifications of Israeli-Jewish grammar instruction lead to errors and conflict with the way the material is presented in standard Israeli-Arab instruction. In some situations where alternative morphological variants coexist, the full gamut may be overlooked and a single variant flagged as the correct one. In other situations where correct morphological practice involves subtle differences in different grammatical conditions these subtleties may be ignored leading to the sanctioning of incorrect practices. In situations where the logic of Arabic differs from that of Hebrew, the differences may be downplayed, leading Jews to misunderstand Arabic constructs.

One example is the issue of how to render the light hamza at the beginning of complex verb structures of the 7th to 10th paradigms. The Hebrew textbooks render those as a strong hamza when the verb stands on its own, and a hamza that is substituted by a *waṣla* when the verb is preceded by a vowel. There is no such thing as a weak hamza in this way of thinking (on the weak hamza see Riding 2005, 19–25).

In fact, throughout their instruction at school Jewish students acquire the sense that it is the letter ا (*ʾalif*) that is being vocalised. The underlying assumption is that that letter is the identical Arabic equivalent to the Hebrew א (*ʾalef*). Jewish students are taught that when an *ʾalif* is vocalised it must always be with a hamza. They are taught that to vocalise an *ʾalif* without a hamza sign is a mistake.

For example, the classic high school textbook of Arabic, *Madāriǧ* (Einat n.d.), presents a verb and proceeds to explain that

> ה إ של הבנין השביעי היא וצלאית, כלומר, אם תבוא לפניה אות, או מלה מקבלת וצלה.
>
> The إ of the seventh form is a *waṣla*-type *ʾalif*, that is, if the *ʾalif* is preceded by a letter or a word, will get a *waṣla*.
>
> EINAT n.d., vol. b, 116–117

Note that the relevant letter here is the *ʾalif* not the hamza. This approach continues with Landau's advanced book of verb morphology.

By contrast, in the Arab texts the letter in question is the hamza and not the *ʾalif*, and the distinction is drawn between the همزة القطع (*hamzat al-qaṭʿ*—rendered here as the strong hamza) and همزة الوصل (*hamzat al-waṣl*—rendered here as the weak hamza). In other words, it is the hamza that is the *waṣla*-type letter in question and not the *ʾalif*. (See for example al-Jarim and Amin [1938] 2005, primary school vol., book 3, pages 43–44.)

The Israeli-Jewish way of interpreting *ʾalif* (ا) as the letter and the hamza (ء) as an orthographic convention that applies when the *ʾalif* is vocalised is consistent with the conventions of the Hebrew alphabet. It does not, however, make much sense of the situations when the hamza changes its orthographic presentation and appears on a *waw* (ؤ) on a *yā* (ئ) or on its own (ء). The Arab way of interpreting the hamza as the letter and the *ʾalif*, *waw* and *yā* as orthographic conventions (as "seats" of the hamza), is a more elegant approximation of the Arabic reality where the changes in vocalisation that are involved in conjugation, for example, can cause the seat of the hamza to change, but the hamza remains *in situ*.

Moreover, the Israeli-Jewish oversight of the difference between the two types of hamza makes things simple, but leads to further orthographic inconsistencies with prevalent practices in Arab instruction. Israeli-Jewish instruction requires that whenever an *ʾalif* is vocalised, it should have a hamza accompanying it. For Arab instructors the weak hamza is fundamentally different from the strong hamza, and is merely there by default for lack of a vocalisation immediately preceding the word that it opens. Consequently, Arab textbooks usually vocalise the weak hamza without indicating it explicitly (e.g. اِنْتَبَهْتُ، اِخْتَبَرْتُ—in al-Jarim and Amin [1938] 2005, primary school vol., book 1, section III, 43). By the standards of Israeli-Jewish Arabic instruction al-Jarim and Amin committed a grievous orthographic error of vocalising an *ʾalif* without a hamza.

The same applies to the way this is rendered in *al-ǧadīd*, also with the vocalisation but without the hamza sign when not preceded by a vocalisation, and without any sign when preceded with vocalisation (where Israeli-Jewish instruction would always have the *waṣla* sign explicitly written), although in that book series, written by Arab scholars who are intimately familiar with the Israeli-Jewish instruction at university, both practices are explicitly allowed.[3] Interestingly, Shartuni's conjugation tables indicate the weak hamza explicitly (Shartuni 1986).

From the perspective of Israeli-Arab grammar, then, and in contrast with Israeli-Jewish instruction, the equivalent letter of the Hebrew *ʾalef* is the *hamza*, not the *ʾalif*. The difference between the strong and weak hamza are not related to the *ʾalif* which is an orthographic convention. The weak hamza is a mere auxiliary, and does not deserve the same orthographic respect as does the strong hamza. It can be dropped from writing and just its vocalisation included, and the *waṣla* need not be written at all.

The Jewish student remains oblivious to all this. What s/he learns helps explain when a sound is added, and when a *waṣla* is written. The student will correctly anticipate the pronunciation of a reader of Standard Arabic, and will

---

3 For example
"همزة الوصل تُكتب على شكل همزة القطع (أو تكتب حركتها فقط) وتلفظ في اول الكلام، لكنّها تكتب على شكل صاد صغيرة او تترك دون علامة في درج الكلام، ولا تلفظ."
("The weak hamza is written in the form of the strong hamza (or its vocalisation alone is written) and is pronounced at the beginning of a phrase, but it is written in the form of a small *ṣād* or left without a mark in the middle of a phrase, where it is not pronounced"—Abu Khadra et al 2000, vol. 3 (for 9th grade), 23).

be able to produce one of the acceptable variants of orthographic practice, but will not be aware of alternative, more salient, orthographic conventions. This will not disturb a student who will read unvocalised printed or even handwritten Arabic. It therefore works. But the omission ignores the complexity of linguistic practice, and would become a nuisance for the student if s/he were to interact with vocalised Arab texts, and find them replete with seemingly erroneous practices, or if the student were to discuss grammar with Arabs. Clearly these scenarios did not seem sufficiently likely for those academics who designed the curriculum.

It is specifically the academics whose judgement is crucial here, rather than Arabic teachers. In fact, the current Jewish Arabic teachers with whom I spoke—those who have learned their Arabic through the Israeli education system before becoming teachers—were unaware of the Arab interpretation of the hamza and the accompanying orthographic practices, betraying the very ignorance I am discussing, and reflecting the restricted extent to which Jews engage with Arabic texts and orthography. It is those who teach the Jewish teachers who have made the strategic decision to keep matters "simple" here, and teach on a need-to-know basis.

Moreover, here too we have another indication of the curriculum's priority. The curriculum seeks to create an explanation that works rather than to understand the grammar as such. It appeals to the common sense of Jewish students (through the identification of *ʾalif* with *ʾalef*), and it works because it generates a correct practice. Its arbitrary nature is unlikely to be exposed due to the limited interaction of Jewish students with Arab culture. But this is not consonant with what Arab students learn at school, potentially bewildering Arab university students.

The issue of the meaning of tenses is another example of such a simplification that caters to the limits of Jewish students' understanding, and is probably more significant because it may lead to misunderstanding of the content and intention of a text or an utterance.

Arab grammar conflates tense (e.g. past, future) and aspect (e.g. perfect, imperfect) in its construction of the temporal component of verbs (Ryding 2005, 51–52). Israeli-Jewish grammar ignores the aspectual element of the verbal structure. The Arabic imperfect tense is rendered in Israeli-Jewish instruction as "present/future" or future tense. Jewish students are taught that Arabic, like formal Hebrew grammar, uses the one verb structure to indicate present and future. They are also taught that participles (e.g. breaking, broken—*kāsir*, *maksūr*), which intuitively to modern Hebrew speakers are present-tense verbs, are considered nouns, as they are, in fact, in Hebrew. This point is emphasised in instruction because being nouns, participles (like infinitives) are desinentially inflected, in contrast with verbs which, according to Israeli-Jewish Arabic instruction, are not. (This notion of desinential inflection is another one of the simplifications that distorts Arabic grammar, as I explain below.)

There is nothing wrong with the observation that the Arabic tense that is often referred to in English as the imperfect denotes the present/future. As al-Jarim and Amin point out, this tense indicates an occurrence in the present or the future ("الفعل المضارع هو كل فعل يدل على حصول عمل في الزمن الحاضر او المستقبل ..."—al-Jarim and Amin [1938] 2005, primary school vol., book 1 page 16). However, it is not quite equivalent to the Hebrew sense or usage of tense, and the fundamental distinction between the perfect and the imperfect remains lost on Jewish students. It leaves students at further risk of error and incomprehension.

Thus, following the verbal construction قبل ان (*qabla ʾann*—before) Arabic constructs the verb in the imperfect even if it is set in the past (e.g. هذا قبل ان تظهر الشيعة على الاغلبية بالقيروان), an unnatural construction for Hebrew speakers who would set the verb that follows that construction in the past tense if it pertained to the time before the absolute present. Consequently Jewish students may mistakenly assume that the imperfect structure of the verb following قبل ان (*qabla ʾann*) means that the action it denotes has not yet taken place. And further, when writing in Arabic Jewish students might be tempted to use the perfect tense for a verb following قبل ان (*qabla ʾann*) if it pertains to an action that has occurred in the past.

Further, basing the analysis of Arab verbs on Hebrew common sense leaves Jews in the dark as to the subtleties of meanings of the active present participle (on the complexity and variability see Holes 1995, 122 ff.; Beeston 1970, 34; and Ryding 2005, 103–104). Jewish students learn to treat that participle as a present tense rendition, as a noun, or as an adjective. Completely lacking from the instruction is the much wider range of usages, such as the sense of a completed action (a true active equivalent of the passive participle). I have only seen systematic discussions of the active participle in Hebrew textbooks in two textbooks, both teaching colloquial Arabic: Aryeh Levin's grammar of the Jerusalemite dialect (Levin 1994, 95–99) which is not widely used in classroom instruction, and Yohanan Elihai's course in colloquial Arabic (Elihai 1992) that is not used at schools at all. (However, Elihai's course is used as the basis for some colloquial Arabic instruction at universities and remains unrivalled as a Hebrew instructional text of Palestinian colloquial Arabic).

The way academic instruction approaches tenses—in line with the dominant Israeli-Jewish approach—also alienates Arab students whose modes of classification of tenses, and their significance, differs fundamentally. The formal axis of differentiation in Arab instruction is a combination of temporal and morphological considerations. The imperfect is the *muḍāriʿ* (مضارع—literally "the one that resembles"), and is named so not on temporal grounds but rather on morphological grounds. It is named so precisely because it resembles nouns in that it *is*, in fact, desinentially inflected.

But how could it be that for Jews the imperfect (in contrast with the participle) is a verb because it is *not* desinentially inflected, yet for Arab students it is called *muḍāriʿ* precisely because it *is*? This is part of the broader incommensurability of the two systems of grammar.

Mistranslation and the Different Construction of Nominal Sentences

Most university students of Arabic—both Jewish and Arab—come to university with a sense that they have learned at school *the* grammar of Arabic—rather than *a* grammar of Arabic. The word grammar is multivalent. It may refer to a series of syntactical, morphological and other regularities in a language. It may also refer to the construction and representation of these regularities. To most students the two are one and the same.

This lack of scholastic self-awareness is precipitated by the inherent positivism of both Israeli-Jewish and Israeli-Arab grammatical approaches. Both construct the science of grammar as an empirical study that discovers the reality that lies out there in the real world. The description and analysis they offer are construed as direct, unmediated reflections of this reality. This kind of positivism lacks reflexivity. Their radically divergent underlying theories of grammar are not approached as objects of consideration or instruction in their own right, and are taken for granted. Thus, Arab school students are not presented with the theory of *ʿamal* (governance, dependency)—the theory which underlies much of the Arabic Linguistic Tradition—as but one possible way to conceptualise language. In fact, most arrive at university without having been systematically introduced to the theory at all. Nor for that matter do Jewish students study the theories and conceptual frameworks of their own grammar of Arabic as a historically specific construction. In both instances what are theoretical constructs are reified as they are misconstrued in educational design as inherent aspects of the nature of language, and are therefore not made fully explicit to students.

The result is that while beginning undergraduate students can, to varying degrees, apply theoretical and analytical concepts that they study, they lack the awareness of the theory as a potential object of investigation in its own right. Most remain ignorant of the specificity of the theoretical approach that underlies the conceptual framework that they use. They therefore lack the basic intellectual orientation that would enable them to see that other conceptualisations are also possible, and that theirs is but one, historically specific approach.

This lack of theoretical self-awareness is pervasive in practice, if not always in theory.[4] The Israeli-Jewish and Arab grammars of Arabic are treated by university instructors, and more generally by scholars and intellectuals, as an analogous field of knowledge which is equivalent in nature to the grammars of other languages. The stated aim of dealing in grammar and syntax is to clarify the regularities of the language.

The notion that grammatical concepts can be applied across languages is further predicated on the premises that the grammar of a language is the analytic description of its regularities, and that a single conceptual framework can describe the regularities of all languages. This is not just an abstract idea but part and parcel of an effective strategy of instruction at least on the Jewish side, where teachers commonly cite and highlight the common grammatical features of Hebrew and Arabic in order to demonstrate, clarify and anchor the logic of Arabic in the linguistic common sense of their Hebrew-speaking students.

The sense of grammar as a monolithic metalinguistic framework is further reinforced by the practice of translation of grammatical terms from Arabic into Hebrew. This creates the false impression of identity in the construction of grammar. A common strategy in Arabic-grammar instruction at Israeli universities is to render Arabic grammatical concepts in equivalent Hebrew concepts which are part of the contemporary Israeli-Jewish grammar of Arabic. These translations seem to work in that they generally designate the same objects as the original Arab term. But being rooted in a different system of knowledge,

4 The scholars of grammar who teach and direct Arabic-grammar instruction at Israeli universities are very aware of the historical evolution of the Arabic Linguistic Tradition. Some are leading authorities on the Arabic Grammatical Tradition and are conversant with the nuances of linguistic debates that typified the tradition's golden age. However, these debates are not the core of Arabic grammar as it is taught today. For example, while the classical theory of *ʿamal* continues to form the basis of the Arab approach to desinential inflection, the theory itself is not taught at schools as a theory, or in any systematic way. Rather, its effects are integrated into the formulaic modes of recitation. Historians of the Arabic Linguistic Tradition generally find little value in studying the Arabic Linguistic Tradition of the last few centuries. Their expertise is therefore not quite relevant to contemporary Arab Arabic-grammar instruction. Consequently, Jewish grammarians' deep knowledge of the medieval Arab science of grammar does not normally translate into consciousness of the essential differences between the contemporary curricula of Arabic grammar in Jewish and Arab schools in Israel.

this sense of translatability is misleading. It does not, in fact, translate the original concept at all. The fact that the translation seems to "work" makes it all too easy to mistake the two systems as somehow similar conceptual frameworks that are merely rendered in different languages. They are not.

In fact, the translation does not even "work" as well as participants might think. But the inevitable anomalies are kept invisible by various mechanisms. Israeli university instructors and educators in the Jewish school streams translate concepts from Arabic opportunistically and haphazardly. There is not a systematic translation of terms from Arabic to Hebrew, which would inevitably come up against terms that cannot be translated thereby exposing the limits of translatability. Even when the translation of a particular term seems to succeed, this sense of success may be false. In the example below a term in Hebrew is taken to be equivalent to an Arabic term. But this equivalence is illusory. The Arabic term denotes a set of phenomena which is merely a subset of what is taken to be its equivalent Hebrew term. Because the instructional power relations are such that terms need to be translated from Arabic into Hebrew, but not vice versa, a false sense of equivalence between the two terms can emerge. What the Arabic term designates is also apparently designated by the seemingly equivalent Hebrew term. The fact that the opposite direction of translation would run into contradictions passes unnoticed.

But because translation seems to work, teachers and students on both sides of the language/knowledge divide operate as if the two systems are somehow compatible. This false sense of commensurability then makes it impossible for stakeholders, most significantly baffled Arab university students of Arabic, to make sense of the difficulty that Arabs have with university Arabic grammar.

The areas of basic syntax and verb morphology usefully illustrate these underappreciated limits on translatability. To demonstrate the incommensurability I will describe the way Israeli-Jewish instruction translates and develops some of its basic analytic framework, and how it maintains a sense of consistency and hides some anomalies. I then turn to the way these Arab concepts are developed in the Israeli-Arab approach to show that Israeli-Arab grammar produces a no less coherent and even more elegant analytic framework which nonetheless differs from the Israeli-Jewish framework.[5]

5 The description also seeks to give a flavour of the disorientation by alluding to gaps in the Israeli-Jewish conceptual framework while describing its internal logic. These gaps will be brought together and clarified in the subsequent description of the Israeli-Arab conceptual framework. Readers who may be disorientated by this mode of analysis may wish to refer to table 2 for a schematic analytic juxtaposition of the two approaches.

Jewish students learn that the Arabic terms *fiʿl* and *fāʿil* are respectively the predicate and subject of a verbal sentence, and that the verb normally precedes its subject in Standard Arabic.

This might seem a reasonable equivalent to Arab constructions, such as that of al-Jarim and Amin's *al-naḥw al-wāḍiḥ*: "every sentence that is made up of a *fiʿl* and a *fāʿil* is called a verbal sentence (*ǧumla fiʿlīya*)" (al-Jarim and Amin [1938] 2005, primary school vol., book 1 page 28). But note the lack of mention of word order in this quote. We shall return to the issue of word order below.

Another pair of terms—*mubtadaʾ* and *ḫabar*—are taken by Arabic instructors in the Jewish streams and universities to be the terms that respectively designate the subject and predicate of a nominal sentence.[6] This seems close to the terms' definition in Arab Arabic instruction, but there is an almost imperceptible yet significant difference. Consider "Every sentence that is composed of a *mubtadaʾ* and a *ḫabar* is called a nominal sentence" (al-Jarim and Amin [1938] 2005, primary school vol., book 1 page 30); or "the verbal sentence begins with a verb, while the nominal sentence does not begin with a verb but rather usually begins with a noun"; and "the nominal sentence is a sentence that is headed by a noun (*ʾism*) and is composed of a *mubtadaʾ* and a *ḫabar*" (Abu Khadra et al 2000, volume for year 7, pages 24 and 110 respectively).

What the Arab textbooks are saying is that nominal sentences are sentences that contain a *mubtadaʾ* and a *ḫabar*, which is different from saying that *mubtadaʾ* and *ḫabar* are the subject and predicate of a nominal sentence.

And from here begins the departure of the systemic logic of the two doctrines. Jewish students are presented with the observation that Arab grammarians distinguish between nominal sentences and verbal sentences according to the first word in the sentence. If the first word is a verb, the sentence is called a verbal sentence and Arabs use the terms *fiʿl* and *fāʿil* to denote subject and predicate. If the first word is not a verb, usually a noun, then the sentence is called a nominal sentence and the terms *mubtadaʾ* and *ḫabar* are used to indicate the same terms, namely subject and predicate. Together these two sentence structures form the major components of the universe of sentences in Arabic.

6 For example, see Iron n.d. vol. 1 page 1:

"הנושא במשפט השמני נקרא مُبْتَدَأٌ (مُبْتَدَأٌ بِهِ כלומר המלה שבה מתחיל המשפט), ואילו הנשוא במשפט זה נקרא خبر (خبر—ידיעה, ידיעה על הנושא), כגון: زَيْدٌ حَكِيمٌ. زَيْدٌ הוא ה مُبْتَدَأٌ; حَكِيمٌ—خَبَرٌ."

(Iron n.d., vol. 1, 1)

Jewish students see this as an interesting contrast with the syntax of Hebrew grammar, where the difference between nominal and verbal sentences depends on the nature of the predicate and not its position in the sentence relative to the subject. If the predicate is a verb, the sentence is verbal. If the predicate is not a verb, the sentence is nominal.

That Arab grammarians should focus on something trivial like which word opens the sentence, while grammarians of Hebrew should focus on something systemic and complex like the nature of the predicate, confirms to many Jewish students and their Jewish Arabic school teachers a prejudicial sense of the relative simplicity of Arab scholarship.

These are, however, misconstructions based on mistranslation. *Mubtadaʾ* is a concept rooted in the syntactic theory of *ʿamal* (which is normally translated as "the theory of governance" or "the theory of dependency" in the historiographic research into the Arabic Linguistic Tradition), and is not defined in any way as subject.[7] But once translated as subject, classroom instruction continues using the terms of subject and predicate in Hebrew, even in areas where Arab terminology differs. This consistent (mis)translation of the Arabic term *mubtadaʾ* as subject of a nominal sentence creates a false sense of security in Jewish students of Arabic, and their teachers, that they understand the Arabic term, and that they are dealing with equivalent concepts, when in fact they are not, as will shortly become clear.

When discussing two groups of prepositions and auxiliary verbs that begin nominal constructions with abnormal desinential inflections, the conscientious Jewish-sector teacher might also present the seeming relevant Arabic terms for the subject and the predicate. The groups are named in both Arab and Jewish-sector instruction after their prototypical member and are called *ʾinna* and her sisters (i.e. *ʾinna* and the prepositions that behave similarly) and *kāna* and her sisters (i.e. *kāna* and the auxiliaries that behave similarly). The terms

7 As the discussion below will clarify, a more accurate way of rendering the relationship between the concepts would be to point out that the word which is the *mubtadaʾ* in the nominal sentence functions as the subject of the sentence. In other words, if we looked for a subject in a sentence with a *mubtadaʾ*, the *mubtadaʾ* would be it. But this would only beg the question of what a *mubtadaʾ* actually is. And given the concept has no equivalent in the Western orientated Israeli-Jewish grammar because it is part of a heuristic system that is completely different from the European system—the two apparently similar terms differ in their structure, their function, and the role they play within the broader intellectual culture—the only way to explain it would be to acknowledge the radical conceptual alterity between the two systems, and start presenting the Arab terminology as an alternative, integrated system of grammar.

that are normally presented by Jewish-sector teachers as the subject and predicate are the *ʾism* of *ʾinna* or *kāna* and the *ḫabar* of *ʾinna* or *kāna*. The term *ḫabar* seems familiar. It is the same term that is translated as predicate of a normal nominal sentence. This gives a continually reassuring sense of parallel between the Arabic and the Hebrew terms, but what happened to *mubtadaʾ*? It is no longer used here by Arab grammarians to denote the word that functions as subject. Rather, the term is now replaced by the term *ʾism*—literally "noun"—to create the constructs of "the noun of *ʾinna*" and "the noun of *kāna*". The significance of the fact that in this context the term *mubtadaʾ* is no longer used to denote the word that functions as subject is overlooked by such teachers, or shrugged off as an unfortunate terminological infelicity of Arab grammarians.

With this bit of oversight, the mistranslations of *mubtadaʾ* and *ḫabar* seem to work in that the translated terms seem to designate the same instances as the original ones. Nonetheless, conceptual cracks keep appearing, demanding some additional patching up.

Topicalised sentences—in particular those where it is the subject of the predicative clause that is topicalised—are usually classed in Jewish-sector schools and university classrooms as normal nominal sentences. Iron's textbook, the most advanced on syntax that is used at schools, discusses topicalisation as a complex sentence in which the *ḫabar* may be a verbal sentence (vol. 1 pages 2–3). But it focuses on sentences in which the subject of the topicalised sentence is an object of the verbal sentence. The example given is "زيدٌ مَرِضَ أبوهُ" (*zaydun mariḍa ʾabūhu*)—literally, "Zayd, his father fell ill". Significantly, the concept of topicalisation is exemplified with sentences whose verbatim translation into Hebrew inevitably produces a sentence that is topicalised, too. This further reinforces the false sense of conceptual compatibility between the two systems of grammatical theory. Iron does not canvass sentences that to Arab grammarians are topicalised, yet may be translated as simple Hebrew sentences (see below). This further confuses things as Jewish students assume that their intuitive notion of topicalisation applies to Arabic topicalisation. By the same token Arab university students are also led to believe that when they discuss topicalisation they mean, in fact, the same thing as their instructors and fellow Jewish students.

The problems would become apparent if instructors chose to foreground topicalised Arabic sentences in which the subject is identical in both the topicalised sentence and its predicative clause. The sentence "زيدٌ مَرِضَ" (*zaydun mariḍa*) would appear to the Jewish student as "Zayd fell ill", where in fact it is best translated as a topicalised construction, something like "Zayd, he fell ill". This construction may be used to indicate meanings that are constructed in English as "It is Zayd who fell ill" or any number of other constructions that foreground and emphasise the fact that the person who fell ill was Zayd. By contrast, "Zayd fell ill" would be conveyed in Standard Arabic by the simple verbal sentence "مَرِضَ زيدٌ" (*mariḍa zaydun*) with the verb preceding its subject. (I will shortly discuss the Israeli-Arab parallel grammatical construction.)

Sentences like "زيدٌ مَرِضَ" (*zaydun mariḍa*) which I glossed as "Zayd, he fell ill" are presented in the Israeli-Jewish classroom as inverted simple sentences, a kind of unusual construction that is reserved for specific stylistic contexts like newspaper headlines. Students learn that notwithstanding such unusual constructions Arabic generally prefers to have the verb appear before its subject. The latter point needs to be emphasised to Jewish students because contemporary Hebrew stylistic preferences would normally have the subject precede the predicate in contrast with the preferred construction in Standard Arabic. Hence the need to reiterate to students the practice of putting the verb first.

However when instructors at Israeli universities and in Jewish schools wrongly identify such topicalised sentences as simple nominal sentences, they open up a new can of worms for the teachers and students of Arabic, namely the problem of inconsistency in agreement in number between verb and subject.

This involves another mistranslation, as it were, of the conceptual framework of Arabic grammar into the Israeli-Jewish grammar of Arabic. Or rather, in this case, it involves ignoring the difference between the two scholastic traditions in the designation of the analytic boundaries of verb morphology. In contrast with the Arab construction of syntax, the dominant approach in Jewish schools and in Israeli universities sees the pronominal suffixes of verbs as part of the verb conjugation, as a matter of morphology, that is, rather than as a matter of syntax. And so, those schooled in Israeli-Jewish grammar of Arabic treat the pronominal affixes of conjugated verbs as an integral part of verb morphology, that is, as one of the dimensions along which verbs are conjugated.

This leaves us with the following anomaly. When the subject seemingly precedes the verb, as in the sentence "الاولاد مرضوا" (*al'awlādu mariḍū*)—"the children, they fell ill", the verb appears to agree in pluralisation with the subject. The "u" sound at the end of the verb "*mariḍū*" is a pronominal suffix that indicates masculine, third-person plural. In other words, when the subject is plural, dual, or singular, the affixes of the verbs will indicate plural, dual or singular respectively. But when the subject is stated explicitly after the verb as in "مرض الاولاد" (*mariḍa al'awlādu*) "the children fell ill"—the verb lacks a pronominal affix, seemingly appearing in the singular.

So from the perspective of Jewish students and instructors in university Arabic grammar classes, Zayd and his friends can fall ill in various grammatical ways. One of these ways, "مرض الاولاد" (*mariḍa al-ʾawlādu*) "the children fell ill", appears to have a verb in the singular preceding a plural subject; while the other, "الاولاد مرضوا" (*alʾawlādu mariḍū*), appears to convey the same meaning, but with the verb, now following the subject, appearing in the plural.

As a result, Jewish students of Arabic learn that a verb that precedes its subject will always come in the singular, but a verb that follows its subject, will agree with the subject in duality and pluralisation.

These syntactic irritants, namely the preference to begin a sentence with a verb and the inconsistent agreement between subject and verb, are major hurdles for Jewish students. The paucity of composition and free writing exercises that Jewish students are required to prepare and submit throughout their academic careers both hides the extent of the problem and hinders them from internalising proper syntactic style in Arabic writing.

Still, this construction of Arabic syntax and grammar seems basic to Jewish teachers and students of Arabic. Academic instruction in Arabic assumes that students are already familiar with these aspects of Arabic, yet they can be thoroughly bewildering to Arabs, many of whom had never encountered the rule about the verb's erratic agreement with the subject. Their bewilderment is no less bewildering to the few Jews who are made privy to their bewilderment.

It would have been much less bewildering all round if it were recognised that the seeming translation of syntactic terms, although appearing to work, is a mistranslation. The syntax that Jews acquire during their schooling—a contemporary variety of Orientalist grammar—is fundamentally different from the grammar that Arabs learn at school, to which I now turn.

For their part, Arab students arrive at university having learnt a set of observations that are rooted in a science of dynamic relations between words and particles that produce specific desinential inflections and structures in specific contexts.

At its core, the science is constructed around the theory of *ʿamal* ('governance' or "dependency"). This theory is effectively a social theory of words and parts of words, and it underpins the conceptualisation and instruction of desinential inflection. It involves a power inequality among elements of speech, and a system of rights and influences, as words and parts thereof vie for power and influence (Levin 1995; Versteegh 1978, 262–263). The field of desinential inflection is perceived as the heart of Arabic grammar in the Arab tradition, and the theory of *ʿamal* is the core heuristic of that field. The stylised declamation of the analysis of desinential inflection is the ultimate manifestation of knowledge of grammar, and both the position of desinential inflection and its stylised manifestation are fixed in their iconic position by the inertia of tradition.

TABLE 2 *A schematic approximation of some differences between the two systems*

The Arab perspective	The sentence	The Jewish-sector perspective
Meaning: the children fell ill	مرض الاولاد *mariḍa al-ʾawlādu*	Meaning: the children fell ill
A verbal sentence because it contains a predicative verb		A verbal sentence because it opens with a verb
The verb (which never conjugates by number), *mariḍa*, precedes a noun, *al-ʾawlād*, which is a plural noun.		The verb, *mariḍa*, precedes its subject, *al-ʾawlād* and is therefore in the singular in disagreement with the plural verb.
The preceding verb governs the noun *al-ʾawlād* and puts it in the *rafʿ* which is marked by *u*		The noun *al-ʾawlād* has the mark *u* of the nominative case[8] because it is the subject of the sentence.
Meaning: the children, they fell ill	الاولاد مرضوا *al-ʾawlādu mariḍū*	Meaning: the children fell ill
A topicalised sentence without a verb (and therefore a complex nominal sentence) where the predicate is a clause, which is itself a verbal sentence.		A nominal sentence because it begins with a noun (which is followed by a verb).
The verb (which never conjugates by number) *mariḍa* is followed by its subject, the suffix *ū*, to construct a full sentence, *mariḍū* (they fell ill), which serves as a clause in the topicalised construction where it is preceded by an explicit noun.		The subject is *al-ʾawlād* and its predicate is *mariḍū*. The verb follows its subject and therefore agrees with it in number.
The principle of *ibtidāʾ* governs the noun *al-ʾawlād* and puts it in the *rafʿ* which is marked by *u*.		The noun *al-ʾawlād* has the mark *u* of the nominative case because it is the subject of the sentence.

8 Normally glossed as "the first case"—*hayaḥsa harishona* (היחסה הראשונה).

TABLE 3 *Aide-memoire—approximations of some Arab grammatical terms*

Arabic term	Approximation in European terminology
fiʿl	verb; a predicate that defines a verbal sentence and governs the *fāʿil*
fāʿil	the agent in a verbal sentence; governed by the verb
mubtadaʾ	the topic in a nominal sentence; a word governed by the principle of *ibtidāʾ*
ḫabar	comment on the mubtada'; a predicate that defines a nominal sentence
rafʿ	nominative case or indicative mood
naṣb	accusative case or subjunctive mood
ǧarr	genitive case
ǧazm	jussive mood

This approach differs from the conceptual framework that underlies European grammatical analysis. The logic of the concepts of subject and predicate, or in their more appropriate Arabic translations of *musnad ʾilayhi* and *musnad*, derives from a different approach and are therefore different kinds of things from the concepts that are part of the theory of *ʿamal* which dominates the Israeli-Arab grammar of Arabic.

According to the Arab grammatical approach, the verb always precedes its subject and acts upon it in such a way that it produces the *rafʿ*, or what European grammarians have construed as the desinential inflection that marks the nominative case.

Ironically, perhaps, for Arab grammarians no less than for grammarians of Hebrew, a verbal sentence is a sentence whose predicate is a verb. Word order as such is not what defines the type of a sentence. This is in contrast with the understanding that is propagated among Jewish students of Arabic according to which Arab grammarians define the sentence by the nature of its first word.

As far as canonical Arab grammarians are concerned, verbs always precede their subject. The subject can take the form of a separate word (noun or pronoun)—e.g. "مرض الاولاد" (*mariḍa al-ʾawlādu*—"the children fell ill"), a pronominal suffix—e.g. "مرضوا" (*mariḍū*—"they fell ill"), or be implicit in the verb—e.g. "مرض" (*mariḍa*—"he fell ill") which can strictly speaking form a complete sentence entirely on its own (see e.g. Abu Khadra et al 2000, volume for seventh grade, 163).[9]

9 Within the European approach the verb "مَرِضَ" (*mariḍa*) is a past tense in the third person

Significantly, in the Arabic Grammatical Tradition the pronominal suffixes are not part of the verb, and verb morphology does not include a dimension of plurality (cf. Shartuni 1986, 9). Rather, pronominal suffixes that indicate pluralisation are elements of syntax. They are but one of the three ways mentioned above (the other two being implicit pronouns and explicit nouns) to connect subject to verbal predicate in order to render a grammatically complete sentence. Not surprisingly, then, when verb conjugations are discussed in Arab texts, pluralisation is not emphasised, and often not even included in systematic discussions of the morphology of conjugation or in conjugation tables.

Now, some sentences have no verbs. These are nominal sentences. In these sentences subjects are not preceded by verbs. Instances where a subject is not preceded by a verb posed a theoretical challenge to theorists of *ʿamal*, namely the need to explain what gives such a subject the desinential inflection of the *rafʿ*. According to the theory, the governing element must precede the word it governs. In a verbal sentence the verb precedes its subject and produces the subject's *rafʿ*. But in nominal sentences the opening words are not preceded by a word like the verb that in the verbal sentence would put the agent in the *rafʿ*. How can the fact that such words have the mark of the *rafʿ* be explained? The explanation that emerged was that it is the principle of *ibtidāʾ*—of initiation or of beginning—that governs these words and inflects them with a mark of *rafʿ* (Levin 1995, 222–224).

Arab educators have typically avoided explicitly elaborating on the theory of *ʿamal* in treatises and works that were aimed at the general public, or textbooks aimed at the general population of school pupils. Their definitions tend to be rather laconic, as in: "the *mubtadaʾ* is a noun in the *rafʿ* at the beginning of a sentence" (al-Jarim and Amin [1938] 2005, primary school vol., book 1 page 25). This is typical of the reluctance to elaborate on the underlying logic of grammar, and the preference to keep instruction to a "need-to-know" basis, which contribute significantly to the invisibility of the incommensurability between the Arab and Orientalist approaches to grammar.

In any event, in contrast with the way it is presented in Israeli-Jewish instruction, *mubtadaʾ* is not a subject in a nominal sentence. It is rather a word whose

---

singular regardless of whether it appears in the sentence "the children fell ill" (*mariḍa al-ʾawlād*) or "he fell ill" (*mariḍa*). Instructors within the Arabic Grammatical Tradition would interpret the former instance as a verb stripped of any indication of subject (because the subject is explicitly indicated following the verb), and the latter instance as a verb plus the implicit third person singular subject.

desinential inflection is in the *rafʿ* (i.e. nominative according to European grammarians' scheme) by virtue of the principle of initiation for lack of an apparent alternative cause.

Not surprisingly, then, if a nominal sentence should be preceded by *ʾinna* or *kāna*—using Iron's (n.d.) examples we have "كَانَ زَيْدٌ مَرِيضًا" (*kāna zaydun marīḍan*—"Zayd was ill", p. 80)[10] and "إِنَّ زَيْدًا عَالِمٌ" (*ʾinna zaydan ʿāliman*—"Zayd is indeed a scholar", p. 98)—the word that had been *mubtadaʾ* is no longer referred to as *mubtadaʾ*, but rather as *ʾism ʾinna* or *ʾism kāna* (the noun of *ʾinna* or the noun of *kāna* respectively) because now its desinential inflection is governed by *ʾinna* or *kāna* respectively, and not by the principle of *ibtidāʾ*.

The way the *ḫabar* is defined in Arab Arabic-grammar instruction fits in this scheme and differs fundamentally from the approach that prevails in Jewish-Israeli instruction. "[T]he *ḫabar* is a noun desinentially inflected in the *rafʿ* [indicating the nominative case according to European grammar] that together with the *mubtadaʾ* forms a complete sentence" (al-Jarim and Amin [1938] 2005, primary school vol., book 1 page 25). *Ḫabar* according to this quote is a noun and not a verb, and if a nominal sentence is one that has a *mubtadaʾ* and a *ḫabar*, then a sentence with a subject followed by a verb cannot possibly be a simple nominal sentence. (This is in contrast with the way Arab Arabic grammar is presented in Jewish education, whereby if a sentence begins with a noun it is nominal even if the noun is followed by a verb.)

From an Arab perspective, sentences like "زَيْدٌ مَرِضَ" (*zaydun mariḍa*) "Zayd, he fell ill" cannot be defined as sentences with a subject followed by its verb. These are not simple nominal sentences. Rather, they are complex, topicalised sentences with a subject followed by a clause, which may itself be a verbal sentence, in which case it requires its own subject and this will follow the verb (e.g. Abu Khadra et al 2000, seventh grade, page 111).

A topicalised sentence is classed as a *ǧumla ʾismīya kubra* (literally "a great nominal sentence"). The first word in the sentence is the nominal subject that is also a *mubtadaʾ*. The *ḫabar* that follows in such a sentence is itself a clause, composed of one word or more. When the *ḫabar* appears to be a verb, the verb is in fact a full verbal sentence that can be decomposed into a subject (be it a noun, a pronominal affix or an implicit subject) following its verbal predicate, in a way totally consistent with the fundamental rule that a verb always precedes its subject.

---

10 I include Iron's vocalisation marks. These are not quite the way most standard Arabic textbooks in the Arab would have them (he indicates short vowel marks before *matres lectionis*).

Thus, "الاولاد مرضوا" (*al-ʾawlādu mariḍū*—"the children, they fell ill") has a topicalised subject "الاولاد" (*al-ʾawlādu*—"the children") followed by a complete sentence, namely "مَرِضوا" (*mariḍū*—they fell ill), which in its turn is composed of the verb "مرض" (*mariḍa*—"fell ill") and its following subject, the pronominal suffix *u* which indicates "they". By contrast, "مرض الاولاد" (*mariḍa al-ʾawlādu*—"the children fell ill") is again a sentence with the verb "مرض" (*mariḍa*—"fell ill") and its following subject, in this case an explicit noun namely "الاولاد" (*al-ʾawlādu*—"the children").

But the clause that to Arab grammarians is a complete sentence composed of a verb and its pronominal subject ("مرضوا"—*mariḍū*, They fell ill) would be approached by a person schooled in the Israeli-Jewish European-style grammar as a conjugated verb ('they fell ill'—past tense, third person, masc. pl.), which appears to be a straightforward predicate to the subject that precedes it. This is why it is so easy to confuse it as a verb that is pluralised in agreement with its preceding subject.

In the Arab grammatical interpretation of topicalised sentences, then, the main sentence has no independent verbal predicate; the inconsistency in agreement between verb and subject never arises; verbs always precede their subjects; and verbs have no inherent quantity and do not conjugate along a dimension of quantity or number.

What is an elementary syntactical rule to Israeli-Jewish students—namely that if a verb precedes its subject it is rendered in the singular, and if a verb follows its subject it agrees with its pluralisation—makes no sense in this scheme of things. The closest Arab equivalent in the Arabic textbooks is the observation that "The *ḫabar* agrees with the *mubtadaʾ* in number and gender" (al-Jarim and Amin [1938] 2005, primary school vol., book 3, p. 4), which is quite a different statement.

These differences are fundamental in that elements of one system cannot be reconstituted in terms of the other system. The two systems cannot be reconciled. The differences are shrouded in metacognitive blindness. None of the students, Arab or Jewish, that I spoke with was aware of the extent of the incommensurability of the two approaches on this particular issue. These differences, precisely because they pass unnoticed, are quite insidious. They lead to inevitable confusion and bewilderment among Arab university students who have internalised one system and need to operate in terms of the other system.

As mentioned earlier, the fundamental reason these limits in translatability escape the consciousness of participants in educational exchanges has to do with the direction of the translation which is itself a reflection of the power politics of language in general and Arabic instruction in particular. The significant translation goes from Arabic to Hebrew, Hebrew being the language that is usually used in university educational exchanges. The instances that are classed as *mubtadaʾ* in Arabic are a subset of the instances that are classed as subjects of nominal sentences in Hebrew, and in Orientalist grammar of Arabic more generally. This is why translating the term *mubtadaʾ* as subject of a nominal sentence seems to consistently work, but translating a subject of a nominal sentence into Arabic as *mubtadaʾ* does not always work (as was the case with the nouns of *ʾinna* and *kāna*). And because in the context of university grammar instruction it is the Israeli-Jewish perspective that is the dominant structure in that Arab students need to adapt to it rather than Jewish students needing to adapt to the Arabic grammatical approach, this mistranslation remains impervious to these anomalies and further reinforces the false sense of commensurability between the systems.

Verb Morphology: Structuring Knowledge at Cross Purposes

As mentioned above, the two approaches differ in the range of linguistic phenomena that are treated as verb morphology. This difference is particularly important because verb conjugation is the most significant area of Arabic-grammar instruction in the Jewish sector. It attracts more teaching attention than other areas, and is highlighted in both matriculation exams and in entrance exams to departments of Arabic. This central position that is occupied by verb conjugation in Arabic-grammar instruction in the Jewish sector is paralleled by the centrality of desinential inflection in the Arab instruction of grammar.

The differences in the scope of what is designated as verb morphology indicate how the reality that is conceptualised by the two traditions is carved up quite differently. What the Israeli-Jewish approach constitutes as a single issue, namely verb conjugation by tense and person, cuts in the Israeli-Arab approach across verb morphology (changes in tense/aspect) and syntax (adding a subject to a verb, the subject being a noun, a pronoun or a pronominal affix).

The fact that in the Arab sector verb conjugation in the strict sense of the word excludes pronominal suffixation,[11] coupled with the lower priority

11 In Shartuni's words

"يكون تصريف الافعال بنقلها من الماضي الى المضارع والامر [...] ويكون تصريف الاسماء بنقلها من المفرد الى المثنى والجمع وبتصغيرها والنسبة اليها."

allotted to verb conjugation in the allocation of drilling and exercise time, may explain how Arab students become habituated to thinking about verb conjugation and performing verb-conjugation exercises without focusing on changes in suffixes. This may leave them ill-prepared to confront common conjugation exercises which Jewish students are extensively drilled at, namely abstract formulaic conjugations of isolated, decontextualised verbs.

In such conjugation exercises a word is taken and changed independently of context along various dimensions. The inclusion of persons or shifts from singular to plural are, from an Arab grammatical perspective, quite arbitrary aspects of the exercise because in the Arab scheme of things these are elements of syntax rather than verb morphology. By contrast, from a Jewish perspective these are both meaningful and logical components of the exercise because in the Jewish scheme of things person and number are integral elements of verb morphology. This might go a considerable way towards accounting for the difficulties that Arab students exhibit in formal, decontextualised verb conjugation exercises.

But even when approaching the common area that both Israeli Jewish and Arab systems of grammar instruction treat as verb morphology proper, there are fundamental differences in outlook and sensibility.

Israeli-Jewish instruction of verb morphology, in a way typical of European grammatical approaches, focuses on the taxonomic level of individual paradigms—*Binyanīm* (בניינים) in Hebrew, and *ʾawzān* (أوزان) in Arabic.[12] In Arab textbooks these individual paradigms are nested within a taxonomy with several superordinate levels of classification, two of which are particularly alien to the Israeli-Jewish construction of verbs. The higher level of the two distinguishes between simple verbs and augmented verbs. The simple verbs correspond to what Israeli-Jewish grammar textbooks class as the first paradigm. The simple verb is subdivided in Arab grammar instruction into sub-groups according to the vocalisations of the middle element. Rather confusingly, these subdivisions are called *ʾabwāb* (أبواب) in some textbooks, and *ʾawzān* (أوزان) in other textbooks. Figure 1 is a chart of these superordinate levels that was adapted from *al-ǧadīd*.

("The conjugation of verbs is in their transition from the perfect to the imperfect and the imperative [...] while the conjugation of nouns is in their transition from the singular to the dual and the plural and in their diminution and adjectivisation," Shartuni 1986, 9).

12 The literal equivalent of the Hebrew term *binyan* (בניין), the Arabic *bināʾ* (بناء), has been used in the course of the evolution of the Arabic Grammatic Tradition (Owens 1997, 52), but is obsolete and not part of the textbooks that I have seen.

The lower of the two superordinate taxonomic levels divides the augmented forms into three groups—augmented by one letter (includes the paradigms that Israeli-Jewish grammar normally counts as second, third, fourth); by two letters (fifth, sixth, seventh, eighth and ninth); and by three letters (tenth and beyond). Thus, what Israeli-Jewish grammar instruction might gloss as the transition of a radical from the first paradigm to the fourth paradigm, is construed in at least some Arab textbooks (e.g. al-Jarim and Amin [1938] 2005) as the augmentation of a simple verb by one additional letter.

Thus from the formal perspective of Jewish grammar the difference between the first paradigm and the other paradigms is not a different taxonomic level from the difference between any two paradigms. In the Israeli Arab grammar this difference is a higher order difference than that between the different augmented forms.

The contrast between, on the one hand, the Israeli-Arab focus on the taxonomic level of "augmented vs. simple", and more significantly, the level of "augmented by one, two or three letters"; and on the other hand, the Israeli-Jewish exclusive focus on the level of specific paradigms, is typical of some general differences in approach. The taxonomic level of specific paradigms—the level on which Jewish pedagogy focuses—is what one must master in order to conjugate verbs correctly. It is the ideal generative focus in that mastery of that level is the precondition for generating correct usage. By contrast, the Arab focus is the most efficient level for the elegant description of the linked underlying logic of seemingly distinct phenomena. The levels of augmentation and size of augmentation—the focus of Arab instruction—lend themselves to subsequent accounts of related morphological, syntactic and semantic phenomena, such as different structural patterns of noun derivations or the links between morphology and semantics in verbs.

Furthermore, there are good reasons to view the difference between the first paradigm and the other (augmented) paradigms as more fundamental than the differences among the augmented paradigms. There is a greater variability in inflection of verbs in the first paradigm, and its sub-groups (distinguished by the vocalisation of the second letter of the radical) carry with them different nuances of meaning. In fact, the division of the first paradigm into subgroups can be seen as equivalent to the division of augmented verbs into different paradigms. Morphologically, too, the rules and structures of noun derivation from verbs also serve to distinguish the simple from the augmented verbs. So, for example, there are commonalities among the morphological structures of the participles that are derived from all augmented verbs that are distinct from the morphological structures of the participles that are derived from the first paradigm (see, for a more systematic discussion, the chapter "Arabic Noun Types", in Ryding 2005, 74ff.).

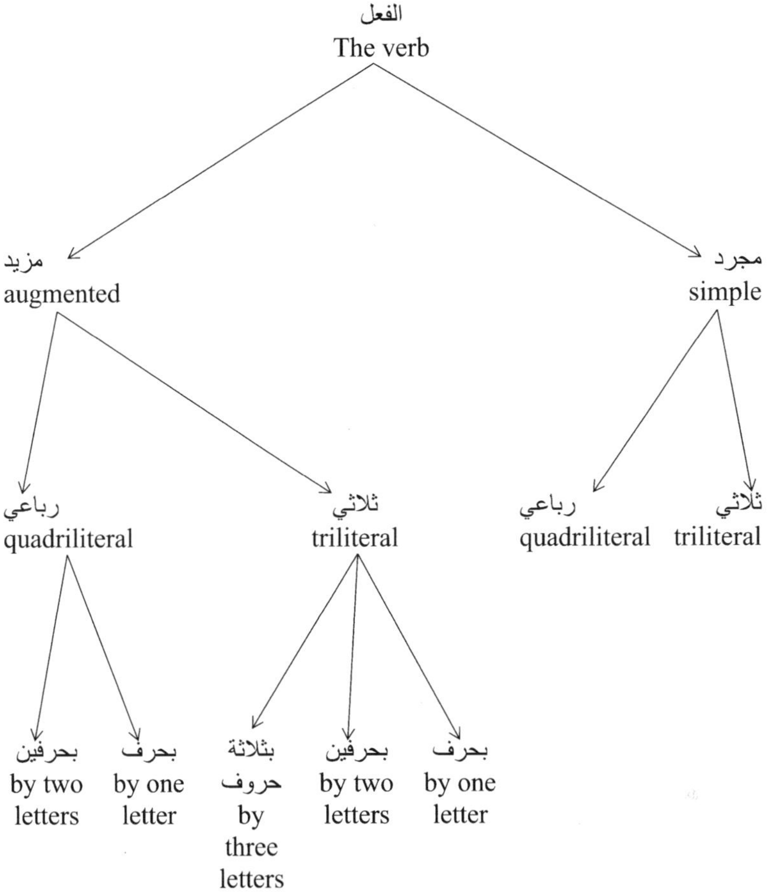

FIGURE 1 *Verb—simple and augmented. Adapted from Abu Khadra et al 2000* (al-ǧadīd), *eighth grade volume, page 111—English translations are added below the Arab terms, but otherwise the exact hierarchical structure is reproduced as it appears in the original.*

In the formal grammar of the Hebrew language there is a distinction between heavy and light paradigms (משקלים קלים וכבדים), but this distinguishes the paradigms that have a doubled consonant with a dagesh from those that do not. This is a different distinction from the Arab one. Moreover, the Hebrew distinction between heavy and light paradigms is not emphasised in the grammatical instruction of Hebrew in the Jewish sector, where the emphasis is placed squarely on individual paradigms. Still, the structure of verb conjugation in Hebrew could also lend itself to the Arab distinction between the augmented and the simple, and an account like that given by Arab grammarians of verb morphology could have also made sense of Hebrew verbs if it had been applied to Hebrew grammar. Clearly, then, it is not the inherent differences between the structures of Arabic and Hebrew that create the differences between the Israeli-Jewish and Israeli-Arab approaches, and in fact, the similarity between the languages might have led us to expect that the two approaches should be mutually intelligible on this point. But they are not.

It is rather the pedagogical aims of the two approaches that accentuate their differences. We see here how Israeli-Jewish grammar seeks to provide the most efficient mechanism to generate correct usage, while the Israeli-Arab grammar induces through analogy the more parsimonious and elegant description of morphological phenomena. This applies to the syntactic formulation of the relationship between subject and predicate that I described above no less than to the different levels of analysis of verbs (cf. Versteegh 1997b, chapter 6).

The chart above depicts yet another instance of the difference between the approaches that prevail in Israeli-Jewish instruction, and those that prevail in Arab pedagogy. The distinction between triliteral and quadriliteral is here used at a superordinate level to the actual paradigms. In the Israeli-Jewish instruction this distinction is part of the broader classifications of radicals (*gᵉzarōt*—גזרות) rather than a way of classifying paradigms. The way the two approaches to grammar integrate the distinction between triliteral and quadriliteral verbs into their explanatory schemes is mutually counterintuitive and confusing.

The generally consistent nature of the differences between Israeli-Jewish and Arab grammars reflects a different analytic orientation between the two approaches. Arab linguistic education seeks to generate the most logically coherent and elegant models *of* linguistic reality, while the Jewish approach seeks to define rules as efficient, functional models *for* linguistic reality.

Hence Jewish textbooks rely heavily on generative conjugation tables that bring together many different phenomena into one analytic framework. Such conjugation tables, for instance, are comprehensive and seek to integrate as many dimensions as possible—person, pluralisation, gender, mood, tense, type of radical, paradigm—into what is effectively a multidimensional prescriptive model projected onto a three dimensional space. Each page provides a two dimensional chart. The third dimension is achieved by reiterating the two dimensional charts with systematic variation in radical type. In other words, the presentation over successive pages of the conjugation of progressively more complicated radical types constitutes a third spatial dimension of presentation.

Typically, each page is dedicated to a radical type in a given paradigm and explores dimensions such as number, tense and mood. The analysis is then repeated in subsequent pages for other paradigms, and then the process is repeated for a more complex radical type, where complexity is measured by the extent to which the radical type departs from the standard of simple radicals. In one central textbook, Landau's *madriḫ bi-šviley ha-poʿal ha-ʿaravī* (Landau n.d.), the only textbook exclusively dedicated to verbs, the tables form the core substance of the instruction. Table 4 is an example of the first conjugation table that Landau presents.

This structure is repeated in subsequent pages, and each iteration presents the conjugation of a particular paradigm. The paradigms of one class of verbs are presented one page after another. The book does not cover the regular verbs which are supposed to have already been taught to students by the time they are presented with the book, and so the first class that is presented is the germinate verb root (גזרת הכפולים, الفعل المضعّف) and the presentation continues from there to the more complex variants.

Typically, each page has a table where the vertical axis lists the person of the verb beginning with the singulars, moving to the plurals, and then the duals.[13] Within each category the movement is from first to second to third person, and within each of these, where relevant, masculine is presented first and then feminine. In other words, the persons are presented in this order: first person singular; second person singular masculine; second person singular feminine; third person singular masculine; third person singular feminine; first person plural; second person plural masculine; second person plural feminine; third person plural masculine; third person plural feminine; second person dual (masculine and feminine); third person dual masculine; third person dual feminine.

Interestingly, if the logic of morphological consideration were carried to its natural conclusion, the order would have been different. The third person masculine singular is the morphologically unmarked variant. Indeed, the third person singular masculine form is what is used to class and name the different paradigms. The other persons are marked variants of the third person singular, whereby a pronominal affix is added to the verb. As it happens, conjugation charts that begin with the third person singular can be found in Arab textbooks. In the schematic conjugation tables that conclude Shartuni's (1986) book, the initial persons listed are the third persons, followed by second persons and cul-

13 Presumably the duals are given following the plural because they are constructed on the basis of the plural, thus *hum* (هم) is the pronoun indicating "them", that is, third person masculine plural, while the third person dual is *humā* (هما).

TABLE 4 *Conjugation table reproduced and adapted from Landau n.d. (page 91)*

גזרת הכפולים, בניין ראשון, משקל فَعَلَ يَفْعُلُ

	עבר	עתמ"ר [עתיד מרפוע]	מנומ"ג [מנצוב ומג'זום]	עתמ"ג [עתיד מג'זום]	עבס"ב [עבר סביל]	עתס"ב [עתיד סביל]	מגס"ב [מג'זום סביל]
أنا	دَلَلْتُ	أَدُلُّ	أَدُلَّ	أَدْلُلْ	دُلِلْتُ	أُدَلُّ	أُدْلَلْ
أنت	دَلَلْتَ	تَدُلُّ	تَدُلَّ	تَدْلُلْ	دُلِلْتَ	تُدَلُّ	تُدْلَلْ
أنت	دَلَلْتِ	تَدُلِّينَ	تَدُلِّي	تَدُلِّي	دُلِلْتِ	تُدَلِّينَ	تُدَلِّي
هو	دَلَّ	يَدُلُّ	يَدُلَّ	يَدْلُلْ	دُلَّ	يُدَلُّ	يُدْلَلْ
هي	دَلَّتْ	تَدُلُّ	تَدُلَّ	تَدْلُلْ	دُلَّتْ	تُدَلُّ	تُدْلَلْ
نحن	دَلَلْنَا	نَدُلُّ	نَدُلَّ	نَدْلُلْ	دُلِلْنَا	نُدَلُّ	نُدْلَلْ
أنتم	دَلَلْتُمْ	تَدُلُّونَ	تَدُلُّوا	تَدُلُّوا	دُلِلْتُمْ	تُدَلُّونَ	تُدَلُّوا
أنتن	دَلَلْتُنَّ	تَدْلُلْنَ	تَدْلُلْنَ	تَدْلُلْنَ	دُلِلْتُنَّ	تُدْلَلْنَ	تُدْلَلْنَ
هم	دَلُّوا	يَدُلُّونَ	يَدُلُّوا	يَدُلُّوا	دُلُّوا	يُدَلُّونَ	يُدَلُّوا
هن	دَلَلْنَ	يَدْلُلْنَ	يَدْلُلْنَ	يَدْلُلْنَ	دُلِلْنَ	يُدْلَلْنَ	يُدْلَلْنَ
أنتما	دَلَلْتُمَا	تَدُلَّانِ	تَدُلَّا	تَدُلَّا	دُلِلْتُمَا	تُدَلَّانِ	تُدَلَّا
هما	دَلَّا	يَدُلَّانِ	يَدُلَّا	يَدُلَّا	دُلَّا	يُدَلَّانِ	يُدَلَّا
هما	دَلَّتَا	تَدُلَّانِ	تَدُلَّا	تَدُلَّا	دُلَّتَا	تُدَلَّانِ	تُدَلَّا

ציווי أُدْلُلْ (دُلَّ) دُلِّي ؛ دُلُّوا أُدْلُلْنَ ؛ دُلَّا

ביפ"ו [בינוני פועל] دَالٌّ دَالَّةٌ ؛ دَالُّونَ دَالَّاتٌ ؛ دَالَّانِ دَالَّتَانِ

ביפ"ע [בינוני פעול] مَدْلُولٌ مَدْلُولَةٌ ؛ مَدْلُولُونَ مَدْلُولَاتٌ ؛ مَدْلُولَانِ مَدْلُولَتَانِ

מצדר دَلَالَةٌ מצדרים אחרים حَلٌّ ، مُرُورٌ ، فِرَارٌ ، مَلَلٌ

minating with the first. In other words, the presentation begins with the basic verb and proceeds to introduce the morphological variations when pronominal affixes are added moving through the second person and culminating in the first (which has the added idiosyncrasy that it is gender neutral). This contrasts with the Israeli-Jewish conjugation tables where the egocentric individualist worldview of European conjugation matrices trumps morphological elegance and the worldview that inheres in Arabic verb morphology.

The horizontal axis of Landau's conjugation tables begins with the active verbs—moving from the perfect to the imperfect *marfūʿ* (approximated in European grammar as the indicative mood), imperfect *manṣūb* (approximated in European grammar as the subjunctive mood), and imperfect *mağzūm* (approximated in European grammar as the jussive mood)—and then repeating the same forms for the passive voice—beginning with the perfect and then moving to the three imperfect states. The use of the Arab terminology for the moods is noteworthy. Jewish students are not familiar with the concept of moods from their Hebrew syntax instruction, and so the Arabised terms are used, reinforcing here, too, the false sense of commensurability between the Israeli-Jewish and Arab grammars of Arabic.

Below the set of conjugation columns follows the presentation of the imperative (which applies to a limited number of persons), and the nominal forms—the participles (whose conjugation is by gender and number, but not by person) and the verbal nouns.

Conjugation tables like Landau's are examples of generative models *for* reality that are central to the pedagogical approach of Jewish grammar instruction. These are formulas that the student can use to combine relevant variables and produce a correct outcome for a given linguistic task. While such models exist in Arab grammatical formulations, the dominant pedagogical approach is quite different.

Shartuni's volume provides examples that further reinforce and exemplify the distinct Arab emphasis on descriptive elegance rather than generative efficiency. The conjugation of verbs is defined to occur by tense, in contrast with the conjugation of nouns which are conjugated by number and some other aspects (Shartuni 1986, 9, see discussion above).

Not surprisingly, when discussing the morphological effects of pronominal suffixes (pages 29–32), the focus is very strictly morphological, and the issue of concern is the effect different letters in the pronouns have on the vocalisation of the verb, and not how to indicate a specific person or number. Thus the explanation of the morphological effects of suffixes follows not the different persons or numbers, but the different letters that make up the suffix. (Typically, as indicated above, the ways to indicate person and number are in his approach a matter of syntax, not morphology, and these are discussed by Shartuni elsewhere).

TABLE 5 *Conjugation table reproduced from Shartuni 1986 (conjugations appendix page 5)*

تصريف الفعل المضاعف

	الماضي المعلوم	الماضي المجهول	المضارع المعلوم	المضارع المجهول	الأمر
الغَائب	مَدَّ مَدَّا مَدُّوا	مُدَّ مُدَّا مُدُّوا	يَمُدُّ يَمُدَّانِ يَمُدُّونَ	يُمَدُّ يُمَدَّانِ يُمَدُّونَ	
الغَائبَة	مَدَّتْ مَدَّتَا مَدَدْنَ	مُدَّتْ مُدَّتَا مُدِدْنَ	تَمُدُّ تَمُدَّانِ يَمْدُدْنَ	تُمَدُّ تُمَدَّانِ يُمْدَدْنَ	
المخَاطب	مَدَدْتَ مَدَدْتُمَا مَدَدْتُمْ	مُدِدْتَ مُدِدْتُمَا مُدِدْتُمْ	تَمُدُّ تَمُدَّانِ تَمُدُّونَ	تُمَدُّ تُمَدَّانِ تُمَدُّونَ	مُدَّ مُدَّا مُدُّوا
المخَاطبَة	مَدَدْتِ مَدَدْتُمَا مَدَدْتُنَّ	مُدِدْتِ مُدِدْتُمَا مُدِدْتُنَّ	تَمُدِّينَ تَمُدَّانِ تَمْدُدْنَ	تُمَدِّينَ تُمَدَّانِ تُمْدَدْنَ	مُدِّي مُدَّا أُمْدُدْنَ
المتكلم	مَدَدْتُ مَدَدْنَا	مُدِدْتُ مُدِدْنَا	أَمُدُّ نَمُدُّ	أُمَدُّ نُمَدُّ	

المزيدَات

مَدَّدَ	يُمَدِّدُ	مَدِّدْ	تَمْدِيدًا
مَادَّ	يُمَادُّ	مَادِّ	مُمَادَّةً
أَمَدَّ	يُمِدُّ	أَمْدِدْ	إِمْدَادًا
تَمَدَّدَ	يَتَمَدَّدُ	تَمَدَّدْ	تَمَدُّدًا
تَمَادَّ	يَتَمَادُّ	تَمَادَّ	تَمَادًّا
إِنْمَدَّ	يَنْمَدُّ	إِنْمَدَّ	إِنْمِدَادًا
إِمْتَدَّ	يَمْتَدُّ	إِمْتَدَّ	إِمْتِدَادًا
إِسْتَمَدَّ	يَسْتَمِدُّ	إِسْتَمِدَّ	إِسْتِمْدَادًا

اسم الفاعل
مَادٌّ—مَادَّةٌ

اسم المفعول
مَمْدُودٌ—مَمْدُودَةٌ

Here is how Shartuni presents the pronominal suffixes:

> الضمائر البارزة ستةٌ وهي:
>
> - "التاء" مضمومة للمتكلم مذكراً ومؤنّثاً نحو "ضَرَبْتُ". ومفتوحة للمخاطب نحو "ضَرَبْتَ". ومكسورة للمخاطبة في الماضي نحو "ضربتِ". ومضمومة ملحقة بعلامات التثنية والجمع لمثنى المخاطب وجمعه مطلقاً نحو "ضربتُما" و "ضربتُم" وبالنون المشددة لجمع الاناث نحو "ضربتنَّ"
> - و "نا" لمثنى المتكلم وجمعه نحو "ضَرَبْنا"
> - و "الالف" لمثنى الغائب المخاطب ومؤنثهما في المضارع والامر نحو "يضربان" و "اضربا"
> - و "الياء" للمخاطبة في المضارع والامر نحو "تضربينَ" و "اضربي"
> - و "الواو" لجمع الغائبين في الماضي والمضارع نحو "ضربوا" و "يضربون" وجمع المخاطبين في المضارع والامر نحو "تضربون" و "إضربوا"
> - و "النون" لجمع الغائبات في الماضي والمضارع نحو "ذهبن" و "يذهبن" وجمع المخاطبات في المضارع والامر نحو "تضربن" و "اضربن"
>
> SHARTUNI 1986, 29–30

Here is a rough translation of this passage.

> There are six explicit pronouns as follows:
>
> - the letter "*ta*" which is vocalised with "*u*" for first person singular masculine and feminine, e.g. "*ḍarabtu*"; and with "*a*" for second person singular masculine, e.g. "*ḍarabta*"; and with "*i*" for second person singular feminine, e.g. "*ḍarabti*", and with "*u*" followed by the letters indicating dual and plural for the second person dual and plural in general, e.g. "*ḍarabtumā*" and "*ḍarabtum*", and by the doubled letter "*nūn*" for the feminine plural, e.g. "*ḍarabtunna*".
> - The combination "*nā*" for first person dual and plural, e.g. "*ḍarabnā*".
> - The letter "*ʾalif*" for the dual of the second person and third person both masculine and feminine in the imperfect and the imperative, e.g. "*yaḍribāni*" and "*ʾiḍribā*".
> - The letter "*ya*" for the second person feminine in the imperfect and the imperative, e.g. "*taḍribīna*" and "*ʾiḍribī*" [the *ya* is absorbed into the *ī* in the two transliterated examples].

- The letter "*waw*" for the third person plural masculine in the perfect and the imperfect, e.g. "*ḍarabū*" and "*yaḍribūna*" and the second person masculine plural in the imperfect and the imperative, e.g. "*taḍribūna*" and "*ʾiḍribū*" [the *waw* is absorbed into the *ū* in the two transliterated examples].
- The letter "*nūn*" for third person plural feminine in the perfect and the imperfect, e.g. "*ḏahabna*" and "*yaḏhabna*", and second person plural feminine in the imperfect and the imperative, e.g. "*taḍribna*" and "*ʾiḍribna*".

This quote conveys the bewildering effect, from the perspective of those used to European-style conjugation tables, of using morphology as the organising principle for the explanation, rather than the syntax. Instead of telling us *when* to use *what*, the author tells us *what* is used *when*.[14]

Yet this mode of analysis is typical of two fundamental aspects of Arab Arabic-grammar instruction. First, the complexities of attaching pronominal affixes to verbs are a matter of morphology rather than the syntactical concern of indicating the verb's subject, the discussion of which is reserved for a different context, namely that of syntax.

Second, the way the material is presented is consistent with descriptive elegance at the expense of generative efficiency. For example, the first subsection groups the different uses of the letter *ta*—ت—and explains how different inflections are associated with different persons. This mode of organisation does not present the different persons in a systematic and easily internalised way. It is therefore of little generative value—it will not help those who seek to learn how to conjugate a verb along the dimensions of person and number. It is, however, very useful as a summary of the different effects to which different letters are put in constructing pronominal suffixes.

This prioritisation of descriptive elegance at the expense of generative efficiency is seen in other aspects of the presentation. In line with the traditional Arab scholarship into Arabic, when considering multi-literal suffixes it is only the first letter of the suffixes that is considered the pronominal suffix, while

14 By way of analogy, this is intuitively similar to presenting the cases and the article marks in German not in a way that follows syntactic logic (by case gender and number) but rather taking the actual article (e.g. der, die, das) and specifying when each occurs (e.g. der—in the nominative singular masculine, in the dative singular feminine, in the genitive singular feminine; die—in the nominative singular feminine, in the accusative singular feminine, and in the nominative, accusative, dative and genitive plural masculine, feminine and neuter.)

the other vocalisations and letters are treated as indicators of quantity. So, for example, the suffix *tumā*—تُمَا—is considered a pronominal suffix followed by an indicator of non-gendered duality. This mode of analysis is of little value for those wishing to generate correct usage, yet privileges the interests of those who seek to provide maximum nuanced justification for morphological and idiographic phenomena down to the finest minutiae.

The two grammatical approaches further use rules and models quite differently. Arab textbooks tend to define rules and models of specific phenomena across different contexts. Thus desinential inflection cuts across the verb/noun divide treating as one phenomenon what Jewish grammar treats as different morphological expressions of the distinct phenomena of case and mood (see below). Israeli-Arab textbooks isolate particular phenomena in different contexts, and emphasise analogy in the explanations and exercises it promotes. Taxonomies are often analogically constructed and fulfil a specific explanatory goal rather than acquire a reified, enduring existence independently of their specific context.

This is visible in the way the two approaches differ in the strictness of their adherence to the grouping of verbs according to radicals and paradigms. Israeli-Jewish grammar sees the distinction by radical and paradigm as a fundamental, inherent aspect of the language and seeks to show how it motivates the behaviour of verbs. Arab grammatical texts deploy the distinction as a heuristic device that serves to demonstrate or summarise morphological regularities, rather than as the very basis of these differences. These Arab texts therefore invoke these distinctions on what seems to be an ad hoc basis as they summarise and exemplify the regularities of language.

For example, in describing the quadriliteral and quinqueliteral verbs, Arab textbooks like *al-naḥw al-wāḍiḥ* often do not distinguish between, on the one hand, verbs with quadriliteral and quinqueliteral radicals, and, on the other hand, verbs of triliteral radicals which contain four or five consonants in their elementary form (perfect, masculine, third-person singular) as a result of the paradigm in which they are. Thus, when writing about the *mujarrad al-rubāʿīy* (مجرد الرباعي—the simple quadriliteral verbs), *al-naḥw al-wāḍiḥ* discusses verbs like بعثر (*baʿthara*) which are of quadriliteral radicals. But only four pages later, when distinguishing different types of *hamza*, the authors refer as رباعي (*rubāʿīy*—quadriliteral) to verbs of triliteral radicals in the fourth paradigm such as أرسل (*ʾarsala*) which are, strictly speaking, triliterals augmented by one letter, rather than quadriliterals. (This example is taken from al-Jarim and Amin [1938] 2005, primary school vol., book 3, pp. 40, 44).

The morphological changes that the authors of *al-naḥw al-wāḍiḥ* sought to demonstrate when they cited the common triliteral verb *ʾarsala* (أرسل) as an example, happen to affect verbs with four consonants regardless of whether they are triliterals augmented by one letter or quadriliterals. Therefore *ʾarsala* (أرسل)—a commonly used familiar verb—was a convenient choice.

Similarly, Shartuni in his discussion of the formation of the imperfect tense includes words such as *taʿallama* (تعلم) and *inṭalaqa* (انطلق) as "non-triliteral" (*ghayr ṯulāṯiy*—غير ثلاثي). This is in point 9 in pp. 11–12. But only very briefly later, in pages 18–19, both these words are classed as augmented triliterals (*mazīd al-ṯulāṯiy*—مزيد الثلاثي).

The prevalence of this approach to taxonomies is not surprising given what Suleiman (1989) has described as the realism of the Arabic tradition of grammar. Thus Israeli-Arab textbooks tend to use conjugation tables for descriptive efficiency and mnemonic reinforcement rather than as a generative device. These tables never constitute an actual explanation, but are rather illustrations of the narrative.

Differences in Language Ideology and the Construction of Learning

The difference in orientation between the Israeli-Jewish generative approach and its Israeli-Arab descriptive counterpart reflects several significant cognitive dimensions that distinguish between the two approaches. The two grammatical approaches differ in the underlying schemas that animate the grammatical and syntactical imagination of students and scholars alike. The Jewish approach sees sentences as schemas or formulas of sorts, a set of pregiven functional relationships into which words are inserted, thereby acquiring their syntactical roles. Arab notions of syntactic relations construct them as effects visited upon one word by another. The Arab metaphorical constitution of these relationships among words and smaller semantic units relies heavily on social theory and jurisprudence. Thus words may claim rights over other words in certain situations, such as the right of precedence (*ḥaqq al-ṣadāra*—cf. al-Ansari 2003; Versteegh 1978). This imagery is alien to the logic of Israeli-Jewish syntax.

In essence, then, the Israeli-Jewish approach can be seen as schematic and functional. Grammatical relationships between words are mediated through their function in the sentence. These relationships precede and exist independently of the actual variables that are inserted into them. This is how the morphology of verbs is approached, and this is how the syntax of sentences is described. Each element (be it a radical or a word in a sentence) is conceived of as independent of the function it fulfils when inserted into the pregiven relationships. This approach affects both instruction and the exercises that are used.

By contrast, the Israeli-Arab approach, in line with the traditional Arab approach, sees the syntactic relationships as unmediated relationships between words. So, as Owens points out, one never finds in Arabic grammars phrases like *fāʿil al-ğumla*, that is, the subject of the sentence (Owens 1997, 52). Arab Arabic grammar shuns the distinction between the substantive item and the abstract relationships it enters in areas where such a distinction is fundamental to Jewish grammatical conceptualisation. There are, of course, regular types of relationships such as between a *fiʿl* and a *fāʿil*, but those, in Arab grammar, are determined through substitution—if you can put a word into the position another word had occupied, these words belong to the same class and have a similar relationship to the common agent that precedes them (Owens 1997, 50–55).

Thus, in Israeli-Arab grammar it is the verb that affects the noun that follows it. The verb may put the noun in the *rafʿ* or *naṣb*—construed in Western grammar of Arabic as the case marks of the nominative or the accusative. Except that in Arab grammar this is not construed as an issue of case, and it is not envisioned through an image of a fixed set of relationships between predicate and subject into which one inserts the specific words to produce a specific sentence.

This leads us to a subtle point of difference about agency. The Israeli-Jewish approach takes a typical European perspective that sees the speaker as agential. S/he puts words together in accordance with rules in order to achieve an effect. The Israeli-Arab approach ascribes agency to words that produce an effect on other words. While one can find remnants of the agency of words in Israeli-Jewish instruction, and while one can find appeal to the agency of the composer of a sentence in Israeli-Arab instruction, the two approaches differ in the primary image of agency in syntax.

This difference is part of a host of contrasts in the schemas that animate the grammatical imagination and their underlying scientific and linguistic ideologies. The Westernised and Arab ontologies of language, which are expressed in turn in the Israeli-Jewish and Israeli-Arab grammars of Arabic respectively, are quite different.

The Western approach sees language as the set of generative rules that are typically discovered by a linguist. Specific actual instances of language use are mere actualisations of the language. By contrast the Arab approach identifies language with a specific body of instances of usage—namely a corpus made up of the Qur'an, early poetry and early Arabian usage—and the grammatical rules it defines are mere descriptions of that language, or mnemonic devices.

The fact that Israeli-Jewish education identifies language with abstract rules while Israeli-Arab instruction derives from a tradition that identifies language with a set of canonical texts underpins two distinct epistemological postures and preferred modes of reasoning. Arab textbooks and analyses lean heavily towards an inductive posture, leading discussions of specific topics with several instances of usage and proceeding to derive rules. Western textbooks by contrast move deductively from rule to exemplifying actualisation. While induction and deduction can be found in both approaches, the difference in preference and in instructional posture is stark. This is reflected in the organisation of textbooks. Israeli-Arab textbooks begin chapters with examples, and proceed to derive rules, whereas Israeli-Jewish textbooks tend to begin with statements of rules and proceed to exemplify them. This leads the Arab textbooks to emphasise the process of discovery in instruction. The student is presented with a sample of language in use that demonstrates the point to be taught, and is invited to discover the rule by finding the regularities in the examples. This is the way chapters are organised both in *al-naḥw al-wāḍiḥ* (al-Jarim and Amin [1938] 2005) and in *al-ǧadīd* (Abu Khadra et al 2000). By contrast, the Israeli Jewish student is provided with a set of rules and is then invited to apply them in different contexts. This is clearly the way Landau's and Iron's textbooks are organised.

The instrumental epistemology of European grammar (Suleiman 1989), that is, the notion of grammatical rules being the language, requires that Israeli-Jewish grammar rules and definitions should cohere into a consistent unified structure. By contrast, Arab rules need not cohere and can remain tentative, descriptive observations that are linked to specific phenomena, because from the Arab perspective the language is the canonical body of texts and quotes and not the rules that describe their regularities. And so, having distinguished noun from verb, Israeli-Jewish grammar textbooks discuss the desinential changes of nouns and verbs separately. The term that translates desinential inflection—*niqqud sofī* (ניקוד סופי)—is reserved for the discussion of case in nouns. The morphological indicators of that which Western grammarians define as mood are discussed separately as one of the morphological variables that affect verb conjugation. Cases and moods are not constructed as a single phenomenon and hence, as far as Jewish students are concerned, it is only nouns that have desinential inflection.

By contrast, Arab textbooks begin by distinguishing between verbs and nouns as part of a general typology of words and parts of speech. But this distinction does not then condition the rest of the conceptual structure. Subsequent discussion of desinential inflection cuts across the divide between verb and noun. Arab analysis ignores the division between mood and case which is not, in the Arab scheme of things, the cause of desinential inflection. The *rafʿ* (رفع) and *naṣb* (نصب) in both nouns and verbs are considered essentially the same phenomenon with the partial caveat that most nouns have the *ǧarr* (جرّ) or *ḫifḍ* (خفض) (glossed as the genitive case by Western grammarians), and the verbs have a *ǧazm* (جزم—the jussive mood in the Western scheme of things) (see e.g. Shartuni 116 ff.). And so, what to Jewish students appears as the conjugation of the imperfect verb along what we could class as mood (from *marfūʿ* through *manṣūb* to *majzūm*), is to Arab students a change in desinential inflection. As I mentioned above, the very reason the imperfect is named *muḍāriʿ* is that it resembles nouns in that it is, in fact, desinentially inflected.

Furthermore, the verbal structure itself forms the model for the class of nouns classed by Western scholars as diptotic (غير منصرفين ,الممنوعون عن الصرف or غير متصرفين)—nouns that do not get nunation, and the *ǧarr* (جر—equivalent to the genitive case) takes the same form as the *naṣb* (نصب—equivalent to the accusative case) when they are indefinite.[15] Part of the rationale is that some of them resemble verbs (cf. discussion in Versteegh 1997b, 82–83).

The contrast in the way desinential inflection is approached further demonstrates that the different grammars carve out reality differently, and constitute incommensurable conceptual frameworks. In the Israeli-Jewish grammar the desinential inflection is an outward manifestation of the underlying rules of case. The Israeli-Arab grammar sees desinential inflection as the essential issue, rather than an epiphenomenon of a latent systematic attribute, and seeks to account for the sentential social dynamics that produce this variation. Arabic grammar textbooks in the Israeli-Arab sector do not, in fact, use a terminology equivalent to case or mood. (Hebrew textbooks use the word יחסה (*yaḥsa*) for case, a concept that students would not have encountered in their Hebrew grammar instruction, and as I mentioned before, there is no term that translates as mood.)

The differences are far greater than incommensurable analytical modes. Arab grammar instruction aims to do much more than teach correct usage. It is preoccupied with inculcating grammatical analysis, most notably the

15 Indefinite nouns commonly have their desinential inflection end with an "n" sound. That phenomenon is called nunation. The word "house"—*bayt*—will therefore be declined as *baytun, baytan* and *baytin* in what European grammarians define as the nominative, accusative and genitive cases respectively. Some nouns do not get a nunation and the sound mark of the genitive (the *ǧarr*) is the same as that of the accusative. The dual ending is one example of that class of nouns. The word for two houses is thus declined *baytāni* in the nominative and *baytayni* in the accusative and genitive.

stylised, declamatory form of analysis of desinential inflection. So much so, in fact, that substantial pedagogic energy is spent on analytical and recitational sophism with no immediate practical consequences, such as *ʾiʿrāb maḥallīy*—the hypothetical inflectional analysis of invariable elements. (Curiously, with this topic Arab grammar comes close to the Western grammatical style that separates a word from its position. In *ʾiʿrāb maḥallīy* the position the word occupies is given its hypothetical inflectional analysis.)

The term *ʾiʿrāb* (إعراب) is multivalent and conflates desinential inflection, the act of desinentially inflecting, and the highly elaborate, stylised, formulaic recitational analysis of desinential inflection.[16] Mastery of the latter symbolises mastery of grammar in the Arab tradition. As I describe in chapter three above, *ʾiʿrāb* has acquired a significance in its own right, well above and beyond signifying grammatical mastery.

This inherent significance that is ascribed to *ʾiʿrāb* contrasts with the utilitarian approach of contemporary European grammar where syntactic and morphological approaches are judged on instrumental grounds. Grammatic knowledge structures, according to the European approach, should serve to systematise practice and inculcate correct usage, and has little inherent value in its own right. Thus, in his academic textbook of Arabic, Peled has no qualms about modifying standard classifications and terminology to suit the method he has developed which links syntactic analysis to translation and interpretation of texts (Peled 1998). It is hard to imagine Arab textbook writers taking such liberties with the established grammatical terminology.

To generalise this point, European grammarians tend to see grammar and its instruction as elements of language inculcation. By contrast, Arab Arabic-grammar instruction has not positioned itself as an element of instruction in language usage, but rather as an investigation into the unique genius of the Arabic language. This is reflected in the consistent preference in Arabic-grammar instruction for descriptive elegance at the expense of generative efficiency.

The emphasis on stylised accounts of desinential inflection may be attributed to the phonocentric sensibilities that inhere in the 'pre-modern' origins of contemporary Arab instruction of Arabic grammar that are described in chapter three. To briefly recapitulate the main points here, Eickelman's analysis of Qurʾanic instruction describes how the standards for evaluation of successful

---

16 At the end of his book Shartuni provides an aide memoire that outlines exactly what elements need to be mentioned in a proper declamation, how and in what order (1986, 387–390). Each and every particle needs to be mentioned in turn and ritualistically described.

mastery differ from the way contemporary school instruction in secular subjects is usually evaluated. It is not the capacity to explain the true meaning of the words that is the hallmark of the successful learner. Rather, the true virtuoso knows how to recite a verse in the opportune situation pushing its range of meaning to the limits. This phonocentric orientation sees meaning as not quite textually fixed, but rather as embedded in an interaction between reader, reality, and text, and as always open to a rediscovery through greater penetration of deeper layers of significance and through an increasingly nuanced and contextual appreciation. The words, rather than the meaning, are what is fixed. This view, in turn, motivates a pedagogical approach whereby the body of knowledge is encoded in fixed texts and internalised through memorisation and stylisation of performance. It is in the interpretation and application of the text where one finds the genius of the virtuoso, and the effects of changing times and sensibilities (Eickelman 1978; 2002, 278–285). It is in fact through this continuous interpretation and application of the text that knowledge acquires its flexibility, adaptability and endurance.

Likewise, on the assumption that over the generations desinential inflection was read but not necessarily used in writing or speech, it would appear that the Arab focus on *ʾiʿrāb* does not reflect a primary concern with the inculcation of correct usage. Rather the capacity to toy with the meanings of words, and push Qurʾanic and other canonical texts to the limit might have been a more significant aim, or mark of virtuosity.

This set of motivations changes with modern schooling, but the conservatism of the field has not encouraged major transformations in pedagogy to match the shifting priorities of formal education. In Arab schools in Israel it was only with the new curriculum of *al-ǧadīd*, that the systematic instruction of desinential inflection was pushed to high school level, and even so this reform is only partially followed in classes.

The elevated status of *ʾiʿrāb* is further embodied in a general attitude that includes aesthetic values and dispositions. One inevitably assimilates not just grammar, but whole attitudes, from the aesthetic values that inhere in the presented material. Underlying humour is a case in point. There is a whole worldview that is folded into elaborate discussions of such humorous transformations as that expressed in the fate of the fish head in the sentence *ʾakala al-samakata ḥatta al-raʾs*—أكل السمكة حتى الرأس. The sentence is ambiguous. It starts with "he ate the fish", then comes the word *ḥatta*, then "its head". The fish was unambiguously eaten. But what happened to its head?

The fate of the fish head hangs in the balance. Will it be eaten or will it be spared? It is all up to a single sound at the end of the last word—a small vowel that, in fact, would not even be uttered because one does not normally pronounce the desinential inflection of the word that ends a sentence.

One can spare the head by treating *ḥatta* as a preposition and inflecting the last word with *kasra*, rendering it as *ǧarr* (equivalent to genitive), to create *ʾakala al-samakata ḥatta al-raʾsi* (أكل السمكة حتى الرأسِ), "he ate the fish up to its head". But the fish head will come to a diametrically opposed end if one inflects the last word with a *fatḥa*, thereby putting the fish head in the *naṣb* (equivalent to accusative) and vocalising the sentence as *ʾakala al-samakata ḥatta al-raʾsa* (أكل السمكة حتى الرأسَ). This rendition treats *ḥatta* as equivalent to the English adverb "even" and views the relationship between the fish and its head as a case of apposition. It produces the sentence "he ate the fish, even its head". And the rich image of the hapless fish head and its gastronomic fate hanging in the balance provides the touch of humour to top up the whimsical example. Such playfulness accentuates an aesthetic acquired through instruction, a disposition that is quite specific to this approach. Virtuosity here is a poetic control of meaning through seamless application of desinential inflection.

The Israeli-Jewish grammar instruction—not least by virtue of its acknowledged position as second language instruction—adopts a deductive functional approach that is focused on producing correct usage, rather than any stylised analysis. This, too, is accompanied by a sense of aesthetics and virtuosity. One can toy with the rules that govern verb conjugation and seek the most complex combination of specific rules. The radical w.ʾ.y. (وءي) is a case in point and is analysed in the final table on the final page of Landau's book. It is described as the radical category of first letter w, second letter hamza, and third letter y ("גזרת פ"ו, ע' המזה ו-ל"י") that is a category unto itself.

The word—a rare, arcane classicism—was fished out of a dictionary of classical Arabic, and was included in the book for no other reason than its sheer complexity. It is not expected that it would be of any practical use to students, other than an exercise in simultaneously integrating different types of radical complexities. Students will almost certainly never use this verb in speech or writing nor are they likely to ever encounter it in texts. Again, here, there is a sense of whimsical artistry, in offering, for instance, an analysis of the uniliteral imperative—*ʾi* (إ), or its even stranger biliteral variant—*ʾih* (إه)—both of which are variants of the first paradigm imperative of the verb *waʾa* (وأى).

We see here, then, two instances of humorous elaboration in grammar instruction that highlight differences in aesthetic values. The Arab approach values the elegant, seamless, effortless control of meaning through nuances of syntax. The Israeli-Jewish approach values pushing the morphological rules to the limits of their logical consistency independently of context and meaning.

TABLE 6 *Conjugation table reproduced from Landau n.d. (page 137)*

גזרת פ״ו, ע׳ המזה ו-ל״י

עבר	עתיד	ציווי	ביפ״ו [בינוני פועל]	ביפ״ע [בינוני פעול]	מצדר
وَأَى	يَئِي	إِ ، إِه	وَاءٍ	مَوْئِيٌّ	وَأْيٌ
تَوَاءَى	يَتَوَاءَى	تَوَاءَ	مُتَوَاءٍ	مُتَوَاءًى	تَوَاءٍ
إِتَّأَى	يَتَّئِي	إِتَّئِ	مُتَّاءٍ	مُتَّأًى	إِتِّئَاءٌ
إِسْتَوْأَى	يَسْتَوْئِي	إِسْتَوْءِ	مُسْتَوْءٍ	مُسْتَوْأًى	إِسْتِيئَاءٌ

The Israeli-Jewish and Arab approaches also seem to differ in the emotional and aesthetic tones that they invoke. The Israeli-Jewish approach emphasises cold intellectual engagement. When rendered positively, the material is interesting. When rendered negatively, it is boring or difficult. Arab discourse about grammar instruction tends to emphasise the emotive aspect. Rendered positively, the student loves grammar. Rendered negatively, the student dislikes or hates grammar. These differences are pervasive, and can be found, for example, in the way people evaluated their own experiences of learning grammar and in the way curricular documents envisage the educational encounter and set out the targets of instruction.

This difference in emotional tonality is not easy to interpret. The cold, calculated approach might reflect a deep emotional detachment of Jewish students from Arabic. The highly emotive valuation by Arabs may also be linked to the traumatic nature of Arabic-grammar instruction in the Arab sector and the high stakes that are involved in it. The differences might also reflect a broader difference in discursive practices between Arabs and Jews whereby Arabs rely on emotive metaphors to construct their educational experience to a greater extent than do Jews, who might draw more heavily on intellective imagery.

Whatever may be the explanation of the emotional tonality, the systemic differences in aim, material and approaches raise the question of whether the Jewish and Arab systems of grammar instruction, and their theoretical underpinnings, are truly equivalent and therefore comparable fields of knowledge and instruction in the first place. Indeed, their embeddedness in different historical trajectories has made them substantially different intellectual projects.

Improbable Role Reversals

While the situation whereby Jewish students are subject to Arab instruction of Arabic does not normally arise, such encounters may occasionally happen, with predictable results. I directly encountered one such situation in the course of my research.

Haifa University has an exceptionally large intake of Arab students compared with the other universities inside Israel, reflecting the demography of its catchment area. Arabs are the overwhelming majority among those enrolling in the undergraduate program in Arabic Language and Literature, to the point that some academics were wondering whether it might become an exclusively Arab department.

Arabic-grammar instruction at Haifa University was split in the first two years between classes aimed at graduates of Arabic speaking schools, and classes aimed at graduates of the Hebrew school system. The former were taught by Arab adjuncts, and the latter were taught by Jewish academics in the department. The third year advanced grammar of Arabic brought together graduates of both streams. It was normally taught by one of the grammarians in the department, adopting a Western Jewish orientation, and reproducing the overachievement of Jewish students and underachievement of Arab students.

Following the death in 2004 of its leading grammarian, the department was forced to rationalise its grammar offerings. This led to an extraordinary situation whereby the second year grammar course for Jewish students was not offered, and Jewish students were required to take the Arab course—a course taught in Arabic and focused on the theory of *ʿamal* (عمل), or in its more common rendition in the Arab sector, the theory of the *ʿāmil* (عامل).

The Jewish students were completely overwhelmed. I followed some of the interactions inside and outside the classroom. The three Jewish students who had enrolled in the Arabic-grammar course were struggling to keep up with class. The department took the unusual step of appointing a tutor to help the students with additional advice and support. The tutor, a Jewish Arabic high school teacher who was employed as an adjunct, would confer in between classes with the instructor of the Arabic course, himself an Arab adjunct, and would then meet the Jewish students for a weekly remedial session where she would help the students by reviewing the material with them. The tutor would also attend the classes of the grammar course itself.

While it is tempting to flag the complete disorientation of the students as the result of the incommensurability of grammatical approaches, there were other dynamics at play here as well that compounded the Jewish students' difficulties.

First, the Jewish students' Arabic was not good enough to keep up with the class. This forced the instructor to interpose explanations in Hebrew in the class, and often move to slow, highly simplified Arabic. The Jewish students struggled with the most basic aspects of instruction. At times when examples were given to demonstrate a grammatical point, e.g. a verb and its object, the examples needed to be translated into Hebrew and explained, as did such elementary grammatical concepts as transitive and intransitive verbs.

The interruptions of these Jewish students to the flow of the class were quite frustrating to the overwhelmingly Arab majority of students. This interference to the normal flow of instruction contributed to a current of mild hostility on the part of Arab students many of whom, with the safety of being part of a collective, would snigger or groan as one of the Jewish students would ask questions or require an explanation of the most basic nature. The ethnic/communal aspect of this conflict was not articulated but was never in doubt. In one class I observed, this was aggravated by some gender undertones. It was a Jewish female student who seemed most lost and who most persistently slowed down the progress of the lesson with what to Arab students were most trivial questions. Her hyper-trendy attire coupled with a high pitch tone which was perceived as comically "prissy", and her extreme difficulties in pronouncing basic Arabic sounds, added a strong gendered dimension to the explosive dynamics of the situation. The class ended in tears on the part of the Jewish student and in a fair bit of frustration on the part of some Arab students.

In essence, then, the problematic integration of the Jewish students into the Arab classroom was compromised by several factors in addition to the incommensurability of grammar, factors that include the Jewish students' poor proficiency in Arabic in general and lack of familiarity with basic concepts in Arabic, along with the intercommunal political underpinning of the classroom encounter between Arabs and Jews.

Still, the regular meeting sessions that the Jewish tutor had with the Jewish students clearly brought out the incommensurability in grammatical instruction, this time from the perspective of Jews trying to come to terms with Israeli-Arab grammar of Arabic. In the lead-up to each such session, the tutor would attend the Arabic grammar classes and get her own individual instruction and material from the Arab instructor of the class. She functioned in effect as an additional instructional intermediary between the Jewish students and the

Arab instructor. During the tutorials both she and the students would review the material and try to make sense of it, often struggling with the material together.

The tutor herself was not entirely new to the Arab way of doing grammar. The high school where she taught had absorbed many children of members of the defunct South Lebanese Army—Israel's proxy militia in southern Lebanon. She had therefore had experience with students who had had some instruction in Arab schools in Lebanon.

However, even she found it hard to follow the logic of some of the material that was being taught in the Arab course. Occasionally she and the students would go over the material, give up on trying to understand the rationale behind it, and focus on a pragmatic approach of "What do we need to know in order to pass the exam?" The disorientation was so profound that at times the students and the instructor struggled to even formulate specific questions to be raised with the Arab instructor that could help them understand the material.

The possibility of fundamental incommensurability was not raised in those sessions of teacher and students, and possibly therefore the basic questions that might have led to an understanding were not raised. This metacognitive blindness left the Jewish students, along with their Arab instructor and fellow Arab students, in a frustrating morass of inexplicable incomprehension.

The incommensurability remained stubbornly invisible to all those concerned, including the academic leaders of the department. This time the alibi was the inadequate Arabic proficiency of the three Jewish students. In other words, it was too easy to explain away the underperformance of the Jewish students by their poor Arabic skills. And in any event, there was no urgency to delve too deeply into the challenge of discovering the barriers that prevent Arabs from excelling at Arabic grammar. The whole situation was unusual and a temporary pragmatic accommodation to the unusual situation following the death of the department's senior grammarian. Still, in this context, both the extent of the lack of Arabic proficiency among Jewish students and the profound and fateful incommensurability between the two systems of grammar, were brought into sharp relief, even if they were not fully appreciated by those involved.

Systemic Incommensurability as Personal Failure

The instance of Jews struggling in an Arab class of Arabic grammar is an improbable temporary result of anomalous circumstances. In the normal course of events the incommensurability of grammars is an acute problem for Arabs, as we see in the saga of grammar instruction at universities. The differences between the two grammars and the systemic nature of these differences tend to pass unnoticed, or at least, not fully appreciated, by academics, teachers and university students, even those who struggle with the material. This is partly because almost all Jewish scholars who specialise in Arabic-grammar instruction—including many academic specialists in grammar—have never themselves undergone Arab Arabic-grammar instruction, and thereby have not experienced firsthand the disorientation that is involved in shifting from one pedagogic orientation to the other. This applies even to the Israeli Jewish scholars of the Arabic Linguistic Tradition who are fully conversant with the grammatical scholarship that underlies the Arab grammar instruction, but not with its contemporary curricular and pedagogic actualisation in educational practice.

The fact that such systemic differences do tend to pass unnoticed or unacknowledged is particularly pernicious. It accentuates the very alienation because what are essentially systemic differences in reasoning and instruction are reconstituted and experienced as individual difficulty in comprehension.

The experience could be quite traumatic. One Arab academic I interviewed recounted that he decided to study Arabic at university because he loved grammar at school. In one of our discussions he used the Hebrew word *muqsam*—enchanted—to describe his love for grammar. He bemoaned the lack of preparation for what he was to encounter in the university grammar classroom. He was completely disorientated at the Arabic grammar class at university, and "did not connect" to the material. The comparative grammar he was taught did not appeal to him at all. He could not even recount which areas he found more problematic, or remember anything about the content of the course. He simply struggled to survive that course, and once completed, he put it behind him and proceeded to specialise in Arabic literature. The themes of total shock at the encounter; of the inability to recollect much about the content of the course or the problematic areas; and the motif of struggling to survive the class, all recurred in interviews and conversations I had with Arabs who had successfully completed their undergraduate studies in Arabic, including successful academics in the field of Arabic, Arab school teachers, and other Arab university graduates and students. Remarkably, none of these interviewees offered a general systemic view of the differences in grammatical knowledge, beyond observing that they had thought they knew grammar before the course, but whatever grammar they did know did not help them through the course itself.

CHAPTER 5

Arabic-Grammar Instruction: Systemic and Cognitive Implications

The preceding chapters describe the field of Arabic instruction in Israel and analyse two of its unintended systemic consequences. One is the inability of Arabic instruction to inculcate proficiency among Jewish students notwithstanding the relative abundance of necessary resources and the high priority that the powers that be in Israel accord Arabic instruction to Jews. The other is the underperformance of Arab university students at Arabic grammar, a situation that reflects and accentuates the broader alienation of Israeli Arabs from Arabic grammar and its instruction.

Both phenomena result from the same constellation of forces that typifies the field of Arabic instruction in Israel. The ongoing containment and marginalisation of Arabs in Israel and Israel's confrontation with its surrounding environment—often glossed as the Arab-Israeli conflict—create the institutional imperative that drives and structures Arabic instruction, even as they produce the dynamics of its subversion on both the Jewish and Arab sides.

On the Jewish side, the very particularist, securitist rationale that drives Arabic instruction hinders the very success of Arabic instruction. It makes the language a less attractive subject than it might otherwise have been, and it makes it harder for those who choose to learn Arabic to master it. More generally, the communal conflict between Jews and Arabs that anchors the securitist rationale also creates an institutional dynamic, most notably in academia, that devalues Arabic proficiency and neutralises the comparative advantage that Arabs enjoy by virtue of their native mastery of Arabic, thereby buttressing the dominant position of Jews and the Jewish educational agenda. The communal conflict also disrupts the integration of Arabs into the enterprise of Arabic instruction to Jews, thereby foregoing a critical resource. Ultimately, the Zionist agenda that creates the securitist rationale also drives the devaluation of Arabic as cultural capital in Israel, thereby undermining any initiative to promote and deepen Arabic instruction to Israel's Jews.

On the Arab side the dynamics are different but the results quite comparable. The institutional structure of Arabic instruction in Israel responds to the needs of Jewish students and consequently disrupts the coherence of Arabic grammar instruction to Arabs. It hinders Israeli Arabs from achieving a measure of autonomous control over Arabic grammar instruction to Arabs by

 | DOI: 10.1163/9789004349957_006

pursuing tertiary curricula that are not entirely relevant to Arabs, and by preventing the formation of an Arab tertiary space that can develop and reform linguistic knowledge, shaping teacher training and the Arab educational enterprise accordingly.

But the disruption of Arab students' relationship with grammar reflects not only the peculiar politics of knowledge, language and instruction within Israel. The effects of Israel's institutional structure merge with the broader crisis in Arabic linguistics in the Arab world in general and with the marginalisation and disempowerment of Israeli Arabs within the Arab world, to alienate Arab students from the grammar of the Arabic language.

The analysis in the previous chapters uses three fundamental approaches. One is a systemic perspective that sees the functioning of the field of Arabic instruction as a whole whose effects are a product of the way its parts interact. The consequences of the field are not simply a reflection of the intentions of the most powerful stakeholder, nor are they a wilful compromise between stakeholders. Rather, the volitional action of each and every stakeholder is always mediated, at times even subverted, through the actions of other stakeholders, through the endogenous dynamics of the field, and through the general conditions in which the field is embedded. The field produces its own effects that are most notably expressed in the field's unintended consequences. This is how the field can produce results that are generally suboptimal and do not serve anybody's interest. In other words, we can envisage numerous outcomes that would be universally seen as much more satisfactory than the current state of affairs. However, the dynamics of human systems are such that their outcomes are not a direct linear reflection of the intentions of their constituent parts.

The systemic perspective on the field of Arabic instruction makes it possible to explain the conundrums of unsuccessful Arabic instruction as unintended consequences that are nonetheless direct products of the field and not mere aberrations. The two seemingly inexplicable predicaments of underachievement in Arabic instruction to Jews and Arabs emerge from the analysis as the unwitting outcome of the combined effect of different stakeholders whose interaction is conditioned by the overarching configuration of power across society. Significantly, the influence of the overarching political structures is decisive, although by no means predetermined. Rather, it produces political imperatives that run through the field of Arabic instruction to which stakeholders must respond within the constraints, opportunities and logic of the field. Two obvious imperatives are Zionism's commitment to the invention and maintenance of a distinct Jewish ethnicity, and Arab linguistic conservatism. The overarching political structures also affect the power structure of the field of Arabic instruction. This is manifest in the political economy of linguistic mastery, and in the balance of power between the local school community (parents, students, teachers and principals) and the bureaucratic authorities (e.g. Ministry of Education and the security apparatus).

The second fundamental approach that informs the analysis in this book is a non-objectivist realism that is applied to knowledge. In essence, systems of knowledge are seen not as direct, unmediated reflections of the reality they seek to apprehend, but rather as the product of two processes. One is the interaction of the apprehended reality with the cognitive and ideological structures of knowledge. In other words, the perception of reality is an active process of apprehension whereby the internalised cognitive structures of the knower mediate whatever objective reality exists "out there". The other process is the social distribution of knowledge and authority. In other words, the apprehension and comprehension of reality draw on accumulated knowledge which is socially differentiated and organised. Social differentiation and organisation have their own effects on knowledge formation and circulation. Indeed, it is impossible to ignore the socially, culturally and historically situated nature of knowledge if one accepts that two distinct grammars of Arabic can co-exist, because the two owe their differences to the historical context of their production and transmission, rather than to differences in the subject matter that they seek to capture. Both are, after all, distinct grammars of the one language.

The third fundamental approach seeks to identify patterned habits of thought and knowledge *in situ*. In other words, I focus on a specific area of knowledge and learning without seeking to make general statements about pervasive culture-wide cognitive styles, and without defining general rules of how people learn. My approach treats patterns of thought, learning and reasoning as habitual practices, rather than as an inherent mode of learning and thought. Such habits normally pass unnoticed. In the case of Arabic-grammar instruction they are continuously inculcated and reinforced in the course of educational interaction. They become part of a person's intuition. In the normal run of events people have little need or reason to become conscious of such habits of thinking and learning. But Arabic-grammar instruction is not a normal situation, as it pits two alternative systems of knowledge and learning against each other. The lack of cognitive self-awareness renders both the profundity of the differences between Arabs and Jews in habits of learning and thinking grammar, and the fateful consequences of these differences, all but invisible to participants in Arabic grammar instruction. In other words, the lack of appreciation by both Arabs and Jews of the extent to which either side's way of thinking grammar is historically and culturally bounded renders participants unable to account in systemic terms for the difficulty that Arab university students face in assimilating university Arabic grammar instruction.

Part of what accounts for the contextual specificity of learning habits is the way the peculiar subject matter in a given context is constructed. Some constructions may lend themselves to particular styles of learning. Moreover, some constructions may have affective ramifications that influence the way the material is taught and learnt. Thus, my proposition that the securitist agenda disrupts the Jewish acquisition of Arabic proficiency implies that some emotional and ideological states of mind facilitate the acquisition of linguistic proficiency, and others disrupt it.

As a point of departure for further research I suggest that the acquisition of proficiency in a foreign language—one that covers the full gamut of linguistic and paralinguistic skills—may depend on a learner's capacity to entertain inner speech (cf. Vygotsky 2012) in the target language in non-threatening contexts. For the purpose of the current discussion, inner speech can be understood as imaginary role play and dialogues that learners can enact in their minds as they toy with the language that they learn and seize control over its expressive capacity. To entertain inner speech, one must be able to envision oneself participating in such an interaction, and internalise through identification different performances that are observed in native speakers of the language. This cannot happen unless the interaction in the target language can be imagined as non-threatening in that one's interlocutor is not a threat, and in that one's self worth is not compromised by engaging in interaction in the target language. A language constituted as the that of a predatory enemy, and an inferior one at that, would therefore be harder to assimilate because it is much harder to imagine non-threatening and non-demeaning contexts of interaction in such a language.

The remainder of the chapter seeks to draw out two broader implications of Arabic instruction in Israel. Previous chapters have taken an empirical approach to cognition, observing *in situ* how people think and learn, and situating this cognitive behaviour within a broad systemic perspective. I draw out the implications of this empirical stance for broader trends and debates in the scholarship. I argue that theories that typify entire cultures with particular cognitive styles and theories that draw generalised links between cognition and culture have reached an impasse. Thankfully, viable analytic alternatives to these approaches do exist. This book elaborates one such alternative tendency, namely that of inductive studies of how people think, reason and learn in practice. I argue for the urgency of studying cognitive functioning not in contrived situations like the psychologist's laboratory or the sociologist's questionnaire, but in real life, performing real tasks. This kind of study must also take into account the relevant objects and the physical and social contexts of people's cognitive functioning. It is only through the progressive accumulation of such holistic, localised empirical studies of cognition *in situ* that we can develop a broader understanding of cognition as a social and cultural phenomenon.

Furthermore, by highlighting the profound hold of habits of thought that are acquired in the course of learning in a particular domain, this study joins with those who see context specificity as a crucial aspect of cognitive behaviour. The rationale that drives this position is that cognitive tasks are linked to contexts, and people acquire habits of thought through continuous habitual engagement with specific cognitive tasks. The empirical study of cognition must therefore focus on given domains, rather than on decontextualised cultural styles of thought. All this does not preclude the possibility that there are cross-domain commonalities in styles of thought in a given culture, but such commonalities should be discovered empirically through synthesis from different domains rather than assumed a priori.

The discussion of the empirical approach to cognition is followed by a consideration of the book's systemic approach and mobilisation of Bourdieu's heuristic framework of field to examine how reality imposes itself on social agents through these very agents' endeavours to act upon reality. The discussion further seeks to account for the perplexing historical continuity in the field of Arabic instruction in Israel. This is a substantial challenge. Attempts to account for continuity run into an inevitable methodological difficulty. The lack of historical change makes it impossible to find empirical evidence to demonstrate the forces and dynamics that fix the field in its current state of apparent equilibrium—hence the need to find alternative analytic means that go beyond description of historical events.

I seek to meet the challenge by offering grounded hypothetical speculation in the final section. I raise some non-radical practices that might have improved the outcome of the field from the perspective of stakeholders and evaluate what prevents such changes from coming to pass. Significantly, these measures do not require the complete transformation of the polity of Israel. Their effect would be mostly localised within the field of Arabic instruction, and the forces that prevent them are to be found within the field, too. In other words, I seek to account for the dynamics of non-change in the field of Arabic instruction in a way that may serve as a potential model for the exploration of the dynamics of stasis in other fields of social practice.[1] But first I turn to the empirical approach to cognition.

1 For a broader discussion of the significance of historicising continuity and non-change see Uhlmann 2005.

The Social Variability of Cognition, Scholarship and Learning

Few issues have excited as much contention in modern social sciences as the debate over the extent to which cognition and thought vary across society, and the extent to which they are shaped by socialisation and social interaction. The contemporary debate over the cross-cultural variability in cognition and styles of thought goes back to that originary Lévy-Bruhlian moment described earlier. The debate is commonly seen as a clash between two positions—the hypothesis of the "psychic unity of mankind" as it was once called, and the claim to "cognitive relativity".

The cognitive-unity hypothesis holds that there is negligible cultural variation in the way people think and reason. It is what people know and think rather than how they know and think that differentiates people from different cultures. In other words, the differences in beliefs, knowledge and the like can be ascribed to differences in the contents of the knowledge, which reflect the specific historical experiences of individuals and societies, but not to procedural differences in the way knowledge is formulated, processed, maintained and transmitted. It is the content rather than the process or structure of knowing that differs cross culturally. Thus the differences between what Victorian thinkers called the "primitive" and the "civilised" are not expressions of inherent cognitive characteristics of the different civilisations and their members, but rather the result of some historical coincidence that led to the rise of science in some societies and of magic in others. This has been the majority opinion among anthropologists since the emergence of modern socio-cultural anthropology. This, in fact, was one of the defining features of the radical enterprise of modern anthropology as it displaced the social sciences of the Victorian era—including criminal anthropology, phrenology, eugenics and the like—that sought the explanations for social and cultural differences in inherited physiological characteristics. The cognitive-unity hypothesis remains the dominant view throughout contemporary social sciences.

Lévy-Bruhl's encounter with Chinese scholarship led him to oppose Victorian essentialism with no less vigour, but from a diametrically opposed position (see Cazeneuve 1972 for an overview and a selection of relevant texts). He came to believe that cultural differences led members of different cultures to actually think differently. In other words, it is not simply the content of knowledge, but the underlying mental structures and cognitive procedures of knowledge formation that differ. So much so, in fact, that true empathy—in the sense of being able to see the world through another's eyes—may not be attainable across cultures. What made this position distinctly modern was Lévy-Bruhl's socio-cultural determinism, namely his attribution of cognitive difference exclusively to the social and cultural environments that condition the cognitive ontogeny of humans, and not to differences in some sort of inherited essence be it genetic or some other biological heritage. Moreover, he held that the different mentalities that correspond to different cultures could not be placed on an evolutionary scale, or evaluated against one another. None was an earlier or later version of the other, none was inherently superior or inferior to the other, and none could be taken as a yardstick by which the other could be measured. Different mentalities were simply that, different, and potentially radically so, in that they may well be mutually incomprehensible.

Lévy-Bruhl's theoretical edifice, constructed as it was on the shaky grounds of the anthropological wisdom of his time, was doomed. Lévy-Bruhl postulated that radically different cultural types produced radically different cognitive types. Reflecting the cultural typology of his time, Lévy-Bruhl contrasted a "civilised mentality" with a "primitive mentality". "Civilised mentality" is dominated by Aristotelian logic and scientific rationalism, where the law of contradiction, along with the law of identity and the law of the excluded middle reign supreme. "Primitive mentality" is substantially broader. It understands logic in its classical sense, but also tolerates contradictions. It perceives as consubstantial various entities that to the "civilised mentality" appear as distinct, and tolerates the coexistence of propositions that render each other impossible.[2]

An immensely important analytical step that Lévy-Bruhl took as he continued to develop his theory was to integrate the affective aspects of thinking into the analysis, and to locate much of the difference he postulated within affective motivation. Presumably the outrage of a contradiction affects bearers of the civilised mentality to a much greater extent than it does bearers of the primitive mentality, hence the former abhor contradictions where the latter accept them.

The issue of the affective aspect of cognition has not been sufficiently developed since Lévy-Bruhl, and has not received the attention it deserves. Yet it appears to be one significant means by which cultural sensibilities can affect cognitive behaviour. For example, in a study by Donna Lardiere (1992) Arab interviewees who were able to formulate the "correct" answer to a hypothetical counterfactual question resisted the question and the answer because of an aversion to engaging in frivolous hypotheticals. Confronted with the question: "If all circles were large, and this small triangle 'Δ' were a circle, would it

2 Lévy-Bruhl's formulation of the primitive mentality resembles the subsequent conceptualisation of fuzzy logic. The distinction between the two mentalities is clearly not a completely idiosyncratic illumination of Lévy-Bruhl's, but taps a broad intuitive understanding that formal logical reasoning is not necessarily a good model of the way people think.

be large?" Lardiere's informants reacted uncooperatively, perceiving the question as belittling, even as their remonstrations revealed they fully understood the exact logical argument that was required. Clearly the affective tonality of that situation overwhelmed the entire exchange to the point that respondents refused to offer the logically correct response. In her paper Lardiere makes the case that ignoring the affective aspects of the way respondents reacted to the question might lead scholars to conclude that Arabs have difficulty conceptualising counterfactual situations, where the difficulty is clearly in the resistance to being demeaned by "silly" tasks (Lardiere 1992). Current behavioural analyses of cognition and learning tend to downplay the affective aspects of intellectual processes, yet this specific example, and others like it, would suggest that the affective tonality of subject matter and of instructional contexts might substantially affect cognitive performance such as learning and scholarship.

It is, in fact, impossible to account for the emergent reality of Arabic instruction in Israel without taking the affective tonality into account. The detrimental effects of Arabic's low status and perceived threatening nature are an instance of the profound influence of the affective domain. A "cold" approach to cognition—one that is focused on the formal structures of learning without paying attention to the total experience of learning and thinking—is too limiting.

Earlier I suggested that the acquisition of proficiency in a foreign language relies on inner speech, and that if imagined interaction evokes a sense of threat, it may disrupt inner speech and undermine the attainment of proficiency. Furthermore, comparing Arab and Jewish conventions of discussing and imagining the experience of learning Arabic suggests significant differences in the emotive experience of learning Arabic. The affective dimension of learning and thought is crucial, yet is too easily overlooked by contemporary scholars.

Lévy-Bruhl's challenge to the dominant ideas in social sciences have failed to undermine the accepted dogma of psychic unity, although his challenge could never be entirely dismissed either. It is easy to see why. Social scientists in general and anthropologists in particular have spent decades elaborating the social construction of pretty much any aspect of human existence, from the ideational to the corporeal, from the individual to the collective. To postulate that culture has no influence on perception and on thought processes—given the profound complexity of perception and thought and the tortuous ontogeny of cognitive development—would seem to run against the grain of social and behavioural sciences altogether. Yet if it is accepted that culture does play a role in cognitive ontogeny, how possibly could the position of cognitive unity be justified?

One of the problems to beset the sociological and anthropological investigation of cognition has been the lack of agreement on core questions such as what is actually being studied and what would constitute a persuasive argument one way or the other. Evans-Pritchard's defence of the psychic unity approach is a case in point. Evans-Pritchard relied on his empirical study of the supernatural among the Azande (1976). Setting himself an ambitious challenge, namely the analysis of beliefs he and his readers knew to be unfounded, Evans-Pritchard sought to demonstrate that the thought processes that are involved in magic and witchcraft are no different from those that are involved in the science of the contemporary West. Thus contradictions that reality brings up are explained away by Azande rather than noted and tolerated. For instance, if an oracle produces a result one knows to be wrong, the problem may be attributed to any number of non-systemic failures like a flaw in the particular way the oracle was conducted, very much like a medical treatment which is unsuccessful does not immediately undermine science in the eyes of supposedly rational Western patients.

On the opposite side of the debate, the lure of finding out the cultural construction of the very reality of perception was sufficiently strong to motivate quite a few scholars to continue the search for proof and explanation of cross-cultural cognitive variation. US linguistic anthropologist Benjamin Whorf advanced what became known as the Whorf or Sapir-Whorf hypothesis (Whorf 1941), a bold assertion of linguistic relativity and linguistic determinism. The argument was that the language one speaks conditions one's cognition. Linguistic variation, by this argument, becomes the basis of a radical cross-cultural alterity in cognition and thought. While the possible influence of language on cognition continues to be debated, few accept the strong contention that language determines cognition. A consistent correlation between linguistic differences and habits of perception and thought has never been successfully demonstrated.

In the Soviet Union, Alexander R. Luria and his collaborators (Luria 1976), following Lev S. Vygotsky, continued from where Lévy-Bruhl had left off and pushed his argument further by identifying formal schooling as the main social process that produces the primitive-versus-civilised dichotomy of mentalities. They argued that formal education causes a qualitative break in cognitive development. Luria and his associates conducted a comparative study of different groups of Uzbeks with different levels of schooling, ascribing consistent differences in formal reasoning and logic to length and depth of experience in formal education and training. They further argued that the function and meaning of language changes in the course of maturation, thereby effectively (but not explicitly) emptying the Whorf hypothesis of any significance. This is so because Whorf argued that the structure of a given language imposes itself on the perceptual structures of the speaker. An argument that the effect of language on human cognition is meditated through and varies by social experience undermines Whorf's vision (or in the very least a strong interpretation of Whorf's vision) of individual cognition as an epiphenomenon of the ossified structures of specific languages.

Against studies like Luria's, works such as Edwin Hutchins' Trobriand case study of reasoning (1980) argue that the seeming differences in logic are an artifice of the research methods used, and specifically the artificial context of psychological interviews. In essence, the schooling effect is little more than experience in how to answer exam questions. By this argument, people's logic in different cultures is one and the same. To demonstrate this, Hutchins provides a detailed record of the legal process in a traditional court on one of the Trobriand Islands, where competing claims over garden ownerships were raised and discussed. Hutchins shows that participants in the litigation adhered to Aristotelian logic to no lesser extent than would Westerners involved in judicial proceedings (Hutchins 1980).

But such an argument could not possibly debunk positions like Lévy-Bruhl's original formulation. Lévy-Bruhl never asserted that "primitive mentality" was impervious to logic. Rather he insisted that "primitive mentality" tolerated departures from Aristotelian logic. In other words, demonstrating conformity to Aristotelian logic in "primitive mentality" is neither here nor there. This highlights how difficult it is to agree upon tests that can disprove any of the numerous contradictory positions on the cultural contextualisation of reasoning and thought.

But Hutchins' study offers a particularly significant contribution to the field, one that can advance the scholarship in this area past these deadlocked debates. In this and subsequent studies (e.g. 1995) he refocuses the research on reasoning *in situ*. Unlike Luria and his collaborators, he does not study responses to a research instrument. Unlike Evans-Pritchard, he does not freely deduce putative reasoning processes from practice. Rather, he takes a slice of reality where reasoning and logic can be observed directly, such as the arguments surrounding a court settlement of a land dispute, and proceeds to analyse the structure of these visible processes.

Hutchins' focus on reasoning *in situ* contrasts sharply with the mushrooming literature produced by cross-cultural psychologists who paint broad brush differences between the West and the Rest (e.g. Nisbett 2003) by opportunistically cobbling together experiments and pseudo-experiments to sustain such unsubtle contentions as that Americans are analytic thinkers, while East Asians are holistic thinkers. This line of research can be traced back to the cross-cultural testing of Herman Witkin's dichotomous constructs of field dependence and field independence which purport to capture different styles of conceptual thinking (Berry 1976). I do not propose to revisit the opposition between cultural psychology and cross-cultural psychology, or the debate over the validity of Witkin's constructs and their cross-cultural applicability, except to suggest that more observational studies of cognition in practice are sorely needed.

The field continues to be dogged by many other obscurities, such as the lack of clarity as to what exactly scholars are looking for when they study cognition, and how to measure or describe it. One further complication is a confusion between what might be distinguished as thinking versus reasoning, the former relating to the actual mental processes which are not easily observed or described, the latter to the cultural patterns and conventions of representing these thought processes, patterns that can be seen as the post-fact explanations that people give to interviewers, or the answers that subjects give to questionnaires.

Probably the greatest hindrance to advances in the field is the ongoing domination of a top-down approach, that is, the move from theoretical contention to a controlled observation. Typically, scholars formulate a theoretical position, and then proceed to muster evidence to support or potentially refute their position. What seems to be in short supply in the literature is a bottom-up approach: rich observational studies of cognition in context that are not driven, and thereby constrained, by the desire to defend a specific position in the debate about cognition, but rather add up to reveal general patterns of cognitive behaviour.

Not surprisingly, ethnographers stand out among those who have made the empirical study of thinking and reasoning the main object of their studies, with surprising results. Jean Lave and her colleagues (Lave, Murtaugh and de la Rocha 1984) followed shoppers in action and recorded their internal deliberations and decision-making processes in real time. They found that the thought processes that motivated shopping calculations were essentially different from formal arithmetic—the arithmetic that is taught at school. Their research emphasises the domain specificity of patterns of thought, a fact that should have raised a red flag to those who search for decontextualised, culture-wide modes of thought (not to mention those who study civilisation-wide mentalities such as Western versus East Asian or Oriental). If indeed modes of thought are unique to specific contexts, and if people acquire an arsenal of specific thought habits that are shaped and honed in specific contexts, then we need to study domain-specific rather than culture-wide habits of thought. In fact, under such conditions much of the comparison across cultures that is not restricted to specific, equivalent domains becomes meaningless.

Other ethnographers have sought to challenge the prevalent view of cognition by challenging the notion of cognition as something that happens within the confines of the brain or the mind of individuals. Rather, they moved to situate cognitive processes within the social and physical contexts that they occur (e.g. Bateson 1972, Hutchins 1995). This turns cognition from an individual phenomenon to a social, inter-subjective process and from a purely mental phenomenon to a material and physical one, too. The structure of social relations becomes critical to cognitive processes, as does the technology used in recording, processing and reformulating knowledge. This approach links to the diverse, empirically focused work on literacy and its effect on cognition. Brinkley Messick's study of the phonocentric styles of early modern Yemeni scholastic culture (1993) insightfully applies this approach to a Middle Eastern context.

It is evidently not the lack of theories that has frustrated the contemporary quest for understanding the possible social and cultural variation in cognitive and learning habits and styles. Rather, it is the paucity of concrete focused observational studies of cognition and learning in different yet comparable contexts. Such an exploration of cognition *in situ* is essential not only to provide more information to be dissected by the existing theories, but also to advance our theoretical understanding, which will likely need to move beyond simplistic models of single-cause (e.g. cultural variation), and beyond the consideration of decontextualised traits such as the notion of a cognitive style that is independent of specific domains.

The methodological difficulties of studying cognition *in situ* are nonetheless quite substantial. This is particularly so with regard to the processes that make up learning habits and styles. Following Bourdieu's theorisation of practice, Eickelman's historical-cum-anthropological analysis of the educational biography of a Moroccan judge (1985) sets out to understand cognitive style in a pedagogical context. The study brings together participant observation, interviews and historical analysis to reconstruct the peculiar teaching and learning processes in religious institutions in the late colonial period in Morocco. Eickelman's methodological versatility allowed him to go beyond the educational process as it was formally constructed by participants, and highlight the way education unfolded in practice. Significantly, the way people recall and reconstruct their educational experience differs from their actual experience. The lacunae in educational autobiographies are instructive. A case in point is the significance of peer study groups in carrying out instruction. These are critical and integral to the learning process in advanced, early modern Islamic education, yet they are invariably omitted from formal and retrospective narratives of education by learned people themselves, as demonstrated by Eickelman's Moroccan notable informant. Evidently, people are not generally sufficiently aware of their own cognitive processes to be able to construct a reliable, comprehensive account of their learning experience. Eickelman further historicises the educational process by reconstructing its various dimensions—including the physical, material technology of teaching and learning, the cultural constructions of knowledge, the political struggles over the value of knowledge and so forth—all of which play an important and often contradictory role.

Such nuanced discussions raise further grave doubts about any attempts to generalise a single cognitive style for entire populations. In any event, given that people are such poor witnesses to their own education, we clearly need many more studies of educational exchanges that are embedded in their historical, physical and social contexts, to complement observational studies of cognition in practice.

Arabic-grammar instruction offers a particularly promising area for such intensive studies. The scholarship of Arabic grammar and its instruction in Israel form a natural experiment of sorts. We have two scholastic traditions that seek to conceptualise what is nominally an identical subject matter—namely the grammar and syntax of Arabic—yet do so from different historical and cultural vantage points.

However, close examination complicates the neat construct of a natural experiment. Although they nominally address the same phenomenon, the Arabic scholastic tradition and the Orientalist tradition seek to accomplish different goals. So much so, that I suggested in chapter four that they are not quite comparable fields of knowledge. Yet, this difference in goals, too, is itself significant, as the project that European scholarship and instruction has set itself is different in meaningful ways from the project that is embodied in Arab scholarship. This difference is itself an integral part of the cognitive divide between different grammars of Arabic. In other words, the comparison of cognitive functioning or styles must be broadened to include the aims and meanings of specific knowledge. It should not be restricted to a decontextualised comparison of knowledge structures and modes of reasoning.

The sense of a natural experiment is further complicated by the fact that the two traditions are not entirely distinct. There have been some influences across the traditions, mostly when European scholars appropriated Arab scholarship to develop their own approach. A close examination of how the knowledge is transformed as it is transplanted from the Arab world of scholarship to its European counterpart may offer interesting insights into the historical and cultural variability of knowledge.

The different historical trajectories further strain the comparison of the two traditions. Arab scholarship developed before the European one, and under different conditions of knowledge formation and circulation. For example, Arab scholarship of Arabic peaked before mass printing, imposing different constraints on the production and circulation of knowledge from those that confronted the European scholarship of Arabic when the latter finally emerged. The differences between the two traditions thus may be ascribed not only to cultural differences in the construction of knowledge, but at one and the same time they may also reflect differences in the technology of instruction, the social relations of instruction, the dynamics of evolution of fields of scholarship, and the social function of knowledge in society. In fact, I doubt whether these different factors could be effectively disentangled in practice, or even in theory.

The clear difference in the aim and use of grammatic knowledge in the two traditions makes it impossible to take the duality of traditions of Arabic grammatic scholarship as a straightforward expression of cross-cultural stylistic differences in knowledge construction and information processing, whereby culture is an independent variable and cognitive style is the dependent variable that is observable through the difference in the ways that members of two cultures respond conceptually (with the theory of grammar) to an identical stimulus (the regularities of Arabic). In fact, the situation calls into question the very utility of the psychological notion of cognitive style. How can one distinguish—either empirically or theoretically—differences in conventions of reasoning (an intersubjective fact), in the aims of a system of knowledge (a historical fact), in the social relations and technological infrastructure of knowledge production and circulation (social and physical realities), from a psychologically conceptualised style of thinking?

In fact, the motivations that underlay Arabic instruction in the Arab world and in Europe were sufficiently different to cast doubt on whether the two enterprises are even pedagogically comparable projects. This is so because scholars and teachers in both traditions have approached grammar instruction from within different intellectual projects, asking different questions and applying completely different standards to measure successful learning.

Inevitably, a consideration of cognitive practices and pedagogy must incorporate an understanding of differences in the aim of knowledge acquisition, in the technology and social relations of instruction and in the modes of the expression of knowledge. Reality is constructed by the knower as the first, essential step of knowing, and this construction is inseparable from the knower's intention, the context of knowing and the purpose for which knowledge is constructed.[3]

---

3 As I mentioned in the opening section of this chapter, I am not adopting here a subjectivist

All this may transcend the intuitive, commonsensical understanding of cognition as information processing, or as "cold" mental representations of reality, effectively a human equivalent of computational processes. But this, along with our intuitive neglect of the affective dimension of cognition, attests to the inadequacy of this computational notion of thinking for the purposes of interpreting cognition in context.

Clearly, any hope that comparing the two traditions of Arabic scholarship would be an elegant way to observe differences in modes of mental processing breaks down under close scrutiny. Nevertheless, much valuable insight can be gleaned from the dynamics of university Arabic-grammar instruction where the two traditions clash as Arab and Jewish students share the classroom. Arab students in Jewish grammar classes, as well as Jewish students in Arab grammar classes, seem to exhibit a profound hold of intellectual habits. It is hard to transition from knowledge that is set in one tradition to the other. These habits of learning and thought, whether or not they cohere across contexts and domains to form culturally distinct styles, are both productive in that they facilitate certain approaches to instruction, and restrictive in that they hinder alternative approaches.

Such narrowly contextualised comparisons as that of the way Arabs and Jews think about and learn Arabic grammar may, in turn, enable us to ask broader, cross-cultural questions, albeit couched differently from the way cross-cultural psychology has sought to contrast cognitive styles. Are these differences restricted to a particular area of instruction? Do they reflect broader characteristics? Are there equivalent differences in other areas of instruction such as music, mathematics, and so forth? If so, how do they conform to broad cultural, historical, material or social tendencies? To answer such questions, we must continue with concrete explorations of knowledge in context.

∴

The way the cognitive dramas of Arabic instruction unfold—the Jewish struggle with Arabic proficiency and the Arab struggle with university grammar of Arabic—demonstrates the general point that there are limits to the malleability of human cognition, limits which affect the dynamics of fields of practice. The incompatibility of empathy and a securitist agenda on the Jewish side,

approach to knowledge whereby reality is merely a figment of the knower's imagination. Rather, I adopt a non-objectivist realist perspective whereby reality is constructed through an interaction between the material world and a socially and culturally situated knower (see e.g. Lakoff and Johnson 1980 for an eloquent presentation of such a position).

and the profound, yet imperceptible, hold of incompatible grammar-learning habits on Arabs and Jews, demonstrate how conditions that emerge from the very nature of the way the human mind works can impose themselves on the field and subvert the intentions of participants in the field. These conditions can continue to play this subversive role so long as they remain invisible to participants in the field by an overwhelming metacognitive blindness.

Indeed, people tend to be oblivious to their own mental structures of learning and thinking until such time as they experience an unexpected anomaly, and sometimes not even then. Such an anomaly—potentially a Lévy-Bruhlian moment—is what Arab students experience in university grammar classes. Yet their disinclination to see the cultural clash in structures of knowledge and learning for what it is, and their misattribution of this difference to personal failure, give us an insight into some significant dynamics of the personalisation or internalisation of a cultural political reality. This cognitive dynamic is a component of the broader effect of institutionalised formal education, namely the personal internalisation of social destiny (Bourdieu and Passeron 1990).

The fact that the differences in habits of learning pass largely unnoticed, or at least underappreciated, by both teachers and students makes these differences unique in the constellation of forces that maintain the educational status quo. Unlike more visible elements that constitute the field like the use of Hebrew in university Arabic-grammar classes or the absence of an Arab university, these habitual differences remain impervious to conscious observation and analysis, and thereby escape wilful action. In a sense, they become depoliticised through misrecognition. The misrecognition of the differences is further motivated by a pervasive commonsensical view of scholarship as a matter of capturing an objectively visible reality in a culturally neutral way. The level of metacognitive awareness, metacognitive blindness in this specific instance, emerges as a critical condition of fields like Arabic instruction in Israel.

Circumscribed Freedom within the Field

Formal instruction is a technical practice. It involves a deliberate interaction that is designed to inculcate knowledge and skills in pupils. Instruction is also a political practice in the broadest sense of the word. It is political because the distribution of knowledge and skills across society is part and parcel of the distribution of power. It is political also because different stakeholders engage in deliberate, purposive action to influence the field of instruction in pursuit of broader overarching aims.

The previous chapters take educational practice as political, while also seeing political practice as embedded in concrete cognitive processes. The discussion seeks to avoid the alternative analytical pitfalls of reducing educational practice to an epiphenomenon of political action, or seeing education as an independent affair that is explicable entirely in its own terms. An essential aspect of the analysis of embedded political practice is the clarification of how stakeholders' deliberate actions are shaped, reshaped and reformulated through practice in specific contexts. For example, some of the participants in the field of education are able to mobilise and act collectively in pursuit of perceived collective interests. Collective action of this sort requires some measure of collective control and discipline among members who might also seek to act as individuals outside, and in conflict with, their group. These collectivities do not, as it were, precede the practice. Rather they are formed and maintained through practice. Jewish parents, students, teachers and principals are an example of one such collectivity in the field, able to effectively mobilise at the school level to confront and subvert policies that are formulated elsewhere. By the same token, some agendas of collective action fail to be realised as a coherent collectivity that would drive them does not materialise. The failure of Israel's mighty security apparatus to mobilise Jews in pursuit of effective Arabic learning in defence of the national interest is an example of such a failed project.

The internal dynamics of the field thus have a significant political effect that can be felt within the field and in other areas of practice. The subversion of the avowed aims of instruction is paradigmatic. This subversion is largely due to two reasons. One is that the great number of stakeholders pursuing different agendas creates a complex and uncontrollable environment that refracts and twists the action of individual stakeholders. The other is the limits on the malleability of the objects of the field, not least of which is the cognitive functioning that underlies learning in general, and language learning in particular. Not everything is possible in instruction, and some of the technical and cognitive limits on what can be done help shape the process and outcome of instruction. So, for the matter at hand, an adversarial language-instruction agenda appears to subvert the effectiveness of proficiency acquisition, producing a countervailing dynamic, or to use the language of systems analysis, a balancing loop.

In analysing the systemic logic of Arabic instruction I have drawn, loosely at times and more heavily at others, on Bourdieu's heuristic notion of field.[4] The

---

4 Purely theoretical debates being an acquired taste, I have generally opted to avoid broad

notion of field offers several particularly attractive aspects of systemic analysis. One is that it allows for an exploration of the emergent reality—the overall systemic logic of action and its effects within the field—as an autonomous area of practice which is neither reducible to the "sum total" of participants nor a mere epiphenomenon of broader regimes of power. Another is that it allows for the social agents involved—the primary constituents of this field of practice—to be shaped and reshaped by their very engagement in the field. In other words, the constituents do not precede the field, but are shaped by it at the very same time as their interactions give it shape. Finally, Bourdieu's framework, at least in the way that it is used in the preceding chapters, does not assume that a field has a state of equilibrium to which it gravitates. Rather, both continuity and change can be identified and both must then be explained rather than assumed.

If the cognitive processes of learning affect the dynamics of the field from within, as it were, then the broad field of power conditions it from outside. The constraints that are imposed by the overarching field of power on the field of Arabic instruction in Israel are powerful and apparently irresistible. The ideological imperatives of Zionism are ubiquitous. While these constraints are significant, they by no means determine the field. Within the hard constraints of the broad political economy there is an enormous scope for the field to take many different shapes. The actualisation of the overarching Zionist project in Arabic education is mediated through the complex interactions of different strategies of different stakeholders within the field.

When fields undergo transformation, the underlying dynamics of power tend to become visible. But the field of Arabic instruction in Israel has not undergone major transformations, and the main contours of the field have remained relatively stable since the field's very inception. This denies us the opportunity to observe transformations in the field, and makes all the more significant an analysis of the normally invisible dynamics that maintain the inertia of the field. Under such circumstances one must go beyond empirical investigation in order to understand the structures of power that fix the field in its inertia.

One such alternative strategy is to envisage potential transformations that might have benefited specific stakeholders, and then consider what processes would be required to effect such changes within the field, and finally, what resistance such processes would meet.

---

theoretical disquisitions in this book. For an explicit, systematic discussion of the way I rely on Bourdieu's conceptual framework in dealing with the issues at hand, see Uhlmann 2008.

The rationale of this approach is as follows. If courses of action that are relatively straightforward were to help stakeholders achieve their goals, the stakeholders would presumably engage in them. These may or may not be successful. For example, the attempt to redirect Arab teachers of Arabic to work in Jewish schools was a failed attempt by stakeholders to improve the field, and both the attempt and its failure can teach us about the dynamics of the field. But if there are seemingly straightforward courses of action that stakeholders avoid, this is presumably so because the stakeholders either consciously or not do not expect them to succeed. By this logic, the courses of action that were not taken can also teach us about the constraints and opportunities that are embedded in the field, at least as it seems to be perceived by stakeholders.

In the next few paragraphs I will suggest some transformations that might have helped ameliorate the situation of Arabic instruction. I take the overall structure of the political economy of Israel for granted in order to focus on the specific factors that are internal to the field of Arabic instruction.[5]

If decisions to make Arabic compulsory were enforced, and if Arabic were given extra weight in matriculation examinations, we would see a greater breadth and depth of Arabic instruction. But this would require shifts of power in two areas. First and foremost, a shift would be necessary in political power away from parents and pupils in the Jewish sector towards the bureaucracy and institutional powers. Democratisation and decentralisation of the control over schooling has proven detrimental to Arabic. This is so because it would require students and parents to invest more in Arabic, incurring opportunity costs. Similarly there would need to be a shift in the relative strength of the lobby groups and vested interests that support other compulsory subjects. Currently the compulsory subjects in the matriculation examinations include mathematics, English, and various topics linked to Judaism and civics. Revaluating Arabic would detract from these by diverting finite resources (budgets, teaching hours) away from the privileged subjects to Arabic, and by diluting the symbolic pre-eminence of these subjects. The vested interests that defend these subjects are quite powerful ranging from academia, through government and industry, to subject experts in the Department of Education.

5 The discussion here is concerned with dynamics that are primarily internal to the field, hence the concentration on non-radical changes. Still, one should point out that if Israel were to relinquish its Zionist imperative, and if the local polity were to cease to be defined as inherently Jewish and therefore non-Arab, the whole dynamics of the field might change. Nonetheless, even then not all problems that currently beset Arabic instruction would be resolved, and quite likely different problems would emerge.

Academia plays a decisive role in devaluing Arabic. Arabic is currently not a required topic for entrance into university. Moreover, in evaluating the matriculation-examination results for the purpose of entry scores, universities prioritise a few subjects, like mathematics and English. These subject attract bonus points, thus artificially overvaluing them in comparison with other subjects (see chapter 2 for details). Arabic is not one of these subject.

Arabic could be revaluated by being made compulsory for entrance into university, or by attracting bonus points that are similar to English or mathematics. Such changes would make an educational specialisation in Arabic more valuable when opportunity costs are concerned. It would further reward schools that emphasise Arabic and students who specialise in Arabic, and provide a greater incentive to study the language. These changes might appeal to the institutional proponents of Arabic instruction to Jews, but are unlikely to meet with enthusiastic support from Jewish parents and pupils who might lose a competitive edge over Arab students in a competitive educational environment. Moreover, parents, students and teachers in Jewish schools would generally rather focus their efforts elsewhere—specifically on subjects that promise greater returns on investment—and would resist such an imposition.

The question of bonus points on matriculation subjects reveals much of the arbitrary nature of academic common sense. The argument for revaluing English with extra bonus points rests on the centrality of English publications to Israel's academia. Arabic is not as essential for active participation in the international academic community. But the preferential emphasis placed on mathematics is harder to justify. Many students will not engage with mathematics in the course of their studies, and in many areas mathematics is not relevant to successful participation in the international academic community. Unlike proficiency in mathematics, Arabic proficiency could facilitate Israeli academia's engagement with the region, and possibly allow it to play a meaningful role in shaping and influencing the Arab academic sphere—a significant contribution even from the perspective of the security apparatus. The reason why mathematics should be preferred over Arabic across the board is hard to attribute to any sound, non-prejudicial rationale.

In fact, we see here in the preferential treatment given to some subjects and not others an expression of an underlying ideology that informs Israel's academia. It is a mixture of European orientation and preferences for "hard" sciences. Given the political economy of international academia, an anglophone Eurocentric orientation seems inevitable. This explains the great emphasis placed on English. Likewise, a market-driven world view is projected through the revaluation of mathematics which underlies technical fields and is deemed to have practical utility. Mathematics is also perceived as more demanding and, on an assumption of unidimensional intelligence, a marker of greater intellectual ability than other fields. This market-driven, Euro-orientated approach has little use for Arabic. These underlying ideological commitments shape the behaviour of players in the field and to an extent act as self-fulfilling prophecies. Students who can excel in formal education are pushed towards mathematics and English, confirming the association of these topics with greater intelligence, and helping entrench this ideology in the field. And so, from the dominant perspective, given that the "smarter" students do mathematics, a grade acquired in mathematics is "worth" more than an equivalent grade in literature, for example. And to the extent that the ideological commitments shape the educational choices of pupils, parents and principals, this perception may in fact be an accurate reflection of the reality of the field. In any event, these pervasive ideological tenets greatly limit the scope for change in the field of Arabic instruction.

An additional hindrance to the expansion and deepening of Arabic instruction and literacy among Israeli Jews is the construction of Arabic as a gentile language, associated with a hostile gentile population. Curricula that emphasise the status of Arabic as a Jewish language might go some way towards ameliorating the perception. Medieval Jews adapted the Arabic language to their own intellectual and communicative needs, and significant developments in Jewish thought, arts and culture have taken place in Arabic. Moreover, Jewish communities throughout the Middle East have evolved distinct Arabic dialects, which could add a rich tapestry of language and culture to the curriculum.

Curricular emphases on the Jewishness of Arabic and on Jewish Arabic usages and dialects might change the view of Arabic among Jewish students, and in fact may even challenge the conceptualisation of Jewishness and Arabness altogether. Furthermore, curricula that can successfully de-gentile Arabic and reclaim it as one of the languages of the Jewish experience might help promote the instruction of Arabic even in the flagrantly parochial Jewish religious school stream where current resistance to Arabic instruction runs high. In addition, at schools that are situated in areas with large Arab Jewish populations such curricula could help further naturalise the Jewish aspects of the Arabic language. For example, public schools whose catchment area may include large Iraqi or Yemeni Jewish émigré communities could teach the Jewish Iraqi or Yemeni dialects as their dialect of choice in the colloquial components of the curriculum, and find more pertinent texts in their selection of Arabic texts. This could possibly make Arabic more relevant to Jewish students, and revaluate the traditional knowledge of Iraqi or Yemeni Jewish students.

So why does the Jewishness of Arabic fail to inspire Jewish educators and students? The answer, I suggest, is that such shifts could be quite threatening. As mentioned above, such curricula might, in fact, have the more radical effect of denaturalising the very dichotomy of Jew versus Arab which is foundational to the Zionist political order in Israel. A different possible outcome of such a move, and no-less threatening to many Jews, might be to re-equate Arab Jews with Arabs as a means of devaluing Oriental Jewry. This association of autochthonous Middle Eastern Jewry with the Arab context in which they had lived was, in fact, significant in legitimising Ashkenazi domination over, and emphatic assimilation of Mizrahi culture in the early years of Israeli statehood. This is a significant reason that even activists for a Mizrahi cause in Israel have been reluctant to confront the de-Arabisation process and embrace the Arabness of their Jewish heritage. Considered from a slightly different angle, it is the inability of Arab Jews to come to terms with their Arabness, and more generally the threat of loss of identity that might result from blurring the sharp distinction between Jews and gentiles, that hinder the adoption by Jews of Arabic as a legitimately Jewish language.

Of course, being recognised as a Jewish heritage language cannot guarantee Arabic's attractiveness as a school subject. Yiddish has no meaningful curricular presence in Jewish state schooling. It is therefore quite possible that even if successfully reconstituted as a Jewish language, Arabic's place in the curriculum would not be boosted. This is so for the related considerations of nationalist ideology and practical benefit. Yiddish, being a quintessential language of diasporic Judaism, was rejected in the name of a Hebraic national revival, and there is no reason why the same fate should not befall Arabic. Had there been a drive among Arab Jews towards the maintenance of a pertinent cultural orientation, schools could have lent themselves to such projects of cultural dissimilation, but such an ideological turn is not currently forthcoming.

There is also a more practical reason that rendering Arabic a Jewish language will not break its marginalisation. The dominant imperative that drives students and their parents is integration into Israel's political economy where Arabness—be it Jewish or gentile—is of little value, and where Arabic is of little use. In other words, students and parents respond to the political economy of language proficiency, and this will not change even if Arabic were reconstituted as Jewish.

Implicit in some of the suggestions above is a willingness to disconnect Arabic instruction in the Jewish sector from its securitist rationale (cf. Mendel 2011, 2014). Such a disconnection could be taken further. Military Intelligence's bear hug of Arabic teaching suffocates it and depletes it from a motivating rationale that would drive students to acquire true proficiency. It imbues Arabic with national strategic significance, but the reasons that underlie the national significance deprive Arabic of meaningful personal significance. Under the pressure of the security apparatus's embrace "security Arabic" comes to displace "civilian Arabic" as decoding trumps personal expression in what I have dubbed the Latinisation of Arabic.

Reforming the rationale of Arabic instruction away from the securitist imperative can benefit from the removal of the military from pedagogical policy formulation and implementation in the field of Arabic instruction. The place of the military in the Arabic classroom can be taken by proficient native speakers of Arabic, the vast majority of whom would presumably be non-Jewish Arabs. This would improve the knowledge base from which teachers operate, and would allow a more effective teaching not only of the narrow linguistic aspects of the different registers, but also the way Arabic's diglossia is handled in practice (cf. Ferguson 1963). More broadly, the involvement of Arabs in the delivery of instruction would possibly allow for greater cultural proficiency to emerge among students.

This is not a novel idea. I mentioned above the aborted attempt to train Arab teachers to teach Arabic in Jewish schools. The experiment failed as none of the teachers stayed for long in their new placements. I suspect that the differences between the Jewish and Arab streams in the systems of Arabic grammar that are taught made it harder for Arab teachers to adapt to teaching the Arabic curriculum of Jewish schools. But it was opposition at schools and the inability of those in the Ministry of Education to force the issue at the local level that condemned this initiative to failure. The decentralisation of authority in schooling has left principals with a great deal of autonomy, and has subverted such top-down impositions that might have improved the delivery of Arabic instruction.

There are two specific conditions that could effectively promote the integration of Arab teachers into Jewish schools. One is the willingness of the Department of Education to compel schools to accept such teachers. This can be done through direct confrontation by mobilising the ultimate bureaucratic authority of the Ministry, or through a system of testing the Arabic proficiency of teachers, enforcing minimal accepted standards, and accrediting and ranking teachers. The other would be an increase in the grading standards of the matriculation examination in Arabic to the point that would make the integration of proficient teachers to be a clear advantage to the school. Such action was a major component of the successful reform of English instruction in Israeli schools in the 1970s. Both sets of steps—using bureaucratic coercion and recalibrating the matriculation examinations—rely on the deliberate application of the institutional powers of central authority to force local school communities to change their practice and conform to externally imposed directives. The administrative resources are there, but the Ministry of Education lacks the will to force the issue and confront the local school communities.

The localisation of school control along with the democratisation of educational decision making emerge as major hindrances to Arabic instruction. This is ultimately so because Arabic proficiency is not currently of much symbolic value to individual students. The gains afforded by the integration of Arab teachers are outweighed by the ideological dissonance posed by an Arab teacher in the Arabic classroom, and the consequent subversion of the very securitist rationale of Arabic instruction, the only rationale that allows Israeli Jews to tie Arabic proficiency to their own personal interests by giving Jews access to relatively prestigious employment in the security apparatus and related fields.

Be that as it may, the integration of Arabs into the design and implementation of Arabic instruction to Jews need not be confined to teachers. In fact, there is a case to be made for integrating Arabs into the development of the curriculum on the assumption that they might be better positioned to determine the linguistic and cultural literacy that such a program should aim to achieve. Currently, it is Jews, and in particular Jews whose very professional *raison d'être* is aligned with the rationale of the security apparatus, who come to define and delimit the target skills of Arabic instruction in the Jewish sector, and they do so with a view to best serve the Zionist project's security requirements and worldview. Hence Arabic's continuing Latinisation.

Another step that could be taken to improve Jews' Arabic proficiency—both linguistic and cultural—could be to have Jewish Arabic teachers in training undertake their undergraduate instruction in Arab institutions. There are no arabophone universities in Israel, but there are Arabic-language teachers' colleges, and attending those would enable Jewish teachers-to-be to interact with Arabic and Arabs in an unmediated way and to undertake their studies in Arabic thereby improving both their cultural and linguistic proficiencies and allowing them to develop their classroom management skills in Arabic. This could happen either through imposition by requiring teachers to have completed a degree in the target language, or by the active desire of teachers to reach fluency in Arabic. Neither is likely. Requiring teachers to have completed their studies in Arabic would threaten the very existence of undergraduate Arabic instruction at universities and Jewish colleges. For their part, teachers are unlikely to enhance their career prospects by improving their linguistic skills given the acceptance of poor standards of Arabic proficiency among teachers of Arabic in the Jewish sector, and the tolerance of low proficiency acquisition among Jewish students.

Finding a way to reward linguistic attainment, perhaps by providing bonus pay to teachers who are able to demonstrate higher levels of proficiency, could help nudge teachers in such a direction. However, such an initiative on the part of the Ministry of Education would entail a formal admission that the current trajectories of professional development are inadequate, and would also demand the diversion of financial resources for that purpose. It would call into question the capacity of the tertiary education system to effectively train Arabic teachers, and potentially expose the pitfalls of Jewish domination of Arabic research and instruction in Israeli universities.

If cultural proficiency is an accepted goal of Arabic instruction in the Jewish sector, then obviously it is urgent to help teachers improve their cultural proficiency through interaction with Arabs, but the issue needs to be taken much further. The very curriculum of Arabic instruction should aim to help students learn the conventions and competencies that are required for effective interaction with Arabs in Arabic. This might best be achieved by fostering and enabling interaction between Jewish students and Arabs in as natural a way as possible, and not just, as currently happens, in the occasionally fashionable highly contrived seminars that bring together Jews and Arabs to discuss coexistence. Perhaps such interactions can be achieved through school exchanges across the Jewish and Arab sectors, where there would be controlled instruction in conventions of interaction accompanied by semi-directed interactions that will instruct students to interact in Arabic.

The logic of promoting cultural proficiency as an integral aspect of Arabic instruction assumes that the school curriculum should aim to allow students to interact with the multiplicities of Arab experiences in a broad way, with a greater component of dialogic contact with Arabs in Arabic. In other words, rather than training Jewish students to adopt the posture of an aloof observer (through exclusive focus on passive reading and translation skills), there should be greater curricular emphasis on interactive communications with Arabs, and on the capacity to engage independently in such exchanges. Such independence might also allow students to continue developing their proficiency as a life-long educational process even after they leave the safety of the pedagogical guidance of their schools.

Such a strategy would push Jewish teachers beyond their comfort zone, and will not sit well with the securitist rationale that drives Arabic instruction. Moreover, the promotion of proficient interaction between Jews and Arabs comes up against the segregation of Jews and Arabs in Israel. This segregation makes it hard to create natural spaces for interaction, especially interactions on Arab terms that require Jewish adaptation. Significantly, it is usually enough for one Jew to be present in a group with Arabs for the language of interaction to shift to Hebrew, and the style of communication to shift as well. This is true of university departments of Arabic, of politically radical organisations, and of other contexts, too.

Independently of interactive communications with Arabs, the very material that is presented to Jewish students could be changed to allow a more comprehensive and genuine presentation of Arab narratives and experiences, if indeed students are meant to be able to understand the logic that drives Arab perspectives. The heavily controlled, biased exposure of Jewish students to Arab voices creates caricatures of Arabs, and hinders rather than facilitates a genuine understanding on the part of Jews of Arabs. In general, the educational establishment in Israel has resisted the inclusion of Arab narratives regarding the Nakba (Catastrophe) and similar aspects of the ethnic cleansing and social dislocation that has befallen non-Jews in Palestine. The very mention of the term Nakba is contentious. An Arabic curriculum to Jews that does not include terms like Nakba and does not expose Jews to the multiple and contradictory narratives that circulate in the Arab world could not possibly achieve a minimal level of cultural proficiency. No less significantly, the current curriculum restricts students' exposure to the discussions and different positions in the Arab world on Jews, Zionism and Israel. (One should also note that the current curriculum purports to include themes of the History of Arabs and Islam, but this marginalisation of central Arab narratives of the last two centuries exposes the tendentious nature of the instructional design which teeters on the brink between historiography and stereotyping.)

Exposing Jews to the narratives that drive Arab politics is not only essential to enable communication with and understanding of Arabs by Jews. It might go a long way towards reducing much of the paranoia that accentuates Jewish fears of Arabs. Failing to enable Jews to understand even the very elementary aspects of Arab perspectives makes Jews perceive Arab hostility as irrational and capricious, and as an essential aspect of Arab existence rather than a historically specific response to the emerging situation in Palestine in particular and in the Middle East more generally. If Arab hostility were put into its historical context, it would become comprehensible, potentially manageable, and thereby less threatening. It would become an object of possible transformative action through communication rather than an immutable fact of nature, indelibly branded into the essence of Arab psyche. Such a reduction in the perceived threat might make it emotionally easier for Jewish students to engage with Arabic and Arab themes.

What makes such transformations unlikely is the inability of proponents of Arabic instruction to shield themselves from some of the political pressures around them, and from the securitist agenda that pervades the field, and to place the rationale of Arabic instruction on a civilian footing rather than a militaristic one.

Turning from the Jewish sector to the problematic of Arabic-grammar instruction on the Arab side, some conceivable changes to curricular policy and educational implementation in the Israeli-Arab educational system might go a considerable way towards mitigating the alienation of Arabs from Arabic grammar and its instruction. Here, too, a consideration of the possible effects of such changes and the constellation of forces that are likely to militate against them can help us further understand the immutable nature of the field.

Probably the most immediate change that could be put into effect to alleviate the difficulties that are faced by Arab students in university grammar instruction is the introduction of a metacognitive module into Arabic grammar courses at the university level. Such a module would explicitly compare the two grammatical approaches on given issues, and seek to highlight the systemic differences and incommensurabilities between them. This would make sense of Arab students' incomprehension in a way that does not imply personal failure on their part, and could help redirect their learning in a more productive way. For the Jewish university students of Arabic the introduction of metacognitive themes would have the added advantage of alerting them to the fact that their grammar is not *the* grammar of Arabic but rather *a* grammar of Arabic, and that other conceptualisations are possible. By highlighting the differences between the two systems, instructors would be freed from the need to translate individual concepts from Arabic to Hebrew—a practice that ultimately mystifies rather than clarifies because the essence of grammar is lost in the translation. Ultimately, it would make for a deeper understanding of the grammatical regularities in Arabic to both Arab and Jewish students.

Such a module could, in fact, greatly benefit from the scholarship of Israeli grammarians of Arabic, several of whom are world renowned authorities on the scholarship of the classical Arabic Grammatical Tradition. It would, however, require a systematic comparison of educational and scholastic styles in a way that has not yet been done. It would further relativise the status of both grammatical approaches—as both would be reduced to but one of several possible approaches—a step away from simple commonsensical positivism that would be uncomfortable to many linguists and teachers on both sides.

Presumably the main hindrance to such a step is the lack of awareness among participants in the educational exchanges of the depth of the differences in the construction of the material and the educational process. Also, as long as Arabs are those who bear the brunt of the incommensurability in the form of poor grades, the pressure to alleviate the problem will remain attenuated. Grammar instructors might greatly welcome a solution to the problem, but senior academic decision makers will be under no pressure to fix the situation.

But it is possible to go beyond such immediate measures as adding metacognitive modules to university instruction in Arabic grammar, and envision more systemic changes that could be made. Looking beyond the Arab–Israeli conflict in grammar, one might want to focus on the already problematic situation of grammar instruction in the Arab world, and challenge the dominant approach to grammar instruction in contemporary schools.

A case could be made for shifting the general instruction of grammar in Arab schools away from the Arabic Grammatical Tradition, and integrating the European/Orientalist approach like that which prevails in the Jewish sector. This option was pointed out to me separately by two Arab linguists I had interviewed, both of whom had studied at Arab schools, and then completed their academic studies learning the Western-orientated grammar of Arabic. One taught at the time at an Arab teachers' college, the other taught grammar at one of the Israeli universities.

Significantly, the adoption by Arab schools of Western approaches to grammar does not necessarily mean the extinction of the Arabic Linguistic Tradition. Rather, the two can coexist. The Arabic Linguistic Tradition can remain an integral subject within the major in Arabic grammar, but for those who do not specialise in the language, utilitarian considerations would in fact favour the adoption of a variant of the dominant Western-orientated approach for various reasons.

One benefit of the adoption of a European grammar of Arabic into Arab school curricula is that Orientalist grammar instruction is aimed at teaching Arabic as a second or foreign language, with a greater emphasis on generative rather than descriptive efficiency. This might, in fact, be more suitable to contemporary Israeli Arab students of Standard Arabic than the traditional approach.

Moreover, a European-style grammar would allow for greater coherence across subject matter like that which is enjoyed by Jewish students. Using a grammatical framework that is applicable to both Hebrew and Arabic, and is consistent with the university instruction of Arabic grammar would make it easier for Arab students to transfer knowledge and understanding from one linguistic domain to another. Arab students would encounter the same, coherent, grammatical framework when studying Arabic and Hebrew throughout their educational careers.

Furthermore, those Arabs who major in Arabic will then have the opportunity to experience the two distinct linguistic traditions precisely as they are, two distinct traditions. These students would presumably develop a strong metacognitive awareness in the area of grammar scholarship and instruction. Armed with a deeper understanding of both grammatical approaches, such students might eventually be well placed to redress the Jewish domination of academic Arabic in Israel, and in particular the field of grammar and syntax.

The adoption of the Western, descriptive, comparative grammar of Arabic in Arab schools would open up the way for another major conceptual transformation in the curriculum, namely the inclusion in the curriculum of formal instruction in the grammar and linguistics of colloquial Arabic. Such a reform would contradict the common view among Arab scholars and teachers that colloquial Arabic is merely a corrupt, vulgar, illegitimate variant that should not be formally taught. In fact, a curriculum that explicitly teaches the grammar of colloquial Arabic—if only as a purely descriptive grammar—might help students get a better intuitive grasp of the grammatical conceptual framework. This is so because colloquial Arabic, rather than Standard Arabic, is the effective mother tongue of Arabs. The current practice of depriving Arab students of formal instruction in the grammar of colloquial Arabic is tantamount to depriving students of grammar instruction in their mother tongue, at the very same time as they are taught the formal grammar of an unintuitive register, along with the grammar of other foreign languages. Further, the explicit instruction of the grammar of colloquial Arabic would enable teachers to systematically mobilise students' native proficiency in colloquial Arabic as a backdrop against which they can elaborate the structures and regularities of Standard Arabic.

Admittedly, the assumed results of shifting Arabic instruction in Arab schools to a Western grammatical approach are speculative. There is also no sound empirical basis to estimate the extent to which the integration of the grammar of the colloquial register might in fact help students develop an intuitive appreciation of grammar, and the extent to which the introduction of a formal grammar of colloquial Arabic would translate into a better understanding of the grammar of Standard Arabic. But it stands to reason that teaching the grammar of colloquial Arabic would enhance grammar instruction all-round by providing students with an intuitive understanding of grammar, and with a contrastive framework against which they can compare the grammar of the standard register.[6]

---

6 This raises the question of the effects that formal instruction in colloquial Arabic grammar might have on colloquial Arabic, whose status as an informal unwritten set of communication patterns would be transformed. This question, however, goes beyond the scope of the present discussion.

It is, in fact, possible to take the adoption of a descriptive, comparative, European-style grammar even further, and develop an independent, integrated module of comparative Semitic grammar that can support the instruction of both Hebrew and Arabic. This approach can be applied in both the Jewish and Arabic streams.[7] In fact, such a meta-Semitic approach to grammar is effectively already used informally in the Jewish stream in Arabic instruction—where teachers draw freely on Hebrew to exemplify grammatical points about Arabic. This is part of what gives grammar instruction in Jewish schools its measure of coherence.

The complete transformation of the pedagogical approach to Arabic grammar, however, would come up against entrenched barriers. It may seem efficient, but is essentially a linguistic capitulation to Israeli linguistics. It requires Israeli Arabs to attenuate the intellectual partnership with the Arab world on the one hand, and adopt the linguistic approach of Israeli Jews. It will also devalue the very knowledge that Israeli-Arab Arabic linguists hold, a knowledge that gives meaning to their position. And of course, it will require a retraining of the Arab teachers of Arabic in a grammatical approach that is quite foreign to them. And to further complicate things, all this occurs against a backdrop of a perceived escalating pressure from Hebrew on Arabic.

Extending beyond the narrow scope of the Arabic-language curriculum, Arab schools play a crucial role in shaping the linguistic attitudes of Arab students through the linguistic choices they make. The language of instruction across the curriculum and the language of administration could be fixed at the appropriate register as a matter of policy.

It is hard to get a sense of what the current situation is with regard to the linguistic register that is actually used across the curriculum at Arab schools, and the extent to which teachers emphasise linguistic performance in their evaluation. The teachers and administrators with whom I discussed the issue recounted that the situation is by no means uniform, and generally there is not much emphasis on proper language skills in Standard Arabic. This is consistent with Muhammad Amara's findings from an observational study of three Arab schools, where the dominant register is a generalised colloquial register that he terms Educated Spoken Variety (Amara 1995). However, a concerted effort to prioritise grammatical expression across the curriculum and fix Standard Arabic as the language of classroom interaction and instruction will come up

7 This approach would have the added advantage of providing a measure of support to the possible instruction of other Semitic languages, including Aramaic/Syriac (a fact which might appeal to some religious Jewish and Christian curricula) and the various Ethiopian languages, some of which are taught at schools that cater to Ethiopian Jewish immigrants.

against the strained status of Arabic among Arab teachers, especially those who teach subjects other than Arabic.

As the last few paragraphs show, transformative measures within the field are imaginable, but clearly the reason they have not been adopted in the past and will struggle to materialise in the future is that they come up against the prevalent dynamics of the field. In considering the two sectors of education, the Jewish and the Arab, the power differential clearly emerges. On the Jewish side it is possible to imagine agents who might implement reforms and others who might oppose them. The situation is incomparable on the Arab side. It is impossible to identify centres of power that could naturally formulate and implement fundamental reforms to Arabic instruction in the Israeli-Arab sector. Israel's Ministry of Education has the formal bureaucratic resources to do so but lacks any legitimacy in such major transformations of Arabic instruction to Arabs. Arab intellectuals who might have the intellectual credibility lack the bureaucratic power to effect substantial changes in instruction. They also lack an independent scope for manoeuvre given their marginal position within the Arab world. There is no immediately visible centre of gravity from which Arabic-grammar instruction to Arabs could be overhauled, and from which deliberate transformations could emanate. This is the consequence of the ongoing containment and marginalisation of Israeli-Arabs and their lack of control over their own linguistic destiny.

Moving beyond curricular policy and into the realm of tertiary education in general, one must note the significance of the lack of an Arab university. The Israeli Arab lack of educational autonomy is epitomised in the absence of academic and intellectual frameworks with a global, bird's eye view as it were, that can facilitate debates over grammar and its instruction, and allow for the emergence of solutions that could be translated into teacher training and instructional practice.

A university whose language of instruction was Arabic could also benefit Arabic instruction on the Jewish side. Such a university would be the ideal place for Jewish student teachers to train in Arabic language instruction. Moreover, a good undergraduate program in Arabic would presumably produce proficient graduates who could pursue advanced studies in Arabic with a superior mastery of the language, and form the backbone of a more proficient future generation of Arabic instructors across Israel's tertiary education system.

The absence of an Arab university is not only the result of neglect on the part of Israeli authorities, but also a broader reflection of the disunity and weakness of the Arab intellectual class. I have heard of one instance when a foreign funder was willing to back the establishment of a private Arab university in Israel, but the project foundered when the steering committee which included Israeli Arab political figures and academics was ripped apart by internal disputes and personality clashes. The history of the non-establishment of an Arab university in Israel is a fascinating drama that falls outside the scope of the current discussion.

It is easy to conceive of policy options and courses of action that might have improved the outcomes of the field not only for specific stakeholders, but for most if not all concerned. Yet these do not come to pass. In accounting for why this is so, several themes emerge as ubiquitous. First, the politics of knowledge are decisive in shaping instruction and its consequences, though not in a predictable way. As we see in the problematic aspects of Arabic instruction among both Jews and Arabs—this is not a zero sum game. Rather, what seems to have emerged is a negative-sum game. Both sides are suffering suboptimal results. Thus, for example, teaching university Arabic grammar in Hebrew detracts from the proficiency of Jewish graduates, at the very same time as it alienates Arab students.

The politics of education materialise in many different ways. They can be seen in the institutional structures and functions that shape instruction; they can be seen in the motivations and sensibilities of the people involved; they can be seen in the political economy of knowledge that interacts with the instructional process. Remarkably, some of the dynamics cut across the Jewish-Arab divide. The devaluation of Arabic in Israel affects both Jewish and Arab students' calculus of the opportunity costs that are involved in educational investment in Arabic. Educational policy implementation in both Jewish and Arab classrooms of Arabic faces problems with teacher training and with the capacity to centrally control and shape educational exchange in the classroom. At universities, where the educational environment is mixed, both Jews and Arabs are hindered by performance anxieties attesting to how profoundly personal the political can be. Ultimately, the inability of proponents of Arabic instruction to find a common ground from which to formulate a joint Jewish-Arab agenda to promote Arabic instruction underscores how entrenched the intercommunal conflict is, and how embroiled Arabic instruction is in shaping and perpetuating it.

The inability of any stakeholder, no matter how dominant, to control the field and achieve optimal results is remarkable. The powerful security apparatus, for example, has squandered plenty of resources in achieving underachievement in Arabic instruction in the Jewish sector.

The emergent reality in the field of Arabic instruction in Israel is a good example of a stable field of practice that results from continuous negotiations of many stakeholders, without any stakeholder exercising total control. The field operates as a system. The reality it produces cannot be reduced to the intention of stakeholders who operate within it or the conditions surrounding it. The action of stakeholders and the conditions in which they operate all interact with each other, and it is only through a consideration of the field as a whole that we can account for the emergent reality that is produced within it. Considering the field in its totality, complete with the internal dynamics that amplify or dampen the effect of specific action is not only essential to fully account for the dynamics of Arabic instruction. It is also an important first step towards a considered strategy to change it.

References

Abu-Saad, Ismael 2006. "State-Controlled Education and Identity Formation among the Palestinian Arab Minority in Israel." *American Behavioral Scientist*, 49(8):1085–1100.

Alon, Shlomo 1987. *"Hora'at ha-ʿaravīt be-veyt ha-sefer ha-ʿivrī: maṭarōt, šiṭōt vᵉ-hesegīm.* [Arabic instruction in Jewish schools—Goals, methods and achievements]." *Sugiyōt bᵉḥinnūḫ* 2:68–76.

Amara, Muhammad Hasan 1995. "Arabic Diglossia in the Classroom: Assumptions and Reality." In S. Izre'el and R. Drory (eds) *Israel Oriental Studies* XV: *Language and Culture in the Near East.* Leiden: Brill. Pp. 131–142.

Amara, Muhammad 2015. "Hebraization in the Palestinian Language Landscape in Israel." In B. Spolsky, O. Inbar-Lourie and M. Tannenbaum. *Challenges for Language Education and Policy: Making Space for People.* New York: Routledge. Pp. 182–195.

Amara, Muhammad Hasan and Abd Al-Rhaman Mar'i 2002. *Language Education Policy: The Arab Minority in Israel.* Dordrecht: Kluwer.

Baalbaki, Ramzi 1995. Teaching Arabic at University Level: Problems of Grammatical Tradition. In N. Anghelescu and A.A. Avram (eds) *Proceedings of the Colloquium of Arabic Linguistics, Bucharest, August 29–Sept 2, 1994, part 1.* Bucharest. Pp. 85–101.

Baalbaki, Ramzi 2004. *Grammarians and Grammatical Theory in the Medieval Arabic Tradition.* Aldershot: Ashgate.

Baalbaki, Ramzi 2008. *The Legacy of the Kitab.* Leiden: Brill.

Barazangi, Nimat Hafez, Donald Malcolm Reid, Syed Rizwan Zamir, Dietrich Reetz, Joseph S. Szyliowicz, Akbar S. Ahmed and Anis Ahmad. [2014] "Education." In The Oxford Encyclopedia of the Islamic World. Oxford Islamic Studies Online, http://www.oxfordislamicstudies.com/article/opr/t236/e0212 (accessed Aug 17, 2014).

Bateson, Gregory 1972. *Steps to an Ecology of Mind: Collected Essays in Anthropology, Psychiatry, Evolution, and Epistemology.* Chicago: University of Chicago Press.

Bawardi, Basilius 2012a. "The Teaching of Arabic in Arab Schools." Paper delivered at Bar Ilan University, 5 March 2012. (http://www.youtube.com/watch?v=04AGH78yDIA)

Bawardi, Basilius 2012b. "The Teaching of Arabic as a Mother Tongue in the Arab Schools in Israel: The Current Situation and Future Challenges [in Arabic]." Paper delivered at the symposium "Arabic: A Language in the Eye of the Storm" Jerusalem: Van Leer Institute, 8 November 2012.

Beeston, Alfred Felix Landon 1970. *The Arabic Language Today.* London: Hutchinson.

Bekerman, Zvi. 2009. "'Yeah, it is important to know Arabic—I just don't like learning it': can Jews become bilingual in the Palestinian Jewish integrated bilingual schools?" In C. McGlynn, M. Zembylas, Z. Bekerman & T. Gallagher (Eds) *Peace Education in Conflict and Post-conflict Societies: Comparative Perspectives*. New York: Palgrave Macmillan. Pp. 231–246.

Berry, John W. 1976. *Human Ecology and Cultural Style*. New York: Sage-Halstead.

Blau, Joshua 1981. *The Renaissance of Modern Hebrew and Modern Standard Arabic: Parallels and Differences in the Revival of Two Semitic Languages*. Berkeley: UC Press.

Bohas, Georges, Jean-Patrick Guillaume, and Djamel Kouloughli [1990] 2006. *The Arabic Linguistic Tradition*. Washington D.C.: Georgetown University Press.

Bourdieu, Pierre 1977. "The Economics of Linguistic Exchanges." *Social Science Information* 16(6):645–668.

Bourdieu, Pierre 1985. "The Genesis of the Concept of Habitus and Field," *Sociocriticism* 2:11–24.

Bourdieu, Pierre and Jean-Claude Passeron 1990. *Reproduction in Education, Society and Culture* [second edition]. Thousand Oaks: Sage.

Bourdieu, Pierre 1986. "The Forms of Capital." in J.G. Richardson (ed.) *Handbook of Theory and Research for the Sociology of Education*. New York: Greenwood Press.

Bourdieu, Pierre and Loïc J.C. Wacquant 1992. *An Invitation to Reflexive Sociology*. Chicago: University of Chicago Press.

Brosh, Hezi, 1997 "*ʿAravīt l^{e}-dovrei ʿivrīt b^{e}-yisraʾel—"safa šniya" ʾo "safa zara"?*[Arabic for speakers of Hebrew in Israel—a second language or a foreign language?]" *Ḥelqat lašōn* 23:111–131.

Brosh, Hezi and Eliezer Ben-Rafael 1994, "*M^{e}diniyūt l^{e}šonīt mul m^{e}tziʾūt ḥevratīt: ha-ʿaravīt b^{e}-veyt ha-sefer ha-ʿivrī* [Language policy versus social reality: Arabic in the Hebrew school]." *ʿIyyunīm b^{e}-ḥinnūḫ* 59–60:333–351.

Carter, Michael G. 1981. *Arab Linguistics: An Introductory Classical Text with Translation and Notes*. Amsterdam: John Benjamins.

Cazeneuve, Jean 1972. *Lucien Lévy-Bruhl*. New York: Harper & Row.

Charalambous, Constadina 2012. "Learning the Language of 'The Other' in Conflict-Ridden Cyprus: Exploring Barriers and Possibilities." In H. Footitt and M. Kelly *Languages and the Military: Alliances, Occupation and Peace Building*. London: Palgrave Macmillan. Pp. 186–201.

Charalambous, Constadina 2013. "The 'Burden' of Emotions in Language Teaching: Negotiating a Troubled Past in 'Other' Language Learning Classrooms." *Language and Intercultural Communication* 13(3):310–329.

Eickelman, Dale F. 1978. "The Art of Memory: Islamic Education and Its Social Reproduction." *Comparative Studies in Society and History* 20(4):485–516.

Eickelman, Dale F. 1979. "The Political Economy of Meaning." *American Ethnologist* 6(2):386–393.

Eickelman, Dale F. 1985. *Knowledge and Power in Morocco: The Education of a Twentieth-Century Notable*. Princeton, NJ: Princeton University Press.

Eickelman, Dale F. et al. 2010. *Committee for the Evaluation of Middle Eastern Studies Programs—General Report*. Jerusalem: Council for Higher Education.

Evans-Pritchard, E.E. 1976. *Witchcraft, Oracles and Magic among the Azande* [abridged]. Oxford: Clarendon Press.

Eyal, Gil 2005. *Hasarat ha-qesem min ha-mizraḥ* [Disenchanting the Orient]. Jerusalem: Van Leer Institute.

Ferguson, Charles A. 1959. "Diglossia." *Word* 15:325–340.

Ferguson, Charles A. 1963. "Problems of Teaching Languages with Diglossia." *Georgetown University Monograph Series* 15:165–177.

Fishman, Joshua A., Robert L. Cooper and Andrew W. Conrad 1977. *The Spread of English*. Rowley, Mass.: Newbury House.

Forrester, Jay W. 1990. *Principles of Systems*. Cambridge, MA: Pegasus Communications.

Al-Haj, Majid 1995. *Education, Empowerment, and Control: The Case of the Arabs in Israel*. Albany: SUNY Press.

Hayam-Yonas, Adva and Shira Malka, 2006 *Likrat pittūaḥ toḫnīt limmudīm b*^{e}*-ʿaravīt l*^{e}*-ḥaṭivat ha-beynayīm v*^{e}*la-ḥaṭiva ha-ʿelyona ba-migzar ha-yhudī: meḥqar haʿaraḫa* [Towards the development of a curriculum in Arabic for the middle and high school in the Jewish sector: An evaluation study]. Jerusalem: Henrietta Szold Institute.

Heylighen, Francis and Cliff Joslyn (2001). "Cybernetics and Second-Order Cybernetics." In R.A. Meyers (ed.) *Encyclopedia of Physical Science & Technology* (3rd ed.). New York: Academic Press.

Holes, Clive 2004 [1995] *Modern Arabic: Structures, Functions, and Varieties* [Rev]. Washington DC: Georgetown University Press.

Hutchins, Edwin 1980. *Culture and Inference*. Cambridge, MA: Harvard University Press.

Hutchins, Edwin 1995. *Cognition in the Wild*. Cambridge, MA: MIT Press.

Ilan, Shahar 2008. "*Hatzaʿat ḥoq: ʿaravīt lo tihye safa rišmīt* [Draft legislation: Arabic will not be an official language]." *Haaretz Daily*, 19 May 2008.

Keen, Ian 1995. "Metaphor and the metalanguage: 'groups' in northeast Arnhem Land." *American Anthropologist* 22(3):502–527.

Knesset 1986. "*Doḥ vaʿadat ha-ḥinnūḫ šel ha-kneset* [A report of the Knesset's education committee]" in Yonai 1992, 174–180.

Lakoff, George 1987. *Women, Fire, and Dangerous Things: What Categories Reveal about the Mind*. Chicago: University of Chicago Press.

Lakoff, George and Mark Johnson 1980. *Metaphors We Live By*. Chicago: University of Chicago Press.

Lardiere, Donna 1992. "On the Linguistic Shaping of Thought: Another Response to Alfred Bloom." *Language in Society* 21:231–251.

Landau, Jacob M. (ed.) 1962. *Horaʾat ha-ʿaravīt k*^{e}*-lašōn zara: leqeṭ maʾamarīm*. [Teaching Arabic as a foreign language: An anthology of articles]. Jerusalem: School of Education of the Hebrew University and the Ministry of Education and Culture.

Landau, Jacob M. 1987. "Hebrew and Arabic in the State of Israel: Political Aspects of the Language Issue." *International Journal of the Sociology of Language* 67:117–133.

Landau-Tasseron, E., E. Olshtain, et al. (eds) 2012. *Teaching Arabic: Where Do We Go From Here? Symposium Report.* Jerusalem: the Israel Academy of Sciences and Humanities.

Lave, Jean, Michael Murtaugh and Olivia de la Rocha 1984. "The Dialectic of Arithmetic in Grocery Shopping." In B. Rogoff and J. Lave (eds) *Everyday Cognition: Its Development in Social Context.* Cambridge, MA: Harvard University Press. Pp. 67–94.

Levin, Aryeh 1995. "The Fundamental Principles of the Arab Grammarians' Theory of 'Amal." *Jerusalem Studies in Arabic and Islam* 19:214–232.

Levin, Aryeh 2002. "*Hora'at ha-'aravīt—Niyyar 'emda* [Arabic instruction—A position paper]." *Journal of the Teachers of Arabic and Islam*, 27:174–177.

Lévy-Bruhl, Lucien et al. 1923. "Séance du 15 février 1923—La Mentalité Primitive" *Proceedings of La Société française de philosophie, Philosophie des sciences, V. Sciences sociales*: 22. Pp. 631–662.

Lloyd, Geoffrey E.R. 2007. *Cognitive Variations: Reflections on the Unity and Diversity of the Human Mind.* Oxford: Clarendon Press.

Lori, Aviva 2008. "*Talmidīm marḥaba* [students *marḥaba*]." *Haaretz Weekend Supplement*, 14 November, 2008.

Luria, Alexander Romanovich 1976. *Cognitive Development: Its Cultural and Social Foundations.* Cambridge, MA: Harvard University Press.

Lustigman, Ran 2008. "*Hora'at ha-safa ha-'aravīt b^{e}-vatey sefer 'ivriyīm* [Arabic language instruction in Hebrew schools]." *Šišīm šnōt ḥinnūḫ be-yisra'el.* Jerusalem. Pp. 167–177.

Mandler, Jean M. 1984. *Stories, Scripts, and Scenes: Aspects of Schema Theory.* Hillsdale, NJ; London: Lawrence Erlbaum Associates.

Mendel, Yonatan 2011, *Arabic Studies in Israeli-Jewish Society: In the Shadow of Political Conflict.* PhD Thesis, Queens' College, University of Cambridge.

Mendel, Yonatan 2013. "A Sentiment-Free Arabic: On the Creation of the Israeli Accelerated Arabic Language Studies Programme." *Middle Eastern Studies* 49(3):383–401.

Mendel, Yonatan. 2014. *The Creation of Israeli Arabic: Political and Security Considerations in the Making of Arabic Language Studies in Israel.* London: Palgrave MacMillan.

Messick, Brinkley 1993. *The Calligraphic State: Textual Domination and History in a Muslim Society.* Berkeley: UC Press.

Al-Musa, Nahaad 1984. *Al-luġa al-'arabīya wa-'abnā'uha* [The Arabic language and its offspring]. Riyad: Dar al-Ulum.

Nisbett, Richard E. 2003. *The Geography of Thought: How Asians and Westerners Think Differently ... and Why.* New York, The Free Press.

Owens, Jonathan 1988. *The Foundations of Grammar: An Introduction to Medieval Arabic Grammatical Theory.* Amsterdam, Philadelphia: John Benjamins.

Owens, Jonathan 1990. *Early Arabic Grammatical Theory: Heterogeneity and standardization*. Amsterdam, Philadelphia: John Benjamins.

Owens, Jonathan 1997. "The Arabic Grammatical Tradition." In R. Hetzron (ed) *The Semitic Languages*. New York: Routledge. Pp. 46–58.

Peled, Yishai 2010. "Sibawayhi's Kitab and the teaching of Arabic grammar." *Jerusalem Studies in Arabic and Islam* 37:163–188.

Qashti, Or 2008 "*Misrad ha-ḥinnūḫ ḥazar bo: ha-safa ha-ʿaravīt tišaʾer bᵉ-toḫnīt ha-libba* [The Ministry of Education has retracted its position: The Arabic language will remain in the core curriculum]." *Haaretz Daily*, 14 April 2008.

Rampton, Ben, Panayiota Charalambous and Constadina Charalambus 2014. "Descuritising Turkish: Teaching the Language of a Former Enemy, and Intercultural Language Education." *Working Papers in Urban Language & Literacies*. Paper 137.

Rittel, Horst W.J. and Melvin M. Webber (1973). "Dilemmas in a General Theory of Planning." *Policy Sciences* 4:155–169.

Roffe-Offir, Sharon 2009. "*Sar ha-taḥbura ʾisher ʾet haḥlafat ha-shlaṭīm bᵉ-ʿaravīt vᵉ-ʾanglīt lᵉ-taʿatīq ʿivrī ṭahōr*, [The minister of transport approved the substitution of signs in Arabic and English to pure Hebrew transliteration]." *Y Net*, 13 July 2009.

Ryding, Karin C. 2005. *A Reference Grammar of Modern Standard Arabic*. Cambridge: Cambridge University Press.

Shenhav, Yehouda 2003. *Ha-yhudīm ha-ʿaravīm: lᵉʾumiyūt, dat vᵉ-ʾetniyūt* [The Arab Jews: Nationalism, religion and ethnicity]. Tel Aviv: Am Oved.

Shohat, Ella 1999 "The Invention of the Mizrahim," *Journal of Palestine Studies* 29:5–20.

Shraybom-Shivtiel, Shlomit 1999. "Language and political change in modern Egypt." *International Journal of the Sociology of Language* 137:131–140.

Shraybom-Shivtiel, Shlomit 2006. *Hitḥadšūt ha-lašōn ha-ʿaravīt bi-šliḥūt ha-raʿayōn ha-lʾumī bᵉ-mitzrayīm* [*The renaissance of the Arabic language and the idea of nationalism in Egypt*]. Jerusalem: Magnes Press.

Snir, Reuven 2005. *ʿArviyūt, yahadūt, tziyonūt: maʾavak zᵉḫuyōt bi-ytziroteyhem šel yᵉhudey ʿiraq* [Arabness, Jewishness, Zionism: A struggle of identities in the works of the Jews of Iraq]. Jerusalem: Ben-Zvi Institute.

So'en, Dan and Edna Debby 2006, " "*ʿAravīt—lama ma?" ʿEmdōt talmidīm klapey ha-ʿaravīt u-nḫonutam li-lmod ʾet ha-safa* [Arabic—how come? The attitudes of students towards Arabic and their willingness to learn the language]." *Ha-ḥinnūḫ u-svivo: Šnatōn seminar ha-qibbutzīm* 28:193–206.

Spolsky, Bernard and Elana Shohamy 1999. *The Languages of Israel: Policy, Ideology and Practice*. Clevedon, UK: Multilingual Matters.

Spolsky, Bernard, Elana Shohamy, and Smadar Donitsa-Schmit 1995. "*Ḥinnūḫ lešonī be-yisraʾel: profil lᵉ-horaʾat ha-safa ha-ʿaravīt bᵉ-vatey sefer ʿivriyīm* [Language education in Israel: A profile for the instruction of the Arabic language in Hebrew schools]."

(Dec. 1995); Report submitted to the Ministry of Education, www.biu.ac.il/hu/lpcr/home/ARAFHEB.htm (accessed 5 October 2007).

Spolsky, Bernard, Elana Shohamy, and Sarit Wald 1995. *"Ḥinnūḥ lešonī bᵉ-yisra'el: profil lᵉ-hora'at ha-safa ha-'anglīt* [Language education in Israel: A profile for the instruction of the English language]." (Dec. 1995); Report submitted to the Ministry of Education, http://www.biu.ac.il/hu/lprc/home/ENGLISH.htm (accessed 5 October 2007).

State Comptroller 1996. *"Hora'at ha-safa ha-'aravīt bᵉ-vatey ha-sefer ha-'ivriyīm* [Arabic language instruction in the Hebrew schools]." in *Doḥ šnatī* 46 *li-šnat* 1995 *ul-ḥešbonōt šnat ha-qsafīm* 1994. Jerusalem. Pp. 367–378.

Suleiman, M.Y.I.H. 1989. "On the Underlying Foundations of Arabic Grammar: A Preliminary Investigation" *British Society for Middle Eastern Studies* 16(2):176–185.

Suleiman, Yasir 1999a. "Language Education Policy—Arabic Speaking Countries." In B. Spolsky (ed) *Concise Encyclopedia of Educational Linguistics*. Amsterdam, Elsevier. Pp. 106–116.

Suleiman, Yasir 1999b. *The Arabic Grammatical Tradition: A Study in* ta'līl. Edinburgh: Edinburgh University Press.

Suleiman, Yasir 2004. *A War of Words: Language and Conflict in the Middle East*. Cambridge: Cambridge University Press.

Suleiman, Yasir 2006a. "Charting the Nation: Arabic and the Politics of Identity." *Annual Review of Applied Linguistics* 26:125–148.

Suleiman, Yasir 2006b. "Arabic Language Reforms, Language Ideology and the Criminalisation of Sibawayhi." In L. Edzard and J. Watson (eds.), *Grammar as a Window on Arab Humanism*. Weisbaden: Harrassowitz Verlag. Pp. 66–83

Uhlmann, Allon J. 2005. "The Dynamics of Stasis: Historical Inertia in the Evolution of the Australian Family." *The Australian Journal of Anthropology* 16(1):31–46.

Uhlmann, Allon J. 2006. *Family, Gender and Kinship in Australia*. Aldershot: Ashgate.

Uhlmann, Allon J. 2008, "The Field of Arabic Instruction in the Zionist State." In A. Luke & J. Albright (eds) *Pierre Bourdieu and Literacy Education*. New York, London: Routledge. Pp. 95–112.

Uhlmann, Allon J. 2010. "Arabic Instruction in Jewish Schools and in Universities in Israel: Contradictions, Subversion, and the Politics of Pedagogy," *International Journal of Middle East Studies* 42(2):291–309.

Uhlmann, Allon J. 2012. "Arabs and Arabic Grammar Instruction in Israeli Universities: Alterity, Alienation and Dislocation." *Middle East Critique* 21(1):101–116.

Uhlmann, Allon J. 2015. "The Failures of Translation across Incommensurable Knowledge Systems: A Case Study of Arabic Grammar Instruction," in P.G. Toner (ed) *Strings of Connectedness: Essays in Honour of Ian Keen*. Canberra: ANU Press. Pp. 143–159.

Versteegh, C.H.M. 1978. "The Arabic Terminology of syntactic position." *Arabica* 25:261–281.

Versteegh, C.H.M. 1997a. *Landmarks in Linguistic Thought III: The Arabic Linguistic Tradition*. London, New York: Routledge.

Versteegh, Kees 1997b. *The Arabic Language*. Edinburgh: Edinburgh University Press.

Weisblatt, Naomi 2002 *"Hora'at ha-'aravīt—hirhurīm ve-'etgarīm* [Arabic instruction—Reflections and challenges]." *Journal of the Teachers of Arabic and Islam* 27:170–173.

Vygotsky, Lev S. 2012. *Thought and Language* [Rev.]. Cambridge, MA: MIT Press.

Weiss, Brad 1996. *The Making and Unmaking of the Haya Lived World: Consumption, Commoditization, and Everyday Practice*. Durham: Duke University Press.

Whorf, Benjamin. L. 1941. "The Relation of Habitual Thought and Behavior to Language." In L. Spier, A.I. Hallowell and S.S. Newman (eds). *Language, Culture and Personality: Essays in Memory of Edward Sapir*. Menasha, Sapir Memorial Publication Fund. Pp. 75–93.

Yonai, Yosef (ed.) 1992 *'Aravīt be-vatey sefer 'ivriyīm* [Arabic in Jewish schools]. Jerusalem: Ministry of Education and Culture, Branch of History of Education and Culture.

Textbooks Cited

Abu Khadra et al 2000

'Abu ḫaḍra, fahd et al. *Al-ǧadīd fī qawā'id al-luġa al-'arabīya* [The new program in the rules of the Arabic language] 2nd ed. [7 vols—grades 7 through 12]. Jerusalem: Ministry of Education and Culture, Pedagogical Administration, Curriculum section, 2000.

al-Ansari 2003

Al-'anṣārīy, 'āṭif walīd. Naẓarīyat al-'āmil fī al-naḥw al-'arabīy 'arḍan wanaqdan [The theory of governance in Arabic grammar—A presentation and a critique]. Irbid: Dar Al-Ketab, 2003.

al-Jarim and Amin [1938] 2005

Al-jārim, 'alī and *muṣṭafā 'amīn*. *Al-naḥw al-wāḍiḥ fī qawā'id al-luġa al-'arabīya* [The clear outline of the rules of the Arabic language] [2 vols—one for primary schools and one for secondary schools, each volume containing three books] Beirut: *Al-maktaba al-luġawīya*, [1938] 2005 [Originally published in Cairo].

Einat n.d.

'Einat, me'īr. Madāriǧ: Sefer limmūd la-'aravīt ha-sifrutīt le-vatey ha-sever ule-limmūd 'atzmī [A textbook of Standard Arabic for school and self-learning in Hebrew], vol. B, Tel Aviv, Einatim, n.d.

Elihai 1992

Elihai, Yohanan. *Ledabber 'aravīt* [To speak Arabic]. Jerusalem: Kesset, 1992. [This course of colloquial Palestinian Arabic for Hebrew speakers is based on the 1967

French course by the author. The Hebrew course is currently owned and published by Minerva in Jerusalem.]
Iron n.d.
'Irōn, dov. Taḥbir ha-lašōn ha-'aravīt, [The syntax of the Arabic language] expanded edition (2 vols). Tel Aviv: Dyonon, n.d.
Landau n.d.
Landa'u, ya'aqov. Madriḫ bi-šviley ha-po'al ha-'aravī: sefer limmūd ve-luaḥ neṭiyōt [A guide in the paths of the Arabic verb: A textbook and conjugation tables]. Jerusalem: Ahiever, n.d.
Levin 1994
Levin, Aryeh 1994 *Diqdūq ha-lahag ha-'aravī šel yerušalayīm* [A Grammar of the Arabic Dialect of Jerusalem]. Jerusalem: Magnes Press.
Peled 1998
Peled, Yishai 1998. *Taḥbīr ha-'aravīt ha-ktuva: hebeṭīm te'oreṭiyīm ve-yissumiyīm* [Written Arabic Syntax in Theory and Practice]. Tel Aviv: Dyonon.
Shartuni 1986
Al-šartūnīy, rašīd. Mabādi' al-'arabīya fī al-ṣarf wa-l-naḥw [The principles of Arabic in syntax and grammar] (vol. 4). Beirut: Dar-Elmachreq, 1986.

Other Primary Material

Abraham Fund. http://www.abrahamfund.org/ (accessed 7 June 2008)
Hand in Hand, http://www.handinhandk12.org/ (accessed 14 December 2009).
Journal of the Teachers of Arabic and Islam [in Hebrew], The Ministry of Education Culture and Sport, The Pedagogical Secretariat, The Supervision of Teaching Arabic and Islam, ICC: The Israeli Curriculum Centre, Jerusalem [Appeared regularly under different editorial arrangements and slightly different titles 1986–2008]
Military Intelligence (I.D.F.). T.L.M. (Section on development of the study of Orientalism), http://www1.idf.il/aman/Site/EnterTelem/EnterTelem.asp (accessed 5 February 2004); https://www.aman.idf.il/modiin/general.aspx?catId=60384 (accessed 4 February 2017).

Index

Printed in the United States
By Bookmasters